Scientific Discourse

Two week loan
Benthyciad pythefnos

Please return on or before the due date to avoid overdue charges
A wnewch chi ddychwelyd ar neu cyn y dyddiad a nodir ar eich llyfr os gwelwch yn dda, er mwyn osgoi taliadau

0 1 JUN 2009
1 0 JUN 2009

http://library.cardiff.ac.uk
http://llyfrgell.caerdydd.ac.uk

Scientific Discourse

Multiliteracy in the Classroom

David Ian Hanauer

continuum
LONDON • NEW YORK

Continuum
The Tower Building, 11 York Road, London SE1 7NX
15 East 26th Street, New York, NY 10010

First published in paperback 2008

British Library Cataloguing-in-Publication Data
A catalogue record for this book is available from the British Library.

ISBN:　HB: 0-8264-8959-1
　　　　Paperback: 9781847063533

Library of Congress Cataloging-in-Publication Data

Typeset by Fakenham Photosetting Limited, Fakenham, Norfolk
Printed and bound in United Kingdom by Biddles, Norfolk

In loving memory of my grandparents

Anne and Harry Cole

Alfred and Helen Hanauer

Table of Contents

Figures

Tables

Acknowledgements

This book presents research that would not have been possible without the support of a generously funded research grant from the National Science Foundation. The original research project was part of a wider literacy-science materials development programme entitled Seeds of Science/Roots of Literacy conducted by the Lawrence Hall of Science at the University of California at Berkeley. The research component of this project, part of which is presented in this book, was funded through Subaward Agreement No SA4047-10056 between the University of California at Berkeley and Dr David I. Hanauer of the Graduate Program for Composition and TESOL at Indiana University of Pennsylvania.

In completing the work on this book and research project, I have been helped by a series of colleagues that I would like to thank. Members of the research and development teams in the Lawrence Hall of Science at the University of California at Berkeley essentially made this project and book possible. I thank the project directors Ms Jacquey Barber and Prof P. David Pearson, team members Ms Catherine Halverson, Ms Lynn Barakos, Mr Lincoln Bergman, Ms Kimi Housome, Ms Nicole Parizeau, Mr Craig Strang, Dr Gina Cervetti, Dr Marco Bravo and Dr Elfrieda Heibert for their input and feedback at various stages of this project. I thank Dr Steve Schneider of Woodside Research Consortium and his evaluation team for the collection of the raw data at the research site. I thank the students, teachers and administrators at the research site for their help and willingness to allow data to be collected within their facility.

In analysing the data, I was helped by a research team. I would like to thank my research assistants Mr John Dunn, Ms Kelli Custer and Mr Alec Lapidus all of the Graduate Program for Composition and TESOL at Indiana University of Pennsylvania for their informative responses, assistance and patience in working with me on this project. I thank Ms Dafna Rehavia of Art Therapy Services of Pittsburgh for help in understanding and analysing visual representations within the collected data. Naturally, the responsibility for all positions, analyses, results and conclusions are mine alone.

Chapter 1: Introduction: Situating Science, Literacy and Discourse in the Inquiry Classroom

1.1 Imagine a Classroom

Imagine a classroom. Four second-grade children sit around a table and rummage in a deep, square plastic box. In the box is sand. A variety of objects are hidden in the sand. The children stick their hands in the bucket and extract a variety of things. As they take objects out of the sand, the children bring them close to their faces and look carefully at each. They may turn it around, shake it, show it to a friend or place it next to their ear. On the whole, the children are excited at every object they find. It is like a new discovery of something hidden. If they know the name of the object they call it out – 'shell, I found a shell'. The observed object may find its way back into the plastic box or be placed on the table. At different points the teacher comes over to the table and asks the children what they have found. The children show objects to the teacher and she picks them up and observes them herself. She asks the children to place similar objects in groups and to provide each group of objects with a name. The children continue to rummage and place objects on the table. Objects are placed together and moved from pile to pile. Some objects are by themselves. Sometimes the children argue over which group an object should be placed in or the name of the group. At one point the teacher brings over a set of pencils and asks the children to draw a line round each group and write a name for the group of objects. The children pick up the pencils and draw circles around the objects organized on the table. Later, they make lists of the objects they have identified on a specially designed worksheet.

This, as you have probably guessed by now, is an elementary school science inquiry classroom and the children in this class are learning science and scientific concepts by conducting a series of physical and verbal activities in the classroom. Learning in this classroom has some characteristics that are immediately salient. First of all, the children are physically active throughout most of the science lesson. They are encouraged to use all of their senses in their class work. To a large extent doing is considered to be a major part of learning. Secondly, while they work they talk. The classroom is noisy and the children are excited about their discoveries. They argue over the names of objects and where to place them in groups. Thirdly, the teacher seems not so much to teach the children as to discuss with them their discoveries and point them in the direction of additional activities. These activities lead to further discoveries and discussion. Fourthly, the content of the classroom discussions seems to be directed by the discoveries of the children themselves and not by the teacher. Fifthly, the students use pencils and conduct literacy activities on worksheets. But some of these literacy activities are unusual, such as drawing circles on the table around collected objects. Finally, the students seem amazingly engaged and animated about the activities they are involved with. Even in this brief vignette of the science inquiry classroom, it is clear that science inquiry provides a special and unique environment for learning worthy of consideration.

This brief vignette also raises some interesting questions relating to science, literacy and discourse. There is no doubt that discourse is heavily involved in the science inquiry classroom but what is this discourse and how is it characterized? Does this discourse allow science to develop? What is the role of literacy in this type of science classroom? Is there value in this activity for literacy development and for science learning? What is the role of the physical activities conducted by these students? How do the different modalities conducted by the children work together? Do these promote or hinder learning of literacy and science?

1.2 Social Context, Genre and Task in the Science Classroom: A Theoretical Orientation

This book is designed to explore the relationship between science, discourse and literacy in the early elementary school classroom. At the centre of this exploration is the idea that discourse is a contextualized activity that functions in particular ways in relation to specific contexts. Put simply, the idea behind this book is that we do not know enough about science, discourse and literacy in the elementary classroom. From the viewpoint of applied linguistics research, this question is important because the particular characteristics of scientific discourse and literacy may offer a unique perspective and description of communicative and representational development in this content area. From a science education perspective, this is important because it may provide insights into how scientific knowledge develops through a variety of communicative, representation and physical activities.

The broad theoretical perspective offered here is that discourse, literacy and learning are the result of social practice (Barton 1994; Barton, Hamilton and Ivanic 2000; Gee 1996; Street 1995). This theoretical approach places a significant emphasis on shared and accepted communal ways of behaving, interacting and communicating. Social participation within the community is dependent on learning these accepted and communal ways of behaving. The ramification of this position is that literacy (and any other behaviour or way of communicating) becomes specific to a particular community. Rather than thinking of literacy or discourse as general phenomena, they are conceptualized as socially contextualized activities which are directed by the guidelines of the community. The significance and meaning of any specific discoursal activity can only be understood within the context of the communal activity where this discoursal activity took place. The concept of a community is not limited to ethnic, religious, linguistic and national groupings. Any group of people working together to fulfil some communal aim are considered to be a community of practice. For our own purposes and within this book, the science inquiry classroom is considered a community of practice. The exploration of literacy, discourse and scientific development described in this book can only be understood in terms of the classroom and wider community of scientific practice within which these activities took place.

Social theories of literacy, such as the new literacy theorists and researchers, define literacy as 'a set of social practices; these are observable in events which are mediated by written texts' (Barton, Hamilton and Ivanic 2000: 9). This position coordinates external, observable activity and textual analysis with a social theory of meaning. New literacy theory posits that there are three components to be addressed in a study of social contextualized literacy: social practice, literacy events and written texts. Essentially, this position sees every act of literacy as conducted within an ideological social context that utilizes texts in social interaction. Observable literacy events (such as writing) and textual manifestations are explained in relation to the social context. As recognized by new literacy researchers, the emphasis on social theory is complementary to the actual analysis of the linguistic aspects of the texts that are actually produced. Hanauer (1998), utilizing the construct of genre theory, offers one approach for making the connection between text analysis and social theory explicit. Hanauer (1998), summarizing a variety of genre theories, states that an analysis of a specific genre involves three types of knowledge (Bazerman 1988; Freedman and Medway 1994a, 1994b; Hanauer 1997; Pare and Smart 1994; Swales 1990): functional knowledge of the purpose and use of the genre; structural knowledge of specific characteristic features of the genre; and procedural knowledge of prototypic reading/writing processes. Put simply, a genre is a text used in a communal setting to fulfil the specific aims of that community. Any community may use more than one genre to fulfil the different aims of the community. Through the history of practice each genre has evolved into a specialized format that can be textual and procedurally defined. This means that a community has specific expectations about the graphic and linguistic form of a text and the way this text is cognitively produced and comprehended.

However, while accepting the broad concept of social contextualized discoursal, literacy learning experiences, this book also accepts the idea of individual cognitive development. The basic principle here is one of interaction between the wider experiences in the social context and the internal cognitive system of the individual. The readiness and cognitive development of the individual learner are to be considered important components in literacy and learning in the science inquiry classroom. Learning and literacy are not only social activities; they are also internal, individual cognitive activities. The procedural component of genre theory, while promoting the concept of communally accepted ways of processing, also promotes the idea of cognitive processing as a central component of literacy and learning. Basically, to describe the relationship between literacy and science in the early elementary classroom, the issue of individual cognitive development needs to be addressed as well. Learning in this sense will be defined as the change in cognitive processing of the individual. This change can be considered at different points in time so as to provide a developmental, longitudinal description of cognitive change. In addition, in attempting to describe the elementary school classroom, it is important to consider what is appropriate for the cognitive development of the individual students in the science inquiry classroom.

As seen in the brief vignette presented at the beginning of this chapter, the science inquiry classroom offers specific challenges to the theoretical description presented so far. New literacy and genre theory are valuable for the understanding they bring to this context, but the science inquiry classroom seems to be defined by children conducting a series of tasks. The idea of tasks, as presented within applied linguistic research, connects the development of communicative abilities with the completion of required, real world tasks (Skehan 1998). These real world tasks are collections of communicative, representative and physical activities organized around the completion of a task that has real aims and outcomes. The participants are only interested in fulfilling the tasks, but the actual doing of the tasks involves using a variety of communicative and cognitive resources that the educational process is interested in. Thus the design of the education process becomes the presentation of a series of tasks to students that include the various communicative, physical and cognitive abilities that the educational process is interested in promoting. The idea of tasks works as an organizing principle that mediates between the overall aims of the educational process and the actual activities conducted in the classroom.

The overall theoretical position taken in this book can be summarized through the following basic propositions:

1. Discourse, literacy and learning are situated activities that involve an interaction between specific social contexts and individual cognitive systems.
2. The science inquiry classroom is considered to be a specific community of practice.
3. Within the science inquiry classroom students perform a series of specific tasks designed to fulfil the aims of the science inquiry classroom.

4. The tasks of scientific inquiry can be described in relation to the actions and cognitions that they include.
5. Specific genres are used to complete the tasks of scientific inquiry and fulfil the aims of the science inquiry classroom
6. The genres of science education have identifiable textual characteristics and are cognitively processed in specific describable ways.

When these propositions are combined and applied to the issue of discourse, literacy and science connections in the science inquiry classroom, the theoretical description that emerges is one of a hierarchy. The science inquiry classroom is considered to be a community of practice with specific educational aims. Within this social context, individual students are required to conduct a series of specific tasks. These tasks require discoursal, communicative and cognitive resources that the educational context desires to develop in the individual students. In order to complete these tasks a series of representational resources in the form of genres are required. These genres have specific textual and procedural characteristics that can be described through analysis. Learning these tasks and the associated genres is a developmental process. Over the period of time in which scientific inquiry is conducted, change in the cognitive and representational resources of the individual student is to be expected. This change, if found, will be manifest in the way the tasks are performed and the way the different genres are used. These changes are considered to be evidence of cognitive development.

1.3 The Design of this Book

In discussing the discourse, literacy and science of the early elementary classroom, the overall approach taken in this book is to fully ground any statements made by conducting qualitative in-depth research of a science literacy classroom and basing conclusions on this research. In other words, the description of scientific discourse that is presented here is grounded within a specific study of a science inquiry classroom. The value of this approach is that it provides descriptions that are really tied to the performance of specific activities in the classroom. This avoids the potential dangers of a superficial analysis of science and the broad application of general principles of literacy and discourse without really exploring the specific nature of scientific discourse in this context.

The design of the book closely follows the design of a research monograph as the book itself is based on a two year in-depth qualitative research project that explored the role of literacy and multiliteracy in a specific second-grade science inquiry classroom. The first three chapters of this book explore the theoretical and empirical foundations of scientific inquiry, literacy and cognitive development. The fourth chapter provides the methodological context and considerations that were employed in order to conduct this study. Chapters 5 and 6 provide a detailed qualitative description of the tasks and genres found within the context of this science inquiry classroom. Chapters 7 and 8 analyse the development of scientific and multiliteracy knowledge within the context of this science classroom. The last chapter provides an overview of the characteristics of scientific discourse and scientific inquiry as found within the context of this study.

Chapter 2: From Letter Recognition to Meaning Construction: Developmental Processes in Science and Literacy

2.1 A Neo-Piagetian Approach to the Concept of Cognitive Development

The aim of the current chapter is to provide an overview of the concept of cognitive development in relation to the domains of science and literacy. By attempting to address both literacy and science within the same discussion of cognitive development, this chapter touches on one of the major conceptual questions of the field of cognitive development: the extent to which cognitive development is domain specific. In terms of schools of thought this is the distinction between Piagetian and neo-Piagetian concepts of development. The Piagetian approach describes development as a series of stages which define and limit all cognitive actions performed by the individual child who is at a particular stage of cognitive maturation (Piaget 1954, 1962). The collection of theoretical positions organized under the heading of a neo-Piagetian approach postulates a much more significant role for the environment and domain-specific learning experiences (Biggs and Collis 1982; Case 1978, 1985; Fischer 1980; Fischer and Canfield 1986). The theoretical question becomes to what extent can situated learning experiences change and enhance maturational cognitive trends in development?

The overall theoretical position taken in this book postulates that the situated learning experience produces particular developmental responses in the individual child and, as such, is close to neo-Piagetian thinking. The current chapter considers that the discussion of situated learning is important for both the development of scientific thinking and literacy ability. From an educational perspective, the ramifications of this position are that the type of school experience is considered to play a major role in defining the outcomes of education in terms of cognitive development. At the same time, cognitive maturation is still considered to be a backdrop against which individual cognitive development occurs. The position taken here is that of Flavell *et al* (1993) that what Piaget managed to capture through his description of the stages of cognitive development was not hard-wired neurological realities, but rather broad developmental trends that characterize but do not define children at different ages. The situated experiences of learning interact with the point of developmental maturation that the child is at and have the potential of developing a child's cognitive abilities. This position places situated learning as the catalyst that pushes cognitive development forward and the trends of cognitive development described by Piaget as parameters within which this development takes place. Accordingly, if a child is exposed to a specific set of situated learning experiences, the potential exists for the development of specific cognitive abilities. Within this theoretical context the study presented later in this book provides a description of a specific science inquiry classroom and its particular set of learning experiences that will be seen to lead to particular cognitive developments in science and literacy.

2.2 The Development of Scientific Thinking in Early Elementary School

From a Piagetian perspective, early elementary school is situated within the concrete-operational stage of development. This stage of development is situated within the 7–11-year-old age group and roughly covers the first three years of elementary school. In broad terms, this stage represents the development of rudimentary logical thinking, specifically consisting of a movement from a central reliance on perceptual information to the ability to infer qualities beyond what can be directly perceived. To explain the nature of this developmental stage, Flavell *et al* (1993) summarize four aspects of developmental thinking that characterize the shift from pre-operational thinking to the concrete-operational stage of development:

1. *From limited, exclusive perception to wide, inclusive perception*: The development of cognitive abilities captured in this category relates to how children in the pre-operational and concrete-operational stages differ in relation to their perception of sensory data relevant to a cognitive task. The major difference consists in the development of a more inclusive and balanced approach to the perceptual input for the older children. In relation to Piaget's well known conservation of liquid quantity task, younger children focus on the limited perceptual field of the height of the liquid in the container. This single source of salient perceptual information is used to provide answers to posed cognitive problems. However, older children conducting the same task take into account the width of the container as well as the height of the liquid. In other words, older children understand that a wider more inclusive set of perceptual variables is important in order to provide a

satisfactory answer to the cognitive problem that has been posed. This usage of a wider perceptual frame of focus is a significant change in developmental thinking.

2. *From the perception of state to the focus on process*: The development of cognitive abilities captured in this category relates to how children in the pre-operational and concrete-operational stages differ in relation to their concept of change. When faced with a cognitive task that includes a series of changed states, younger children tend to prioritize the final state over initial states and to ignore the transformative process. This cognitive perspective dehistoricizes the final state and gives it prominence in responding to cognitive tasks. For example, in the well-known liquid conservation task, which consists of pouring equal amounts of liquid into different sized containers, younger children tend to focus on the final perceptual state of the liquid in the container and not on the fact that it was poured from another container. In other words, the final state of the liquid in the container is divorced from the historical process of change that produced the final state. Older children tend to have a more historical perspective of change when faced with a cognitive task that involves changed states. Older children address prior states and the process of transformation in resolving cognitive tasks that involve change. This wider conceptual framework includes the perceptual information of the final state and memorized information concerning prior states and transformative processes. This wider conceptual framework is a significant change in developmental thinking.

3. *From fixed perception to symbolic manipulation*: The development of cognitive abilities defined in this category relates to the ability of a child within the concrete-operational stage of development to rethink and manipulate existing perceptual states. Children within the pre-operational stage of development tend to perceptually and cognitively focus on the existing state of process and to consider this to be a final state that is unalterable. In other words, they dehistoricize and fixate on the existing perceptual state. Older children within the concrete-operational stage of development have the option of symbolically (and hence concretely) manipulating the existing state. As specified by Piaget this manipulation can consist of considering and actualizing the historical process that led to the current state (termed by Piaget 'inversion') or conceptualizing the process of change as movement of a constant mass (termed by Piaget 'compensation'). In problem-solving terms, the child within the concrete-operational stage of development when faced with the liquid conservation task may pour the liquid back into the original container in order to historically reconstruct the process. This type of action is based on the ability to move beyond the existing perceptual state and consider the historical process which created it.

4. *From perceptual estimate to quantitative measurement*: The development of cognitive ability related to in this category consists of an increased

understanding of the role of measurement in solving posed cognitive problems. Although children within the pre-operational stage of development do have rudimentary mathematical thinking they tend to solve cognitive problems through broad qualitative perception. Older children within the concrete operational stage tend to solve appropriate problems by considering options of quantitatively measuring as a method of solving the posed problem. In other words, measurement becomes a tool that can be used to interact with cognitive problems. Thus rather than basing decisions on perception alone, older children within the concrete-operational stage of development may utilize inferential problem solving based on quantitative data as a way of approaching the problem.

Within the Piagetian approach, the four aspects of cognitive development reviewed above present the outer parameters of the concrete-operational stage of development. When compared with the cognitive development during the pre-operational stage, these shifts are significant, specifically in relation to a child's ability to solve problems concerning processes in the physical world. The development of historical thinking concerning process, the ability to handle a wider range of data and the possibility of considering quantitative measures allows the child in the concrete-operational stage of development to infer understanding beyond immediate perceptual content and thus solve problems.

The main arguments against the Piagetian position presented above consist of evidence that children's development is uneven across domains and that children may in different contexts manifest behaviours and thinking patterns that are reminiscent of higher or lower stages of cognitive development (Case 1992). In other words, the argument is that the stage-like description of development does not capture the diversity of children's thinking within specific domains of knowledge and action. Several researchers within the neo-Piagetian context have attempted to explore the role of domain-specific knowledge in child development (Carey 1985; Chi *et al* 1988; Chi *et al* 1989). The results of these inquiries suggest that increased expertise within a specific domain of knowledge does facilitate cognition. For example, in a study of young (4–7-year-old) experts on dinosaurs, these children were found to be able to provide causal explanations based on inferences from specific characteristics of the dinosaurs (Chi *et al* 1989). This type of thinking shows the role of heightened levels of domain-specific knowledge that allows children to focus their thinking on specific aspects of the problem and provide relevant inferences within the context of the domain. From the perspective of the Piagetian description of uniform age-related stage development, this study and others like it provide evidence of the importance of domain-specific knowledge and the way this expert knowledge diversifies cognitive abilities.

One important domain to consider within the current context is scientific thinking. Young children develop theories that they use to interpret the physical world around them. These theories can relate to the scientific fields of physics and biology (Wellman and Gelman 1992). However, the presence of naïve theories of scientific phenomena does not mean that children at a young age have developed the epistemology of scientific thinking. The basic epistemological position of science is that claims are based on evidence. Thus scientific thinking requires clear understandings of the relationship between theory and evidence. There are several aspects in children's thinking which interfere with the development of a scientific epistemology:

1. *Confusion of theory and evidence*: Young children may find it difficult to actually distinguish between a theoretical explanation and evidence (Kuhn 1989; Kuhn and Pearsall 2000). This confusion makes coordination of evidence and claim problematic as theories and claims cannot be evaluated in light of evidence without an understanding of what actually constitutes evidence. The real world manifestation of this situation consists of the use of a tautological argument in which the same theoretical position is used as both the conclusion and the supporting evidence for the conclusion. When asked to explain their theories, children simply repeat the theory itself.

2. *Theory dependence and predisposition:* Children tend to need theories to explain phenomena. The theoretical explanation may relate to the current state of the observed phenomenon as in the case of younger children or, for older children, take into consideration historical evidence of process. But once a theory is in place, children seemed predisposed to holding on to this theory and are reluctant to change or discard it (Kuhn *et al* 1988). The ramifications of depending on a particular predisposed theory concern the coordination of evidence and theory. Once a theory exists, evidence that is relevant to the theory might be ignored if it is discordant with the predisposed theoretical orientation. Data that is addressed may be used in a very selective manner that only looks for supporting evidence. This creates a situation in which the relationship between evidence and theory becomes distorted and unscientific.

3. *Theory certainty:* Children may have difficulty with the idea that theoretical positions are uncertain, constructed and tentative. In relation to epistemic arguments, children up until the age of adolescence tend to take what Kuhn (2001) terms an absolutist position which defines knowledge as objective and certain. This leads to a situation in which children see theories as definite without the need to address factual evidence. The theory itself has the epistemological status of a fact. Situations of theoretical indecision and ambiguity resulting from alternative explanations of evidence cause difficulties for children and run counter to their epistemological understandings and are thus ignored in favour of a certain theoretical position.

These aspects of children's thinking construct a specific epistemological orientation towards scientific thinking. The overall direction of early scientific thinking seems to be situated on supporting existing naïve and partial theories. This tendency results from a limited understanding of the distinction between theory and evidence and the importance of evidence in generating theory. If evidence is used, it is within the context of selecting to address supporting evidence. On a basic level, a change in this epistemological understanding requires a shift in relation to the understanding of the role of evidence in evaluating theoretical positions.

2.3 The Development of Conventional Literacy

Early elementary school is a crucial period in the cognitive development of literacy. From a cognitive viewpoint, the period between first and third grades can be seen as the period in which conventional literacy is acquired (Pressley 1998). This period starts with an understanding of the alphabetic principle and ends with the ability to decode written text in a fluent manner so as to allow the construction of meaning to take place. During this period, children need to acquire the skills that will allow them to partake in the world of conventional literacy. Two basic types of skill are required to be able to read conventionally: the ability to transform written words into meanings in working memory and the ability to integrate multiple individual word meanings into an integrated discoursal meaning (Langenberg et al 2000). For conventional reading to develop both of these skills need to be addressed within the early reading and building fluency stages.

There are two distinct ways in which written words are transformed into meanings (Ehri 1991, 1994). The first way is by automatic sight recognition. This type of reading involves recognizing the word on the basis of its visual graphic format and is called sight reading. This is a very fast form of reading. Good readers have large vocabularies of sight words and these function as an aid in speeding up reading (Adams 1990). The second way words are read is by an analysis of the graphic and phonological information of a word and then the activation of the meaning of the word (Adams 1990; Ehri 1991). This type of reading involves three stages: analysis of the graphic form, analysis of the phonological form and finally activation of the meaning. This is a time-consuming process and requires a large degree of attention. This type of reading is called assembled reading because the task before the reader is the analysis and then assembly of the individual sounds into a sound unit that is recognizable as a word. Assembled reading is sometimes called decoding and mistakenly considered to be 'real' reading. In actual fact, mature readers do very little decoding when they read. This skill is reserved for words that are beyond their sight vocabularies. This is not to say the decoding is not an important skill but rather that it is just a transitional skill. While important in the early stages of reading, as reading ability develops it becomes of less and less value.

At the beginning of the early reading stage, readers have very limited sight word vocabularies and very limited knowledge of the relationship between specific letter forms and their sounds. Reading at this stage involves slow, laborious decoding based on a limited set of letter-sound mapping rules and a limited set of sight words (Ehri 1991; Ehri and Wilce 1987). This type of reading is termed cipher reading and usually involves the use of initial or final consonants as representing the whole word. Meaning construction during individual reading at this stage is difficult because a lot of the child's attention is directed at decoding (Barron 1977). However, with storybooks or connected discourse the child does have the option of using contextual clues in order to help identify the word being read (Ehri 1991, 1994). As the child learns more and more letter-sound mapping rules and the child's sight vocabulary grows the process of decoding becomes easier (Barron 1977). Writing during this stage is characterized by the use of invented spellings based on letter-sound relationships (Henderson 1992; Read 1986). In the initial stages of early reading, many of the invented spellings are incomplete and are based on knowledge of one or two letter-sounds. These are often in the initial or final positions. Development during the early reading stage involves the gradual increase of a series of letter-sound relationships and sight word recognition. Development is accumulative and the result of a literate learning environment and instruction.

By the end of first grade a child should have learnt all the letter-sound mapping rules (Pressley 1998). However, decoding will in most cases still be slow and to a certain extent laborious (Barron 1977). From the middle of first grade, after several letter-sound rules have been learnt, simple orthographic patterns can also be taught (Adams 1990; Stanovitch and West 1989). The acquisition of the understanding that clusters of letters can also be used to produce sounds is considered a stage of development in that the child must to a certain extent 'unlearn' what s/he has just learnt about individual letter-sound rules (Gough *et al* 1992). The orthographic principle is the understanding that clusters of letters form new sound patterns that are different from the individual letters. In other words, a grouping of letters can produce a sound which is not made up of the sounds of the individual letters (Gough *et al* 1992). For the early reader this poses two distinct problems. The first problem is that these clusters have to be remembered as clusters rather than individual letters to be decoded one by one. The second problem is that the child has to learn that letters have more than one sound associated with them. Acquisition of the orthographic principle is an important stage of development because reading by using orthography can speed up the child's ability to recognize words (Adams 1990; Berninger 1994; LaBerge and Samuels 1974).

At the early stages after the acquisition of the orthographic principle the child still relies mainly on letter-sound relationships. But as the child's knowledge of specific orthographic patterns grows, the reliance on letter-sound relationships alone decreases (Gough *et al* 1992). Parallel to this accumulation of recognizable orthographic patterns, the child's sight vocabulary should also be increasing. Readers at this stage use orthographic, alphabetic and contextual information to help them decode specific words in texts (Ehri 1991, 1994). Meaning construction at this stage may still be slow but the child's main concern is to understand the text and not to just vocalize the sounds of the word. Spelling at this stage still involves experimentation with the sounds of letters and letter clusters, however, it is more conventional in that conventional letter sequences are used (Henderson, 1992; Read 1986). During the early stages of the orthographic stage, sections of the letter sequences may be used and not the whole sequence. When orthographic knowledge does not exist, letter-sound relations are used.

By the end of second grade all the specific letter-sound mapping rules and the orthographic rules of the language should have been acquired (Pressley 1998). What is left to do, is the practice of use of these patterns and the gradual increase in word recognition speed. The main emphasis of the child should be on constructing meaning and the decoding process should become less and less effortful. By the end of third grade a child should be able to read approximately 150 words a minute in an age appropriate written text on an issue that the child knows about (Carver 1992). This reading speed is not optimal but allows the child to focus on meaning construction and signifies that the child is not focusing on decoding.

In some ways the development of decoding ability within the early reading and beginning fluency stage can be characterized by the strategy used by the child in recognizing words (Ehri 1991, 1994; Marsh *et al* 1981). The initial stage of word recognition is based on sight. The word is identified by the shape of the word and its visual features. In some cases this will lead to attempting various different words that could be connected to this form. This type of word recognition is usually found before the acquisition of the alphabetic principle. The next stage of word recognition also uses the visual form of the word but in addition makes uses of the initial and/or final consonant of the word. This type of word recognition is characteristic of the initial period after the acquisition of the alphabetic principle. The next word recognition strategy is based on analysing the sounds of the word. This analysis sounds out each of the letters of the word. It is a slow and laborious analysis which may or may not include blending the sounds together. This type of word recognition is characteristic of the early reading stage after a child has learnt a series of specific letter-sound correspondences. The next stage of word recognition is based on the use of letter clusters as well as letter-sound correspondences. This type of word recognition is found after a child has learnt a series of specific orthographic patterns and has begun to use them to read and spell. Finally, the last stage of word recognition is relatively fluent and is based on a large sight vocabulary and solid knowledge of orthographic patterns. Word recognition at this stage is quick and automatic in most cases. It should be noted that children should be encouraged to use all and any resources they have to recognize words. This type of holistic approach may include word analysis on the graphic or phonetic levels and use of the contextual information in the case of connected discourse.

Table 2.1 summarizes the stages of development that are present within the period from first grade to third grade.

To a large extent as seen in the review above the major concern of researchers and educators considering the early elementary school years relates to the development of basic, conventional literacy abilities. This agenda usually translates into directing resources into developing a deep understanding of the linguistic forms of literacy and less attention is directed at the meaning construction.

Table 2.1 Stages of Literacy Development from First to Third Grade

A. Cognitive Development

Alphabetic Principle (An understanding that specific graphic forms represent sounds)	*Orthographic Principle* (An understanding that specific clusters of letters represent sounds that are different from the sounds of the individual letters)

B. Developmental Literacy Ability

Cipher Readers (Phonological decoding stage, the reader uses a system of rules which map specific letters and some letter sequences to phonological form)	*Orthographic Readers* (Readers use letter sequences/blocks as a central aid in the decoding of words)
Letter-Name Spelling (Spelling based on the alphabetic principle. Letters are used to represent sounds but the spelling is incomplete and sounds in the word may not be represented or represented in an unconventional way)	*Transitional Spelling* (Spelling that uses both the alphabetic and the orthographic principle. Letter sequences which are different from the individual letters are used. When the orthographic rule is not known letter sound rules are used)
Form-Directed Meaning Construction (Autonomous meaning construction is slow and laborious with most of the child's attention being directed at the decoding of the graphic forms. Few attentional resources are left for the construction of meaning)	*Meaning-Directed Meaning Construction* (Autonomous decoding is fluent enough that most of the child's attention is directed at the construction of meaning)

2.4 Characterizing Developmental Trends in Science and Literacy in the Early Elementary School

As seen in the review above, from a developmental perspective the early years of elementary school pose options for significant developments in cognitive abilities in relation to both scientific thinking and literacy. As stated above, the overall approach taken in this book towards the issue of development is that of a neo-Piagetian approach that conceptualizes cognitive development as sensitive to environmental, educational experience and more general trends of individual cognitive development. In this sense the current review of literature presents some broad developmental parameters within which the specific potential developments of the elementary science inquiry classroom can be explored. In evaluating cognitive development in the science-literacy classroom the following aspects would seem to be significant:

1. *Understanding the role of empirical evidence*: This essentially consists of an epistemological development in which empirical evidence is given the role of qualifying and evaluating theoretical positions. The development of this understanding would result in the initiation of a scientific epistemology of knowledge.
2. *Widened perceptual abilities*: This consists of being able to recognize and then use, within a problem-solving context, more than one perceptual source of information. Directing attention to several relevant sources of perceptual information allows increased abilities to address and resolve posed problems.
3. *Development of historical understanding of process*: This consists of the development of a historical understanding that present states, although perceptually salient, actually are the result of prior states. This understanding of process is crucial for scientific understanding to develop.
4. *Development of systematic observation*: This consists of the development of methods of observation and recording that allow evidence to be used in theory evaluation. This shift can involve new quantitative methods of observing.
5. *Development of inferential processing*: This consists of a child's ability to move beyond the immediate perceptual context and to infer qualities that cannot directly be observed. The development of inferential processing is crucial for the development of an understanding of process and to construct logical scientific arguments.
6. *Focus on meaning construction*: This consists of a change in the way literacy is understood. Rather than conceiving of literacy as an aim in itself, literacy is understood as a method of generating and exploring meaning. This consists of a shift from a focus on the forms of literacy to the use of literacy to fulfil real world learning tasks. Literacy in this context serves the purpose of enabling learning to take place.

7. *Development of conventional literacy abilities*: This consists of the acquisition of the conventions of reading and writing on the local and global levels. These developments should include increased fluency, use of orthographic patterns of spelling, extended writing abilities and increased understanding and usage of different genres.

Chapter 3: Teaching Science: The Revolution and Ramifications of Elementary School Science Inquiry

3.1 The Historical Context of Scientific Inquiry as a Teaching Method

For the last 15 years, educational researchers in the US interested in science education have been working to change the concept of scientific classroom pedagogy. Fuelled by disappointing results of US students on international science and maths comparisons (NCES 1996, 1998), descriptions of the nature of scientific knowledge and scientific pedagogical practice have widened from an emphasis on factual knowledge and terminology to a consideration of scientific cognition, argumentation, communication and experimentation (AAAS 1993; NRC 1996). At the centre of this shift in pedagogical objectives is the emphasis on students' direct involvement with activity-based scientific learning. The National Science Education Standards (NRC 1996) state that 'scientific inquiry is at the heart of science and science learning' (p. 15). The concept of scientific inquiry is broadly conceptualized as involving a range of activities including making observations, posing questions, using a variety of scientifically informed print resources, designing experiments, reaching conclusions based on empirical data and communicating scientific findings (NRC 1996). However, as pointed out by Anderson and Helms (2002), this shift in perspective brings with it the requirement for research directly addressing the characteristics of inquiry-based scientific learning. Specifically, as identified by Anderson and Helms (2002) there is a need for research that addresses the practical details of scientific inquiry in the classroom, to explore the student roles and cognitions in this learning environment and to consider the roles of the teacher in enhancing this form of learning. Britton *et al* (2000) are even more exact in their identification of the research that needs to be conducted. In a forum designed to promote educational science research, they propose that contextualized research within real classroom settings that addresses the actions, thoughts and roles of students and teachers involved in scientific inquiry needs to be conducted in order for a fuller understanding of what scientific inquiry in the science classroom actually involves. While some research has been conducted on scientific inquiry in the classroom, still little is known about scientific inquiry in the early elementary school classroom.

In a parallel development to the shift of focus to inquiry-based science pedagogy, the role of scientific epistemology and the role of literacy in science education have come to the forefront of many discussions of educational practice in the science classroom. The connection between these two developments resides in the importance of communication and representation in scientific practice and in the science classroom. Groundbreaking work, such as Lemke (1990), has shown the science classroom to be situated within specific parameters of discourse not necessarily accessible to all students. The teaching of science cannot be addressed without an understanding of the discourse of science. More traditional science educators, such as Kuhn (1993), have investigated the role of argumentation in the science classroom and presented the position that without explicit discussion and understanding of the epistemology of science, an inquiry-based classroom is difficult to conduct. The development of scientific epistemology within developmental and educational frameworks underpins any meaningful activity in relation to science inquiry activities. In more recent developments, scientific practice and science education are seen from a multimodal and multiliteracy perspective. Kress *et al* (2001) address the multiple modes and ways in which scientific knowledge is shaped within the classroom and propose that any discussion of scientific literacy must be widened so as to be able to address the multimodality of the science classroom.

3.2 The Inquiry-based Science Classroom

Inquiry-based science instruction is based on the idea that students need to be actively involved in the processes of science in order for scientific knowledge to develop. The roots of this movement towards scientific inquiry are both constructivist and based on a specific conceptualization of what science is and how science is conducted in the real world. Professional scientific inquiry in this formulation is characterized as a problem-solving activity directed towards the process of concept discovery and modification (Qin and Simon 1990). Of particular importance within this problem-solving context is the use of experimental data within the format of hypothesis testing. It is the evaluation of empirical, systematic data collected for the purposes of understanding natural phenomena that is seen as one of the main distinctions of scientific thinking. In the real world of scientific activity, the discovery of new scientific understandings is tied to the scientists' evaluation and interpretation of unexpected empirical findings (Dunbar 1995, 1997).

The educational ramification of this description of science was the requirement that school science reflect the practices of science as it is practised in the laboratories of the world. This shift essentially involves a widening of the school science curriculum to include two different types of knowledge: substantive knowledge informed by current, scientific informed concepts of natural phenomena; and procedural knowledge of the thinking patterns and methodological procedures utilized by real scientists. In this context, the scientific inquiry is seen as a way of developing both these types of knowledge while at the same time engaging the students in interesting activities within the classroom. As summarized in an early statement from the National Science Board, 'students are likely to begin to understand the natural world if they work directly with natural phenomena, using their senses to observe and using instruments to extend the power of their senses' (1991).

Research, mainly focused on middle and high-school students using scientific inquiry, has generally provided positive results for this method of teaching science. The ability to work in the laboratory and interpret data was seen to develop in middle-grade students (Mattheis and Nakayama 1988). A series of conceptual and scientific thinking patterns, such as knowledge of terminology, critical evaluation and understanding of scientific process, was seen to develop in middle and high-school students involved in scientific inquiry (Llyod and Contreras 1987). Scientific inquiry was also promoted as a more inclusive mode of science teaching that may allow students from minority backgrounds greater access to the world of science (Rodriguez and Bethel 1983). Beyond anything else scientific inquiry has been shown to be truly engaging for students from a variety of different backgrounds (Reiss 2000)

However, scientific inquiry has also been questioned as a method of science instruction. In an innovative study, Millar (1998) questions the openness of the school laboratory experiment to alternative understandings of accepted substantive descriptions of scientific concepts. In other words, is the scientific inquiry experience really a case of inquiry-based science? Millar used the metaphor of rhetoric to show how the activities of scientific inquiry are manipulated to provide specific, historically defined answers. In this formulation scientific inquiry as a teaching method is not inquiry-based but rather is a form of simulated demonstration of existing knowledge. Nott and Smith (1995) further show how teachers manipulate the actual classroom demonstrations so that they conform to the accepted position on how they are supposed to perform. This is once again not so much science inquiry as demonstration of a known scientific fact.

Thier and Daviss (2002) propose a more balanced approach to the definition of the science inquiry activity. They propose that scientific inquiry in the classroom is actually a purposely directed and informed activity and not a case of open inquiry. They term this approach to scientific education as *guided inquiry* and define this as 'using a series of structured sequenced scientific investigations that integrate appropriate processes and information chosen through research, to fashion meaningful learning experiences for children' (p. 12). In this formulation, students do conduct a series of inquiry activities, but these are purposely designed to direct the student towards a particular understanding that is accepted as knowledge within the wider community of scientists.

3.3 The Professional and Educational Discourse of Science

Educational and applied linguistic accounts of professional scientific activity significantly modify the description of scientific activity presented above. While the collection of empirical data may be central to the work of empirical researchers, this data is not self-explanatory. Rather, as seen in the descriptions of professional scientists, it is the discoursal construct within which the data is conceived that makes it meaningful to the development of scientific concepts. It is scientific thinking and, by extension, scientific discourse which are crucial to the activity of scientific discovery. Essentially this involves the recognition that science is a field in which theories are socially constructed within a community and that scientific knowledge is heavily dependent on language to provide a tool for the expression of scientific theories, hypotheses and conceptualizations (Kuhn 1962; Taylor 1996). As stated by Osbourne (2002) in this formulation, 'science is a complex interplay of phenomena, data, theories, beliefs, values, motivation, and social context both constituted by, and reflected in, its discourse' (p. 206). Based on this concept of science, a scientific education must involve the acquisition of the discourse and thinking patterns of science as a basic requirement for the participation in the scientific community. Thus, the components of the science curriculum need to be reconceptualized to include patterns of scientific thinking and discoursal knowledge and research needs to be conducted that is sensitive to the discoursal nature of scientific knowledge development.

Analyses of scientific language present the role of language as intrinsic to the scientific endeavour. As shown by Giere (1991), data is transformed into scientific knowledge through a quite complex process of reasoning and argument conducted through linguistic tools. The main task of the scientist becomes the contextualization and interpretation of data within a system of explicit verbal statements. Predictions and results are verbal constructs that are presented, used and manipulated by the researcher in order to transform the data into meaningful scientific concepts. Kuhn (1993), working within the context of discourse argumentation, describes this process of data-based concept development in the laboratory as a coordination process involving reciprocal adjustment in which evidence is used to modify, change and evaluate alternative theories of the phenomenon under discussion. For Kuhn (1993), the pedagogical ramifications of this position are clear: science as inquiry needs to be supplemented with science as argument. The epistemology of science, with its emphasis on language and argumentation, should be an explicit part and aim of the science classroom. This is especially true since most science teachers assume that language is a transparent medium that directly transfers meanings in an unambiguous form (Lemke 1990). A simplistic perception of language and its relationship to science holds the danger of interfering with the students' ability to actually conduct scientific inquiry and by extension to create useful scientific understandings. Thus, not only the language of and epistemology of science needs to be discussed, but the complexities of linguistic negotiation in relation to evidence and data need to be understood and then modelled in the classroom setting.

As pointed out by Osbourne (2002), the verbal statements produced within the laboratory are rarely left in the realm of the spoken word; to claim scientific status they need to be circulated in written form to other members of the scientific community for evaluation. As with any other literate discourse community, the forms of writing used in science fulfil a series of specific functions and take on specific genres of presentation (Atkinson 1999; Bazerman 1988). In this formulation, learning science involves learning the representational resources used within the discourse community of scientists (Kelly and Bazerman 2003). As stated by Osbourne (2002) 'the central goal of science education is to help students to use the language of science to construct and interpret meaning' (p. 208).

The genres of scientific writing have characteristics which take them beyond the usual patterns of literacy usage found within the language arts classroom dominated by an emphasis on the humanities. This position echoes the work of Lemke (1990) on the inaccessibility of scientific discourse, spoken and written, to non-scientists. Scientific writing tends to extract the personal statement from its self-presentation based on the idea that subjectivity has been distanced from the contents of the text. The description, theory or proposed concept is presented to other scientists without the presence of the direct agency of the writer (Osbourne 2002). Scientific writing utilizes specific usages of known words and high concentrations of specific terminology developed within small communities of scientific specialists (Montgomery 1996). Both of these vocabulary aspects cause difficulty for non-scientist readers or writers. Scientific writing, focused on the development of coherent arguments that relate data to evidence through the presentation of argument patterns, tend to extensively use logical connectives (Wellington and Osbourne 2001). While in other forms of writing these may seem superfluous, in scientific writing they serve the purpose of making connections explicit so that the scientific argument and concept can be evaluated. Scientific writing also tends to be multimodal, incorporating a variety of different visual and graphic formats into its written format (Hanauer 1997; Lemke 1998). Lemke (1998) points out that the genre of a science text is a form of primitive hypertext, directing the reader to different information sources such as footnotes, visuals and other sources.

This aspect of multimodality and multiliteracy has been the focus of attention of some of the more recent work on scientific literacy (Kress *et al* 2001; Lemke 1998; Lowe 1993). Much of the emphasis on multimodality has been directed towards the use of pictures and graphic representations within science. In a meta-analysis of science text, Lemke (1998) found that there is at least one graphic/visual representation on every page of a professional scientific text. The relationship between visuals and science can be found in the nature of the information being represented. For example, representing change, fluctuation, degree, quantity, ratio, proportionality and non-linear relationships may be achieved in a more direct and meaningful way through visuals than with words. While the spoken and written word may be crucial for the negotiation of scientific concepts, visual representation would seem to be a major component of actually representing the results of tool-based observations of the world. The ability to comprehend or produce a visual representation is a learnt skill. Lowe (2000) points out that science teachers may assume that visuals are self-explanatory and do not require negotiation or explication. This problem is further compounded as a result of the specialized nature of some visual representations within the realm of science. Knowledge of everyday or artistic visual representation may not help with the comprehension of visuals designed for specific scientific representations. Most teachers have not been prepared to handle this aspect of science education, and very little research addressing the way visuals are used in the science classroom exists (Lowe 2000).

The focus on multiliteracy is not limited to the role of visual representation. Kress *et al* (2001) take multiliteracy and multimodality one step further by proposing that all semiotic resources are functional in the promotion of scientific learning. Lemke (1998) summarizes this conceptualization of science by stating, 'To do science, to talk science, to read and write science, it is necessary to juggle and combine in various canonical ways verbal discourse, mathematical expression, graphical visual representations and motor operations in the world' (p. 87). Within the educational context, recent multimodal analyses of secondary school students have shown how written, visual and physical modes are used to shape the students understandings (Kress *et al* 2001). The development of scientific knowledge is seen to result from the usage of multiple representational resources and is not limited to the spoken, written or visual representation. This direction in research has ramifications on the way science education (and especially teacher training) is understood. In addition to the widening of the science curriculum from an emphasis on the substantive knowledge to the inclusion of procedural knowledge, current positions would suggest a further widening of the concept of representational knowledge to clearly include the variety of semiotic resources used to represent and develop scientific knowledge.

3.4 Directions for Current and Future Research on Scientific Discourse

The research project presented in this book consists of a qualitative study of a specific science unit – 'The Sandy Shoreline' – used in a diverse, second-grade classroom in the California Bay area. As discussed in the theoretical summary above, several forms of knowledge are currently valued as part of educational practice within the science inquiry classroom. These types of knowledge consist of substantive knowledge of scientific facts, processes and concepts; procedural knowledge or methods of scientific inquiry; patterns of scientific thinking and argumentation; and representational knowledge of how to utilize written, visual and physical modalities for the preservation of observation, the development of scientific concepts, the organization of scientific knowledge and the evaluation of data in light of hypotheses and contrasting explanations. The theoretical summary presented above emphasizes the position taken by Britton *et al* (2000) that more in-depth qualitative investigation is required of the way children (especially in the early years of elementary schooling) acquire different forms of scientific knowledge while studying within a scientific inquiry classroom and that these studies should be situated within environments that provide a diversity of linguistic and academic achievement levels. The review also makes it clear that any current study of the science classroom needs to address the multimodality and multiliteracy of science education. The direction of the research presented in this book is to directly address this series of concerns through the in-depth qualitative analysis of a specific, elementary science inquiry classroom. Put simply, this book will attempt to answer the following questions:

1. What characterizes the process of substantive scientific knowledge development in this science inquiry classroom?
2. What characterizes the process of procedural scientific knowledge development in this science inquiry classroom?
3. What characterizes the process of written literacy scientific knowledge development in this science inquiry classroom?
4. What characterizes the process of visual literacy scientific knowledge development in this science inquiry classroom?
5. What is the role of multiliteracy in the development of scientific knowledge?
6. What are the characteristics of scientific discourse?

Chapter 4: Researching Scientific Inquiry in the Elementary Classroom

4.1 Research Methodology

The research design utilized for the investigation of scientific discourse in the science inquiry classroom consisted of a series of qualitative data collection and data analysis stages. The research study was situated within a particular site and essentially consists of a qualitative in-depth study of science education in a specific second-grade science inquiry classroom. The specific science unit that was studied was entitled 'The Sandy Shoreline' and dealt with the shoreline ecosystem. Overall, a grounded, qualitative multiliteracy approach was taken in this analysis. The materials were analysed in a cyclical manner moving among a series of data analysis and data collection stages. These stages included the collection of video classroom data, the collection of written classroom materials and science portfolios, the generation of a coding system, the analysis of a sequence of coded items, the analysis of task components, multiliteracy analyses on the content, genre and cognitive components of the products created in the classroom and a series of interviews with participants. As is required practice with qualitative data, the analyses were checked and rechecked against the raw data and at different points in the analysis were evaluated for reliability with other researchers and then presented to participants for modification and validation purposes.

4.1.1 Site Description

The data for the current study were collected in a second-grade classroom in a low income area in the California Bay region. Sixty-six per cent of the school students were English language learners with 94 per cent of the students qualifying for free or reduced-price lunch. The large number of English language learners in the school and the second-grade classroom in which the data were collected posed educational challenges. Only 2 per cent of the English language learners were found to be proficient

in English/language arts on the 2002 California Language Arts Test.
Only 6 per cent of the English language learners were found to be proficient in maths on the California Standards Test in 2002. The school and
the teaching staff provide English language learner programmes and
individualized support for English language learners in the classroom
setting, including the use of the reading recovery programme, literacy
academy and after-school tutoring. The school defines lower levels of
English proficiency as a major hurdle to educational practice and thus
places English language instruction as a major priority on its educational
agenda.

   The individual classroom in which the data were collected for the
science unit provided a rich environment for the study of science inquiry.
The class consisted of 20 students in all. The classroom was well kept, with
books, pictures and artistic materials in full view and access. The science
unit investigated in the current study was team taught by a member of
the science unit professional development team and the classroom teacher.
Both members of this team were highly experienced teachers with over
ten years of professional teaching experience in public school settings. A
two lesson block within the regular school day was set aside for work on
the science unit. The science unit was taught for five weeks in the autumn
of 2003.

4.1.2 Stages of Data Analysis and Data Collection

The data collection and data analysis stages were intertwined within this
qualitative study. The stages of this process are outlined below:

1. *Stage One: Structural and procedural analysis of class textbook and teacher's
   classroom log:* The first stage of research consisted of an analysis of the
   textbook used by the teachers in this class and the teacher's classroom
   log which described on a lesson-by-lesson basis the development of the
   course. As an initial starting point the analysis provided an overview of
   structure of the course and the series of proposed activities, readings
   and scientific and literacy knowledge that the course covered. The
   analysis provided an overview of the development of the whole course
   as a series of tasks that needed to be conducted by the students and
   a description of the assumed conceptual development of scientific
   and literacy knowledge through these tasks. The practical aim of
   this analysis was to identify potential points of conceptual scientific
   and literacy knowledge development. These were used to direct the
   video data collection process for the current study. At the end of the
   data analysis process the teacher's classroom logs were reanalysed and
   each of the specific analyses was situated in relation to its place in the
   overall science unit development.
2. *Stage Two: Student participant interviews:* Stage two consisted of a series
   of interviews with students at the data collection site. The aim of the

interviews was to identify a group of four children with a range of literacy and language abilities and personality traits that would make them good candidates for focused video data collection. The interviews were preceded and followed by an interview with the teacher in the classroom. A group of four students was formed on the basis of these interviews. The group consisted of students with high and low literacy levels and one English language learner. For the videotaping of tasks consisting of small-group work, this particular group of students was focused on.

3. *Stage Three: Video data collection:* The third stage consisted of video data collection. A camera with an operator was situated in the classroom. The unit of data collection was the completion of the specific task being conducted. The video operator was instructed to capture on the tape the verbal interaction, the physical actions on the table, any use of visual aids (such as drawing) and the social interaction surrounding the task. In addition, an audio microphone was attached to the table to enhance the audio data. Following data collection all the video and audio data was transferred to a DVD format and stored on compact discs.

4. *Stage Four: Coding system development:* The fourth stage consisted of the development of a reliable and valid coding system for the video data. In order to provide a detailed analysis of the video data a coding system was developed for this specific data set. The coding system needed to cover physical, visual and verbal data in the classroom setting while conducting hands-on science-literacy activities. As a starting point for the coding system, a comprehensive literature review of coding systems dealing with science and classroom activities was conducted. This literature review allowed the production of a rich concept map of potential systems of coding. Following this, a series of sessions were held in which the video data was observed and aspects of coding recorded. This produced a rudimentary coding system that was applied to the first video task for analysis. At this stage the coding system in its initial form was written up with descriptors defining its application. Two independent researchers then used this system to code the initial video data. The independent codings were compared and inter-rater agreement evaluated. The inter-rater agreement was 87 per cent. The coding system was then utilized for a full analysis of each of the videotaped tasks. For each task the developed coding system was evaluated for its ability to comprehensively cover all verbal, physical and visual aspects of the video data. For each specific task, additions were made to the coding system. These additions followed the same process of development as the whole coding system. Independent ratings were conducted by two researchers, descriptors were defined and inter-rater agreement was evaluated. Inter-rater agreement ranged from 82 per cent to 91 per cent. Any disagreements among independent researchers were resolved through discussion and

clarification and/or modification of the video data coding system. This cyclical process produced an extensive integrated coding system that comprehensively covered the verbal response, actions and visual representations present within the video data.

5. *Stage Five: Coding of video data:* The fifth stage consisted of the detailed analysis of each of the science-literacy tasks. The video data was transcribed on a separate file. The transcription provided the spoken dialogue, a short form of the actions that were conducted including pictorial representation and a timeline of activity. The analysis using the coding system was conducted on the full transcript. The analysis was conducted while viewing the video and audio data and carefully considering the transcript. A full analysis of each video was conducted that involved comprehensively coding the whole transcript. This process was conducted independently by two researchers and results were compared. Inter-rater agreement ranged from 82 per cent to 92 per cent. The product of this analysis was a fully coded transcript of each of the videotaped tasks.

6. *Stage Six: Analysis of task characteristics:* The sixth stage of analysis consisted of analysing recurring sequences of coded elements in the transcripts. The aim of this analysis was to try and identify the characteristic stages of each task. This process was both a bottom up and a top down process. Recurring sequences of coded items were noticed and recorded and then the meaning of these coded sequences within the wider video data was analysed. This bidirectional analysis provided an analysis of the tasks that combined the micro-level of coded description with the macro-analysis of stages of the task. The product of this stage was a detailed description of the way each task was completed and main stages of that task. In all, six major tasks were analysed in this way.

7. *Stage Seven: Analysis of multiliteracy classroom products:* Throughout the classroom work on the science unit, students produced a series of written and pictorial products. Each of these products for each of the students was collected in a portfolio by the classroom staff. At the end of the teaching of the science unit, these portfolios with the associated classroom products were collected by the research team and analysed. These multiliteracy products covered the entire class on any given day and addressed exercises done as part of the study of the science unit. As such, these materials provided a snapshot of the students' knowledge at different points in the science unit and could be used to document conceptual developments in knowledge of science and literacy. The analysis was conducted on three different levels: content analysis, genre analysis and cognitive analysis. The content analysis addressed the content of the multiliteracy products and was designed to elicit evidence of the structure, depth and extent of the students' knowledge. The genre analysis addressed the representational forms that were used by the students while studying science in

this classroom. The analysis was designed to elicit information on the representational resources of the students and the representational requirements of science-literacy activities. The cognitive analysis addressed the cognitive processes involved in the production of the various products. In all, 12 multiliteracy products were analysed. These products covered all stages of the science unit instruction. Each product was considered and analysed individually, but lessons learnt from each analysis of a specific literacy product were carried over to the next literacy product to be evaluated. The process of analysis was cyclical, in which first the materials were read in an open receptive manner and discussed by two researchers. Then a method of analysis was decided upon. In some cases, this was very straightforward and consisted of identifying content, counting sentences and words, or defining organizational structures. In some cases, expert advice was required. This was especially true for the pictorial representations. In cases such as these, a qualified art educator was contacted and asked to provide feedback and ideas for analysis. This expert was also asked to conduct the analyses in conjunction with the researchers. The result of this process of consultation was the development of methods of analysis for both verbal and pictorial information represented in the various products. Once a method of analysis was established, the analyses were carried out. All analyses were conducted independently by two researchers and then results were compared. Agreement was high between the two researchers, ranging from 90 per cent to 100 per cent.

8. *Stage Eight: Validation processes:* During the data collection and initial analysis stages, a series of meetings was held with the science unit development team. In these meetings, the direction of video data analysis and the coding system used were discussed in light of the specific experience of this team in the classroom used for this study and their wider experience of working with the 'Sandy Shoreline' science unit. All comments and issues raised were taken into consideration in the evaluation and modification of the coding system and analyses. In addition specific meetings were held with the two classroom teachers to get initial input on some of the understandings to emerge from the data analysis. Following the analysis of all the data a draft report was compiled and sent to the science unit development team for consideration and validation purposes.

4.2 The Science Unit

The science unit investigated in the current study was entitled 'The Sandy Shoreline' and was originally developed by the Marine Activities Resource and Education programme of the Lawrence Hall of Science at the University of California at Berkeley. In broad terms the programme was designed to develop scientific knowledge of the sandy shore ecosystem for elementary school (second to fourth grade) children. The programme follows an interdisciplinary, science inquiry approach to the development of scientific knowledge and defines itself as a programme that will 'encourage the acquisition of both science and language, especially among English language learners.' The programme aims at developing knowledge of science as a field of inquiry, specific knowledge of sandy shores as an ecosystem and literacy knowledge associated with science and science learning.

As defined by the science-literacy development team at the Lawrence Hall of Science, the sandy shores unit develops the following National Science Education Standards:

A. *Science as inquiry* (Scientific abilities): Employ simple equipment and tools, use data to construct a reasonable explanation, and communicate investigations and explanations. (Understandings of scientific inquiry): Scientific investigations involve asking and answering, scientists use different kinds of investigations, simple instruments provide more information, scientists develop explanations using observations and what they already know, scientists make the results of their investigations public, and scientists review and ask questions about the results of other scientists' work.

B. *Physical science* (Properties of objects and materials): Observable properties, measurable properties, objects are made of materials that can be described and categorized by the properties, and materials can exist in different states and can change from one state to another by heating or cooling.

C. *Life science* (Characteristics of organisms): Organisms have basic needs and can survive only in environments in which their needs can be met and each plant or animal has different structures that serve different functions. (Organisms and environments): All animals depend on plants, humans depend on their natural and constructed environments and humans can change environments.

D. *Earth science* (Properties of earth materials): earth materials are solid rocks, soils, water and the gases of the atmosphere and soils (and sand) have properties such as colour and texture. (Changes in earth): The surface of the earth changes, some of these changes are due to slow processes and weather changes from day to day and over the seasons.

E. *Science and technology* (Abilities of technological design): Identify a simple problem, propose a solution, implement proposed solutions, evaluate a product or design and communicate a problem design and solution. (Understanding about science and technology): Science is one way of answering questions and explaining, people have always had problems and invented tools and techniques to solve problems, scientists and engineers often work in teams with different individuals doing different things. (Abilities to distinguish between natural and human-made objects): Some objects occur in nature, others have been designed and made by people to solve human problems and objects can be categorized into two groups, natural and designed.

F. *Science in personal and social perspectives* (Types of resources): The supply of resources is limited and if used, resources can be extended by recycling. (Changes in environments): Environments are the space, conditions and factors that affect individuals and populations, changes in environments can be natural or influenced by humans, and some environmental changes occur slowly and others occur rapidly. (Science and technology in local challenges): People continue inventing new ways of doing things, solving problems and getting work done.

G. *History and nature of science* (Unifying concepts): Systems, order and organization; evidence, models and explanation; constancy, change and measurement; evolution and equilibrium; and form and function.

The science-literacy development team at the Lawrence Hall of Science also defined a series of science-related literacy standards appropriate for second and third graders that were to be developed within the framework of the sandy shores science unit. The standards are as follows:

A. *Expand knowledge of concept and process related language in science* – Learn new words and concepts from reading, listening to and discussing conceptually challenging material, use knowledge of prefixes, suffixes and roots to determine the meaning of words, use resources and references to determine the meanings of words and use a standard dictionary to determine the meaning of unknown words.

B. *Participate effectively in discussions of science investigations, texts and personal knowledge* – Listen responsively and critically; respond to speakers by contributing, connecting and asking questions; participate actively; communicate effectively with others, using appropriate vocabulary; and retell and summarize what has been said by another speaker and ideas that are built during discussion.

C. *Follow and give directions* – Give and follow oral and written directions, give oral presentations and/or directions.

D. *Read every day from independent-level and more challenging material across a range of science genres, using comprehension strategies and responding to these texts* – Set purposes for reading and recognize purposes for various texts, use strategies to understand and to monitor comprehension, make well supported predictions and other inferences, and demonstrate comprehension by answering questions and/or in writing or by drawing and discussing visual images based on text descriptions.

E. *Actively make connections in writing and discussions between text and experience* – Move between and compare text-based information, concurrent experiences and personal/prior knowledge.

F. *Engage in second-hand textual inquiry related to scientific concepts/topics under study* – Generate questions, use reference material, gather, record and organize information from text, use structural features to locate information, summarize and retell texts, recognize themes, main points and important details in text, represent information in different ways including story maps, graphs and charts and interpret and use graphic sources of information.

G. *Demonstrate learning in oral and written reports.*

H. *Develop understandings about language and literacy in science* – Know different functions in language; recognizing various science-related genres and their features; understand authorship and point-of-view and capture meaning from figurative language.

I. *Write every day using the processes, conventions and discourses of science* – Choose topics for writing and use pre-writing strategies; write focused and organized texts; write well-supported and descriptive texts; write using the conventions of science genres; write for a variety of purposes; use models of writing; write for a variety of audiences and demonstrate awareness of audience and purpose; use appropriate vocabulary and evaluate and monitor writing.

J. *Evaluate and respond to scientific writing* – Respond to other's writing, evaluate texts and distinguish fact from opinion.

The overall design of the 'The Sandy Shoreline' science unit consists of the definition of five inclusive activities. The specific activities are termed 'Beach Bucket Scavenger Hunt', 'Sand on Stage', 'The Sights that Sand has Seen', 'Build a Sandy Beach' and 'Oil on the Beach'. Each of these activities includes a series of more narrowly defined activities including scientific inquiry, classroom discussion and associated literacy and multi-literacy activities. Table 4.1 summarizes the main components of each activity in the unit and the key educational aim of the unit. In addition, it outlines the context of the video data and multiliteracy products that were collected, analysed and presented in this study.

4.3 Video Data Coding System

As reported in the data analysis section of this chapter a system of coding was developed to analyse the video data of a small group of students conducting a series of science-literacy activities. This coding system was developed to comprehensively cover the range of verbal responses, actions and visual representations utilized by students and teachers in this specific classroom. The coding system was developed in a gradual, cyclical, grounded manner that utilized the video data, transcribed versions of the videos, and theoretical materials and dialogue among researchers and participants. The categories of code that emerged from this analysis provided definitions of the types of verbal, visual, physical and conceptual activity that the students were involved with while conducting science-literacy tasks. In all, 19 categories of code were found that covered the responses of the students while conducting the science literacy activ-ities: noticing, grouping, questioning, argumentation, counter statement,

Table 4.1 Outline of Science Unit Activities, Key Educational Aims and Associated Analyses Conducted

Science Unit Activity	Key Educational Aim	Analysed Video Data	Analysed Multiliteracy Product
1. Beach Bucket Scavenger Hunt			
1.1 Planet Ocean Brainstorm: Class consists of teacher-directed discussion relating to water on the globe and introduction of a notebook for the recording of observations. 1.2 Brainstorm and Concept Map: Working in small groups, the students create concept maps. 1.3 Reader: Classroom reading of expository text and creation of postcards. 1.4 My Buddy Says: Dyad description of beach knowledge and observations.	* Knowledge activation relating to beach and sea *Discussion of role of evidence and observation * Concept mapping * Experience of conducting investigation based on observation * Experience of categorization process * Development of scientific vocabulary and written observations		1.1 Colored world maps; notebook picture covers 1.2 Beach photograph description 1.3 Beach bucket observation sheets; Evidence categorization (human; animals; plants and non-living); Beach bucket Venn diagram; My Favourite shell/rock descriptive essay 1.4 Beach books
1.5 Beach Bucket Explorations: Working in small groups, students observe, sort and categorize found objects in sand buckets. 1.6 Mini Books: Students create mini books based on the concept map.		1. Task One: Development of Scientific Thinking – Categorization (Beach Bucket Explorations)	

Science Unit Activity	Key Educational Aim	Analysed Video Data	Analysed Multiliteracy Product
2. Sand on Stage			
2.1 Partner Parade and Anticipation Chart: Dyad discussion of sand and the mutual creation of a chart that summarizes the dyad's knowledge of sand.	* Concept mapping * Experience of conducting investigation based on observation * Use of scientific tools to provide directed observation using rudimentary idea of measurement		2.1 Sand on stage directed observation page; The unknown sand page; My sand summary (1st and 2nd draft) 2.2 My Inference Worksheets
2.2 Science Inquiry of Sand: Students in small groups observe sand using lenses and microscopes. These observations are written up on an observation worksheet.	* Comparison of observations *Inference in relation to observed qualities * Written report of observations	2. Task Six: Development of Scientific Description: Knowledge of Tools of Measurement (Sand Observation)	
3. The Sights Sand has Seen			
3.1 My Buddy Says: Dyad discussion of the way sand is formed. 3.2 Reader: Shared classroom reading of the reader 'Sandy's Journey to the Sea' and the creation of a story chart. 3.3 Postcard Stories: Individual creation of postcard stories. 3.4 Discussion: Teacher-led discussion of sand as material.	* Development of understanding of a scientific process * Construct causal relationships * Summarization through visual and written modes of representation	3.1 Task Two: Understanding Process Through Shared Reading 3.2 Task Three: Summarization of Scientific Process through Picture Drawing 3.3 Task Four: Summarization of Scientific Process through Narrative Writing 3.4 Task Five: Development of Scientific Vocabulary	3.1 Directed picture drawing in four parts; Postcard Stories – pictures and written narrative

Science Unit Activity	Key Educational Aim	Analysed Video Data	Analysed Multiliteracy Product
4. Build a Sandy Beach			
4.1 Partner Parade: Discussion of animals and plants on the beach.	* Concept mapping * Reading encyclopedic genre * Note taking		4.1 Written report; Beach animals and plants report
4.2 Report Writing – Beach Animals and Plants: Each student using an encyclopedic information page and other informational sources creates a report on a chosen animal or plant from the beach ecosystem.	* Report writing – knowledge of the processes and structures of informative report writing		
5. Oil on the Beach			
5.1 Partner Parade and Class Discussion: Dyad and class discussion of uses of oil and oil spills.	* Knowledge activation and concept mapping * Observation and comparison * Rudimentary experimental design		
5.2 Science Inquiry of Oil on Feathers: Students compare feathers dipped in water and dipped in water and oil. Predictions and observations are recorded.	* Prediction (hypothesis) * Observation reporting		

Science Unit Activity	Key Educational Aim	Analysed Video Data	Analysed Multiliteracy Product
5.3 Tide and Oil Slick Demonstration: The teacher creates a demonstration of how a tide works and what happens when there is an oil spill. Students observe the demonstration and offer descriptions and explanations.			
5.4 Cleaning an Oil Spill: Students working in small groups use different materials to clean up a simulated oil spill. Before the activity they predict outcomes and after the activity write up results.			5.1 Oil on the beach – observation and prediction worksheet

restatement, elaboration, integration of knowledge, world knowledge, word meaning, text discussion, text writing, picture discussion, picture drawing, literacy discussion, active participation, general statement, emotive response and classroom management. This coding system was the basis for the subsequent analysis of the stages of conducting each science-literacy task. In the section that follows each category of response is defined and an example is provided.

Noticing

A noticing response was defined as the process of directing attention to a specific aspect of the phenomenon that was being explored in the science inquiry activity or a science-literacy activity. Noticing processes were in general multimodal responses combining physical pointing (or touching) and a verbal utterance. For example, one student, while exploring a simulated beach in an activity called 'Beach Bucket Explorations' picked out a shell from the sand and announced, 'It smells like paint'. This student drew attention to the shell and a specific attribute of the shell, its smell. Different things were noticed by the students conducting the science-literacy activities. These included drawing attention to physical attributes, noticing the material of the object under consideration and directing attention to an object by naming it.

Grouping

A grouping response was defined as the process of creating a connection among two or more objects. This process of connecting objects could be a physical phenomenon such as picking up and collecting items together or it could be done verbally by providing a general term that defined a collection of objects. The basis for the connection among the objects could relate to a physical attribute shared by the objects, or the type of material that the objects are made of. The grouping of the objects could be based on the students' world knowledge or in some cases through the direct comparison to a written text (or another authority like a teacher) that provided a detailed description or a visual representation. For example, while at the end of the 'Beach Bucket Explorations' activity two students leafed through a science book with pictures, descriptions and names of shells and sea animals. The two students looked at the shell they had found in the simulated beach bucket and at the pictures and descriptions in the book. After a while they found the shell and announced finding it. With the help of the teacher they read the name of the shell as 'a Princely Cone. A cone fit for a prince.' Grouping objects together could be verbal, physical or a collection of both verbal and physical. Not in every case was the collection of objects given a clear verbal reason of being grouped together. In some cases, students would group some objects together and just give a very general terms such as 'things' to designate the grouping.

Questioning

A questioning response was defined as an utterance or an action that questions an aspect of the task being performed or explained. The process of questioning demonstrates the students' critical appraisal and deliberation in relation to decisions that have been made, explanations that have been proposed or the way tasks have been performed. Questions were proposed in relation to the way an object is named, the material of an object, the source of an object and the group membership of an object. Questions were also used by teachers to focus students on specific aspects of a process, a task or a decision that they had made. In this way teachers directed students to consider and evaluate what they know about the phenomenon under discussion or observation. For example, as part of the process of introducing a class reader one of the classroom teachers asked the students, 'What force could work on a shell to make it into sand?' The teacher's questioning of the students' world knowledge made them focus on explanations of how beaches and specifically sand were formed. In this example, this primed the students for the comprehension of the classroom reader that addressed this particular process.

Argumentation

An argumentation response was defined as an utterance that was part of a series of statements that together formed an argument relating to a specific phenomenon. The basic structure of an argument that was addressed in the current data set consisted of a claim that was supported by evidence, especially empirical evidence. The science unit aimed to promote this form of scientific argument. This type of argument was used by the teachers in explaining phenomena and in the design of the different tasks, but was difficult for the second-grade children in the current data set when they worked independently. The development of a scientific argument was mainly part of the teacher–student interaction and discussion with the teachers presenting basic claims and then questioning or directing students so as to elicit types of evidence and support to promote or qualify the specific claims being made. For example, in the development of the understanding of scientific vocabulary relating to the processes of erosion and weathering, one of the classroom teachers asked the students, 'What part of that that you just described was what actually broke her into smaller pieces? What was the force? Remember jolly ranchers? What was the force?' The teacher referred the students to a classroom demonstration that consisted of placing some sweets in a plastic container and shaking it around until they broke into smaller and smaller pieces. This demonstration exhibited the role of different forces in breaking rocks into sand. The general processing claim that is forwarded by the teacher was that forces could break rocks. The evidence she referenced came from the 'jolly ranchers' demonstration and knowledge from the reader relating to specific forces such as waves and the weather which fulfil the same role. Later, as part of the same scientific vocabulary development, the students physically rubbed a soft rock and turned it into powdery sand providing additional experiential and empirical evidence supporting the more general claim of how sand is formed.

The series of potential statements used to create a scientific argument supported by evidence consisted of general claims and processing claims. Both of these propose a hypothesis or a conclusion relating to a phenomenon that is being explored. In addition to claims, an argument can include reference to empirical data or hypothetical data based on prior background knowledge. In the teacher's discourse, the validity of the hypothesis of conclusion may be addressed and statements that may have been made may be qualified. Some of the teacher utterance categorized under the heading argument also made an effort to express the structure of a scientific argument.

Counter statement

A counter statement response is an utterance or an action in which a previous statement, claim or decision is countered by the presentation of a different option. The counter statement comes as a response to a statement of decision that has already been made. This counter statement negates the original statement and offers new options for understanding. This counter statement can be in relation to the naming of an object, the claims proposed in relation to an object or the grouping of an object. A counter statement is an important part of a critical interaction among students and the tasks that they are conducting. It is a process in which the modification and change in understanding is directed. A counter statement is usually a verbal response, but it can also be a physical response as well. For example, while conducting a small group exercise that involved comparing bags of sand in relation to the size of the grains of sand by using a magnifying glass, one student created a rank ordering of bags of sand from small to big. Another student took out her magnifying glass and changed the order of two bags. By so doing the student countered the decision made by a member of the group and offered another option.

Restatement

A restatement response is an utterance or action which reaffirms a statement or decision that has already been made. This restatement is a repetition of a previously made statement or the affirmation of that statement or decision. This reaffirmation may be as a verbal statement or in the form of a physical affirmation such as a nod of the head in agreement. Verbal restatement does not imply that the new statement is a verbatim representation of what was already said. The verbal restatement addresses the deep structure of what has been said and provides a reaffirmation of the statement or decision. Restatement appeared within group work among students and in the interaction with the teacher. As part of the student–teacher interaction, restatement was used as a way for the teacher to reaffirm the student statements and then in many cases to extend these through a subsequent question or elaboration. In small-group work, restatements established group decisions and proposed understandings. For example, while working with a magnifying glass, one student saw a white piece among the grains being observed. She identified this as a piece of bone. Another student reaffirmed this understanding by restating 'bone, bone.'

Elaboration

An elaboration response is an utterance that extends a statement that has already been made. This elaborative statement addresses directly or indirectly a statement, claim or categorization that has been made. This elaboration is achieved by adding new information, ideas or categories to the statement that has been made. Verbal elaboration was found in the interactions in small-group work and teacher–student interactions but was more prevalent in the teachers' discourse. The teachers used elaboration to extend the students' knowledge of ideas and concepts. For example, in a discussion of potential forces that could create sand from rocks a student proposed that a thunderstorm was such a force. The teacher picked up this idea and then elaborated on it by stating, 'A thunderstorm with lightning … so I could imagine maybe lightning striking a tree. The tree maybe could fall and crush a rock'. Elaboration was also an important part of vocabulary instruction in that the meanings of words were extended by elaborating on the students' current understandings of the words being learnt.

Integration of knowledge

An integration of knowledge response is an utterance that connects two or more previously made statements and proposes a more comprehensive understanding of the phenomenon that is being investigated or discussed. As an integration of knowledge utterance takes statements that have already been made and combines them in an inclusive statement, that makes the connection among the different pieces of information salient. Different patterns of knowledge integration were found in the current study. These consisted of the integration of previous statements according to patterns of cause and result, chronology, comparison and contrast and narrative. These integrative patterns were found in the discourse of the students and the teachers. Teachers used integrative responses to summarize understandings that were developed within the classroom by the whole class or by individual students. The integration of knowledge response played an important role in the establishment of an understanding of scientific processes being taught. For example, in a teacher-led class discussion of the forces involved in the formation of sand, a series of options were raised by the students. The teacher addressed several comments that had been made and integrated them using a cause and result pattern into the following summarizing statement: 'OK to freeze and to warm up, to freeze and then warm up. That's really hard on rocks. That causes cracks in rocks to be frozen and then unfrozen and get warm and then freeze again. It causes those cracks to happen. And if a crack happens in a rock, maybe it ends up falling off. And so that rock ends up being a little bit smaller.' When students used integrative statements they tended to use patterns of narrative or chronology.

World knowledge

A world knowledge response was defined as a statement or question that related to a speaker's knowledge of the world or the speaker's personal experience. In making a response of this kind the speaker uses knowledge that is stored in long-term memory and relates to the speaker's knowledge of the world. This is not an analytical response but rather an activation of existing knowledge. This activation of prior knowledge provides additional information that can be used to understand a phenomenon being observed or discussed and to provide inferences relating to this phenomenon. For example, in one of the class discussions, the teacher asked the students what forces could form sand. One student answered, 'people' and when asked how, he continued by saying, 'step on it'. The idea that people create sand was not within the classroom discussion until this point. Essentially the student had used his own experience and knowledge of the world to propose a new option of a force.

Word meaning

A word meaning response was defined as a statement or question referring to vocabulary items and their meaning. As this was a second-grade classroom with a majority of English language learners the learning of vocabulary was a priority for both students and teachers. The vocabulary addressed included words that were specific to the science unit being studied (words such as 'erosion' or 'weathering'), but also included more general items. For example, in the introduction to a classroom reader, the teacher asked the students, 'What does journey mean?' She received the answer, 'An adventure?' and later from another student, 'Does it mean travelling?' During the literacy activities students asked the teachers to help them understand specific vocabulary items.

Text discussion

A text discussion response was defined as a statement or question relating to the content and world described in a written text. As this was a second-grade classroom with a majority of English language learners, discussion of class or individual readings was part of the curriculum of literacy learning as well as the study of the science unit. The response of text discussion consisted of those classroom interactions in which explicit discussion was directed at the different levels of meaning to be found in a text. This response type included discussions of local and global meaning of the text as well as to predictions as to coming content. The category of text discussion was also extended to statements which addressed the purpose of the text. Teachers explicitly engaged in text discussion to enhance both the literacy skills of their students and to ensure that the specific material being learnt was comprehended by students. The discussion of text meaning was achieved through both questions and statements. For example, in an exercise that followed the reading of a classroom reader, students were required to use the reader to write their own narrative. During this activity one student was having difficulty continuing his story. The teacher read what the student had written and asked, 'Now, here's what I want you to tell. I want you to tell how she got from being on the beach to being part of the sandcastle. How did she get moved from the beach?' The teacher's response got the student involved with the content of the text that he was developing.

Literacy discussion

A literacy discussion response was defined as a statement or question relating to the performance of a literacy act. This type of response included discussions of the genre aspects of a text, such as a suitable structure, discussions relating to the author or illustrator, discussions of the potential audience and any intertextual connections that could be found. Most importantly for this second-grade classroom, this category included comments made by the teacher that made students direct their attention to the print or the specific graphic, phonetic or orthographic components of reading and writing. This is an important aspect of any second-grade classroom as it allows basic literacy skills to continue to develop. For example, while working with the vocabulary associated with a shared class reader, one of the classroom teachers introduced the phrase 'beach wrack'. The second classroom teacher then addressed the orthography of the word 'wrack' when she stated, 'And look at the spelling of the "w" and the "r" together. It's different than the "rack" that you hang something on'.

Text writing

Text writing was defined as the observed activity of writing as part of the educational process of learning this science unit. Within the analysis of the video data this was defined as the actual activity of placing pencil to paper and physically writing. Text writing was conducted as part of the recording of observations, as an aid to categorization or in the writing of extended reports.

Picture discussion

A picture discussion response was defined as a statement or question relating to the comprehension or production of a picture or a photograph within the educational setting of learning the science unit. This type of response was mainly found in the teacher's discourse and consisted of directing students' attention to the information in the pictures or photographs. These visual representations were used for informational purposes and through teacher interaction students were directed to consider the local and the global information in the pictures. Discussions of this type were used to summarize information taught in the classroom as well as to direct students to develop their own writing utilizing pictorial information as a cue. For example, as an introduction to a shared class reading, the teacher focused on the front picture of the reading book and said, 'Everybody put your finger on that first picture.' The second classroom teacher then questioned a specific student by saying, 'Starting place. Good. OK, M, try that one again. Where's Sandy starting?' Both teachers used the front picture as a source of information to be discussed in this knowledge activation exercise.

Picture drawing

Picture drawing was defined as the observed activity of drawing as part of the educational process of learning this science unit. Picture drawing was defined as the actual activity of using artistic materials to produce visual images. The analysis of the video data revealed two broad types of picture drawing: drawing which focused on the outer contours of the objects being drawn and pictures which focused on the specific details of the pictorial representation. Picture drawing was used at various stages in the science unit by both the students and the teacher. The teacher used this mode of representation for summarization purposes and the students were required to use pictorial representations to record observations, make comparisons and represent the knowledge they had acquired.

Active participation

Active participation was defined as a series of physical or verbal actions in which children participated in a shared classroom activity. As a scientific inquiry unit in a second-grade classroom many activities required the active physical participation of the students. These included using various instruments, working with various materials and performing those actions required in order to conduct the observations and experiments designed as part of the science unit educational practice. In addition, since this was a second-grade classroom that included classroom readers, there was also active participation as part of the shared reading process. This included reading along with the teacher in a whole class choral reading format. These physical activities by the students were preceded by directives given by the teacher. Active participation was also used by the teachers to teach vocabulary items. For example, while teaching the concept of erosion, the teacher directed the students to rub a piece of pumice against a harder stone. Each student had the experience of physically turning the pumice stone into fine powder.

Classroom management

A classroom management response was a statement that was directed at maintaining appropriate classroom behaviour. As with any second-grade classroom, comments of this type were required in order to make sure that the appropriate behaviour that allowed learning to take place could occur. These comments consisted of redirecting students to the tasks in hand, addressing a series of small interruptions in the classroom and general issues involved with the running of a classroom. For example, during a class discussion, the teacher turned to one of the students and said, 'Ch. You need to look this way and talk to L. later.'

Emotive response

An emotive response is a verbal or physical response in which an emotional reaction is expressed. These emotive responses were found as a reaction to some of the science inquiry activities conducted in the classroom. These responses tended to be either of excitement or disgust (or a mixture of both). For example, in a discussion of the experience of walking on the beach the teacher asked the class, 'Can you imagine what seaweed might smell like when it rots?' Various students responded by making faces and saying 'yuck' or making 'yucky' noises.

General statement

A general statement response was defined as a personal comment made by the students not connected to the learning experience. These personal statements did not help the performance of the activity that the student was involved with and did not promote any additional understanding of the science or literacy material. These comments were extra-curricular and addressed either the social lives or activities of the students, such as programmes on television or sporting activities.

Table 4.2 summarizes the complete coding system used for the analysis of the video data and provides a brief key description of each of the specific codes that were used.

Table 4.2 Category Name and Abbreviation for Coding Science Classroom Video Data

Category Name	Abbreviation	Brief Definition
NOTICING	**N**	Directing attention to a specific aspect of the phenomenon
Noticing Physical Attribute	**NA**	Directing attention to a physical attribute such as sight, sound or smell
Noticing Material	**NM**	Directing attention to material of object
Noticing Object	**NO**	Directing attention to object through naming
GROUPING	**G**	Grouping several objects as a collection
Physical Grouping	**GP**	Picking up and collecting two or more items
Verbal Specification of Series of Objects	**GVS**	Noticing a series of objects in close progression leading to a verbal grouping
Verbal Specification of a General Term	**GGT**	Providing a general term that defines a collection of objects
Grouping through Physical Attribute	**GPA**	Group objects according to a defined physical attribute
Grouping by Material	**GM**	Group objects according to shared material
Grouping through Reference to an Authority	**GRA**	Found objects (or groups of objects) are compared to a written text or another authority providing detailed scientific description
Grouping through Reference to World Knowledge	**GWK**	Observed objects are grouped under headings that come from the student's knowledge of the world
Unspecified Grouping	**GU**	Objects are collected but no verbal definition is given or an unspecified name such as 'things' is applied
QUESTIONING	**Q**	A question is posed relating to an aspect of the task being conducted

Category Name	Abbreviation	Brief Definition
Questioning Naming	QN	A question is posed as to the way an object has been named
Questioning Material	QM	A question is posed as to the material defined for an object or group of objects
Questioning Site	QS	A question is posed as to the physical site of an object or the source of the object
Questioning Categorization	QC	A question is posed as to the term used to categorize a group of objects or in relation to the membership of the objects to the group
Questioning World Knowledge	QWK	A question that is posed in relation to knowledge of the world
Questioning Knowledge of a Process	QP	A question relating to the understanding of a process
ARGUMENTATION	**A**	A series of statements constructing an argument relating to a specific phenomenon
Claim	AC	A new understanding, hypothesis or conclusion relating to a phenomenon is proposed; this understanding attempts to explain what is being investigated
Process Claim	ACP	A new understanding, hypothesis or conclusion that explains the world in the form of a process – cause and result, chronological-procedural
Empirical Data	ADE	Use of observed physical phenomena (facts) as a basis for a proposed hypothesis which students have access to and use
Hypothetical Data	ADH	Address a phenomenon which has not been observed but is used in support of a proposed hypothesis
Warrant	AW	A statement that explains why the hypothesis is a valid conclusion based on the empirical or hypothetical data

Category Name	Abbreviation	Brief Definition
Qualifier	**AQ**	A term used to assign a condition to a hypothesis
Argument Discussion	**ARD**	Statements addressing the form of a scientific argument
COUNTER STATEMENT	**CS**	A statement which counters a previous statement or decision that has been made
Countering Naming	**CSM**	Countering the naming of an object
Countering a Claim	**CSC**	Countering the proposed understanding (claim) of the observed phenomena and proposing a different hypothesis
Countering Categorization	**CC**	Countering the proposed grouping of objects
RESTATEMENT	**R**	A statement or decision that has already been made is restated and reaffirmed
ELABORATION	**E**	Elaboration or extension of a prior statement or claim that has been made; this may involve extending the claim to include new categories
INTEGRATION OF KNOWLEDGE	**I**	Two or more previously stated utterances are connected creating a more comprehensive understanding of the phenomenon under investigation
Cause and Result Integration	**ICR**	Two or more previously stated utterances are connected using a cause and result pattern
Chronology Integration	**IC**	Two or more previously stated utterances are connected using a pattern of chronology
Comparison and Contrast Integration	**ICC**	Two or more utterances or observations are connected utilizing a pattern of similarities or differences
Narrative Integration	**IN**	Two or more previously stated utterances are connected using a narrative pattern

Category Name	Abbreviation	Brief Definition
WORLD KNOWLEDGE	**WK**	A statement or question relating to world knowledge or personal experience
WORD MEANING	**WM**	A statement or question referring to vocabulary items and their meaning
TEXT DISCUSSION	**TD**	Statements and questions relating to the world described in the text
Text Purpose	**TDP**	A statement or question relating to the purpose of the text
Local Meaning	**TDL**	A statement or question relating to the local level of meanings usually related to characters, actions, settings and descriptions
Global Meaning	**TDG**	A statement or question relating to the global meaning of the text usually relating to theme, plot, outcomes, main ideas and resolutions
Predict Content	**TDPC**	A statement or question that requests or is based on a prediction of content that has been explicitly stated
TEXT WRITING	**TW**	The construction of a written representation for educational purposes
PICTURE DISCUSSION	**P**	Statements or question relating to pictures used in the educational setting
Local detail	**PL**	A statement or question relating to a local or specific detail in the picture
Global Meaning	**PG**	A statement or question relating to the global meaning of the picture and/or relating the relations between a series of pictures
PICTURE DRAWING	**PD**	The creation of a visual represen-tation for educational purposes
Drawing Details	**PDD**	The creation of specific details in the pictorial representation

Category Name	Abbreviation	Brief Definition
Drawing Global Contours	**PGC**	The creation of the global contours of the objects being drawn and/or the pictorial representation of global relations such as a narrative or cause and result structures
LITERACY DISCUSSION	**LD**	Statements or questions relating to literacy or the performance of a literacy act
Genre	**LDG**	A statement or question relating to the genre of a text; statements of this type can relate to the structure of the text type being discussed
Author and Illustrator	**LDAI**	A statement or question relating to the author or illustrator of a text or picture
Audience	**LDA**	A statement or question relating to the audience of the text or picture
Intertextuality	**LDI**	A statement or question relating to other texts or pictures
Literacy Comment	**LC**	A statement or question addressing the performance of a literacy act
Attention to Print	**LP**	A statement that directs the students' attention to the print in the written material
ACTIVE PARTICIPATION	**AP**	Physical or verbal actions in which the children participate in a shared classroom activity such as a shared reading
Read Along	**APRA**	Reading along with the teacher
Fill in Blanks	**APF**	Provision of words from the text before the teacher has read them aloud

Category Name	Abbreviation	Brief Definition
Perform Actions	**APA**	Physical acting out of the content of the text or directions given by the teacher; this can include performing a series of actions required for the science unit; clapping, verbalizing or acting in response to a written text; or use of instruments
Action Directive	**AD**	A statement is made directing another participant to perform a physical action
Reference to Active Participation	**APR**	A statement referring to a previous experience of actively participating
GENERAL STATEMENT	**GS**	A personal comment not directly connected to the learning activity
EMOTIVE RESPONSE	**ER**	A verbal or physical response is made which expresses an emotional reaction
CLASSROOM MANAGEMENT	**CM**	A statement is made directed at maintaining expected classroom behaviour

Chapter 5: The Tasks of Scientific Inquiry

The aim of the video data collection and analysis was to provide in-depth information relating to the way the scientific inquiry tasks of the science unit were conducted by a specially selected group of children. The analyses in this chapter provide detailed analyses of the implementation of the 'The Sandy Shoreline' science unit in this specific classroom. The analyses provide a detailed, qualitative account of the tasks and activities of scientific inquiry. The video data related to a series of chosen moments of potential educational growth. As seen in the overview of the unit as a whole and the general description of the programme, these scientific and literacy tasks were multiliteracy tasks that integrated various modes of representation.

5.1 Beach Bucket Explorations: Categorizing Objects

The development of scientific knowledge is dependent on the development of a scientific epistemology of knowledge. One crucial stage in this development is the understanding of scientific observation and categorization. Observation and categorization are basic components of any scientific argument in that they specify the conditions of relevance for the description of a scientific process. As opposed to common knowledge or experiential knowledge of the world, scientific epistemology requires definitional accuracy based upon observable and replicable criteria.

The analysis presented below relates to the classroom activity of 'Beach Bucket Explorations'. This activity is essentially an activity that aims at providing students with an observational investigation followed by a categorization task. The educational aim of the activity is to develop an understanding of systematic observation and categorization. This activity consists of small groups of students exploring simulated beaches, finding objects in the sand and then categorizing them. This process of observing and categorizing involves a movement from a holistic concept of sand to a differentiated understanding of the components of sand and their sources. Figure 5.1 summarizes the main stages defined for this task.

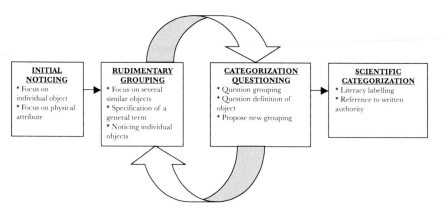

Figure 5.1 Stages of Development of Beach Bucket Exploration Task

As seen in Figure 5.1, four main stages were observed for the development of this task. The middle stages 'Rudimentary Grouping' and 'Categorization Questioning' were cyclical in that these two stages were revisited several times before a categorical decision was made in the last stage of 'Scientific Categorization'. In the following section a detailed discourse analysis is provided for each stage. Each stage is defined by the progression of coded categories found in the detailed analysis. A symbolic notation system based on the coding system presented in Chapter 4 (see Table 4.1) was used to define each stage.

Initial noticing

NA + NO + NM

This stage is characterized by a process of noticing individual objects. The process of observation consists of noticing specific objects by their name, material or physical attribute. No attempt is made to place them in a group. The object that is noticed is presented as an individual case. This is essentially a process that would be expected at the beginning of learning about observation and categorization. However, it can reappear as a process at later stages. See the following sequence as an example of this process.

> *I: These ones look broken.*
> *T: This shell—*
> *M: It smells like paint.*
> *T: That's a shell!*
> *I: Look at this! A brush!*
> *S: [inaudible]*

I: Plastic stuff.
T: Hey look there's noise in here!
I: That's a neat rock! Look at this rock.

In this short section, a series of students notice specific items in the sand bucket. Each item is removed from the box, and a statement is made. Noticing the item consists of recognizing and naming an object, noticing and physically testing its physical attributes or making a decision as to the material of the object. In this example, the students are collecting a series of objects without placing them in groups but clearly differentiating them from other objects.

Rudimentary grouping

N (NO, NA, NM) + GP + GVS + R + QC + GGT

This stage is characterized by the creation of an initial grouping of items. In this stage, items that have been noticed as single items are redefined as members of a group of items. This process of group membership can be achieved by the physical action of placing items together, the verbal redefinition of an item as a representative of a group or the recognition of a series of similar objects. The following example presents one sequence of rudimentary grouping.

I: That's shells.
Teacher: You have a shell group here.
M: We have a fossil … rock.
Teacher: You have a fossil! Where are you going to put that?
I: The rocks.

In this example the students have already noticed individual objects and have picked them out of the sand and placed them on the table. The concept is still essentially of individual objects but the beginning of a group can be identified through the creation of collections of items and the use of the plural in relation to these objects. In this stage the teacher's role is pivotal as she redefines the collected objects as 'groups'. The teacher also uses a question about categorization to force the children to make a decision as to the category and group membership of an object.

The next example shows a case of the students working independently of the teacher in creating rudimentary groups.

I: Sticks … sticks … sticks.
M: Ropes.
I: Sticks.

In this example, the students physically collect noticed objects. The process of noticing includes finding a series of similar objects and placing them together. This is a simple form of grouping that is mainly based on finding similar objects rather than considering the physical attribute or material of the object. In these two examples, the creation of groups and categories is still at an early stage and is conducted through the more salient features of object identification. However, the concept of grouping items does exist at this stage and groups are being formed both conceptually and physically with the objects from the sand bucket.

Categorization questioning

N (NO, NA, NM) + G (GP, GVS, GGT, GPA, GM) + CC + Q (QC, QN, QM) + IK

This stage is characterized by the questioning and/or countering of an existing decision about the category of an object or a grouping. This stage is important in that through verbal interaction the group categories are modified and changed. Decisions made about the nature of an object or the grouping of a series of objects is questioned and decisions made by students are once again revisited for further consideration. This process can be subsequent to decisions that have already been made and may have a cyclical relationship with the rudimentary grouping stage. These two stages in conjunction allow more coherent groupings of objects to emerge. This stage can also come prior to a decision about the nature of an object or the grouping of an object and the questioning and countering function as part of the process of actually deciding what the category of an object is. Consider the following example of questioning the category of a noticed object.

> *I: Look! That one has a crab!*
> *M: Where?*
> *I: A dead crab! That one inside it!*
>
> . . .
> *I: Ew! Ew!*
> *A: That's not feathers.*
> *M: That's not a dead crab.*
> *A: Is it alive?*
> *M: No, it's a baby shell. It's a baby shell trapped in there.*
> *T: Here's the wood.*
> *A: Where?*
> *T: Open it.*
> *I: It looks like sand to me.*
> *M: Yeah, because there's sand in there and the baby shell is trapped in there.*

In this example, a group of students is attempting to define a found object. The object consists of a small shell stuck in a bigger shell surrounded by sand. The smaller shell is noticed by one of the students and identified as a crab in a shell. This categorization of the object is countered by another student and a new hypothesis is proposed. The crab is really a shell. This is followed by additional noticing and ultimately the category is decided in conjunction with the integration of previous knowledge in the form of a more comprehensive hypothesis that explains what is being observed. The final categorization of a shell in a shell is supported by a causal explanation. In the next example, categorization is modified through a teacher's interaction.

> *Teacher 1: — What do you call this one?*
> *M: Things.*
> *Teacher 2: Look at the shapes, you guys.*
> *Teacher 1: Things? What do they all have in common? Why did you put them in this group?*
> *T: Rocks don't go right here.*
> *Teacher: Oh, so T. says rocks don't go there —*

In this example, the teacher questions the students about a group of objects that have been placed together on the table. The name given to this group, 'things', leaves the category very open and essentially has not been well differentiated. A second teacher relates to this situation by directing the students' attention to the attributes of the objects and questions the underlying reasons for grouping these objects together. This question leads one of the students to counter a categorization judgement that has been made and directs a change in the physical grouping on the table. The next example shows a group of students questioning both the nature of an object and the group category.

> *I: What is this little thing? Looks like a goblin!*
> *M: It's a fossil.*
> *I: Why did you put this inside here?*
> *T: Things! Things!*

In this example, one of the students has found an unidentifiable object. She is interested by it but cannot recognize it. The answer is provided by another student. This is followed by the first student asking about group membership of another object. Notice that in all these examples the students are involved in defining an object or creating a group but this process is more sophisticated and complex than the process of initial noticing or rudimentary grouping. The process described in this stage involves consideration, reflection and argumentation to achieve the category of object or group. It is through an interactive group process that the work of categorization is developed.

Scientific categorization

N (NO, NA, NM) + GRA + QN + QC + NO (scientific term for object)

This stage is characterized by the use of a written and/or verbal authority to finalize the decision about the category of an object or grouping of objects. This stage may involve the introduction of scientific terminology and precise definitions. These definitions might be verbal, visual or a mixture of both. Literacy plays a significant role in this stage of the process of learning about categorization. On one level, the use of written material, visual images in books or others forms of description provides the students with an authoritative definition that can be used to categorize an object or group of objects. At the same time, the written material provides a scientific vocabulary for the student to work with. On a different level, the students writing and drawing also forces the student to make a decision as to the category of the object or group of objects. This decision is more binding than the verbal description since it is expressed in a more permanent format and thus involves a weightier decision on the part of the student. In some cases, the teacher is used as an outside authority that provides both the definition of the category and introduces new scientific vocabulary. Consider the following example of scientific categorization:

[M. and I. turning pages of book.]
I: Oh, there it is!
M: Oh, yeah! Hey we found it!
I: We found it! We found it!
M: Hey C, we found it! Look!
Teacher: [inaudible]
I: Teacher, we found it!
Teacher 1: You guys found it?
Teacher 2: You ID'd it! What a match! And what is that called?
I: Let's see. It's a co—
Teacher 2: It's called a cone shell. In fact, it's called a Princely Cone. It's a cone fit for a prince because it's so beautiful. That complicated pattern, isn't it neat?

In this example, two students are leafing through a science book with large pictures of different types of shell and other things found in the sea. The book shows each object in vivid detail and provides a brief description of each object. The students are looking through the book to find the name and definition of a shell they have found in the beach bucket. The students are doing a visual analysis comparing the features of the shell with the pictures in the book. Once the shell is found, the students call over the teacher who makes them focus on the scientific name of the object. The teacher then reads from the book to the students.

Summary: Beach bucket explorations: categorizing objects

In the video data collected for the current study, the task of categorization involved a four-stage learning cycle. The initial stage involves a process of just looking, picking up and noticing individual objects. This stage allows some initial differentiation in the observed phenomenon. The second and third stages involve the creation of rudimentary groupings and then the questioning and modification of these groupings and definitions of objects. The third stage is particularly important in that oral discussion, argumentation and verbal reflection allow the modification and evaluation of the groups that have been formed. The last stage is characterized by the use of literacy, visual representation and scientific terminology. It is at this stage that the decision about the category of an object, its scientific name, its clear definition and its group membership is finally made. It is important to note that in the current data this was a decision mainly made in reliance on an authority.

5.2 Observing Sand: Understanding Tools of Measurement

A central aspect of scientific knowledge development is the development of scientific modes of description. Scientific description involves an understanding of the concept of measurement and the tools which allow such measurements to emerge. As such scientific description has a procedural component of how to actually use the tool and a conceptual component of comprehending the role of measurement in scientific argumentation. Scientific thinking involves the construction of inferential arguments based on observable evidence. The role of tools in this construct is to make the observations as accurate as possible and allow similarities and differences to be clearly observed and if possible quantified.

The analysis below relates to the classroom task of 'Science Inquiry of Sand.' This activity is essentially an activity that provides students with the experience of conducting a tool- and measurement-based observation of sand. The aim of this activity is to develop the concepts of measurement- and observation-based inference as part of the epistemology of science. The activity consists of observing sand using magnifying glasses and microscopes, considering the different types of sand and inferring the components of the sand. This process of utilizing tools to observe sand involves a transformation of the way observation is conducted. In the current task, instead of an open process of just noticing, the method of scientific description is shown to involve a directed observation process based on enhanced visual abilities through the usage of tools. In this context, measurement becomes the process through which similarities and differences can be defined and later used in organizational tasks. Figure 5.2 summarizes the main stages defined for this task.

As can be seen in Figure 5.2, the task of developing scientific description as part of the process of scientific thinking involves the movement from

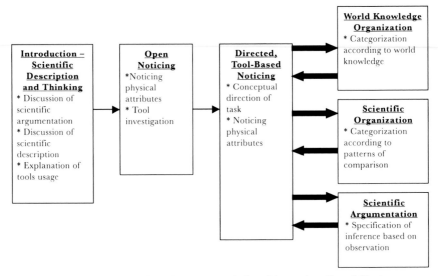

Figure 5.2 Stages of Development of the Observing Sand Task

open noticing to directed noticing and then the usage of the information obtained for the organization of knowledge in world knowledge schema, scientific patterns of comparison and scientific argumentation. The process of directed tool-based observation is pivotal in that this is the evidence that is then used in the organizational scientific tasks. Once a process of conceptual organization has occurred this conceptual information is redirected back to the tool-based noticing process resulting in further empirical observations and conceptual categorizations and distinctions. In the following sections, a detailed discourse analysis is provided for each stage.

Introduction: Scientific thinking and description

Q (QM, QS, QWK, QP) + ARD + AC + WK + AD + CM

This stage is characterized by the development of an initial understanding of scientific argumentation and tool-based scientific description. As an initial stage in explaining the epistemological form of a scientific, observation-based argument, a series of questions to be answered are generated. These questions function as a context against which the issue of the form of a scientific argument can be addressed. This involves a metacognitive turn which is designed to make the epistemological discussion of the form of an argument explicit. The discussion may develop a rudimentary understanding of the concept of a warrant (a statement that explains the basis upon which a claim is being made).

The issue to be addressed is how the questions posed can be answered. The form of the scientific argument should direct the students towards the idea that observable data is the basis for any proposed answer. This epistemological discussion may lead to the development of a discussion concerning the use of tools of observation. The discussion evolves around the presentation of a tool of observation through an explanation of how it works and what its function is. This is followed by detailed instructions on working procedures in the form of directive instructions to be followed. The result of these introductory discussions should be an understanding of the way observation can be made using specific tools and why these observations are important for scientific arguments.

To exemplify the epistemological discussion of scientific argument consider the following classroom interaction:

> *Teacher 1: We're gonna try to figure them out. We're gonna try to figure them out by looking at some sand and seeing if you can find out an answer. If you do find the answer to one of these questions, please share it with the rest of us so we'll know the answer, as well. And if there are some questions that we can't figure out just by looking at sand, how can we figure out the answers to them?*
>
> *...*
>
> *Teacher 2: When you're doing research, what are other resources for you?*
> *Teacher 2: Looking at books—*
> *Teacher 1: Sure—*
> *Teacher 2: —about sand. Talking to experts, scientists. You could make phone calls, you could email. Yeah.*
> *Teacher 1: Well, we're going to look very, very closely at some sand today and one of the ways that you can look very carefully at sand is—you know I'm gonna move over here so everybody can see—One way that you can look very closely at sand, and it's the way that we're going to do it first today is with your eyes. Just with your eyes. Look so carefully. Notice everything you possibly can about that sand and we're gonna use this. You are familiar with this, aren't you? Seems like you use it a lot. You have one at the house, too? So, this is a magnifying glass.*

In this example, the teacher starts by addressing a series of questions that have been generated concerning sand. These questions cover issues such as the structure of sand, its components and its source. Within the teacher's discourse direct observation is presented as the appropriate way to answer the questions that have been generated. The teacher poses a question as to the way these questions can be answered if observation does not provide an answer. These other options all consist of reference to outer authorities whether in the form of books or communication with experts. The teacher then reinforces the idea of empirical observation as the mode to be used. The answer to the questions will come through the very close observation of the sand using the students' own eyes and, at a later stage, tools to enhance observation such as a magnifying glass. Thus the teacher makes it clear that observable data is the way to answer questions in a scientific context.

In the next example, the role of a tool is presented to the students:

> *Teacher 2: So, maybe we need to understand what magnifying glasses do. Do you know what magnifying glasses do? What do they do? Yeah, but what's actually happening? What's happening? Do you have any idea, B.?*
> *B.: It lets you see closer.*
> *Teacher 2: It lets you see things bigger than they actually are. When you see bigger, you can see details. Right. It's as if they're closer 'cause they're much bigger.*

In this example the teacher discusses the function of magnifying glasses. The discussion focuses on what the magnifying glass does and how this will help the students to fulfil the task of observation. The teacher directs the students towards the idea of looking for details and thus widening their options for observation and noticing. This discussion of widened options for observations is part of the larger discourse structure that deals with the epistemological form of a scientific argument. The inference is that through enhanced visual abilities (the ability to see details) the student will be in a much better position to answer the questions that have been posed through the empirical process of observation. In later discussions within the introduction of scientific description and measurement, the procedural issues of the way the magnifying glass and the microscope are to be used are explained. These explanations involve quite detailed instructions and are to be considered part of the introduction to the process of scientific description.

Open noticing

NA + NM + NO + ER

This stage is characterized by a process of physically and visually investigating the qualities of the sand. This is a process of noticing individual aspects of the sand. The process of noticing consists of physically testing the qualities of the sand by weighing and feeling the sand and by looking closely at the sand with a magnifying glass. As part of the same direction of investigation, the magnifying glass itself is also explored as an object. This is a learning process in relation to the tool and its qualities. The following pictures exemplify this process.

In Figure 5.3, a student is seen throwing a bag of sand into the air and then catching it. The sand was thrown several times into the air and its weight compared to other bags of sand. The same student was also seen patting the bag of sand, sticking his fingers into the sand to test its density and tactile qualities. Similar physical tests were observed for a variety of students in the class. All these physical actions served the purpose of directing attention to the physical qualities of the sand and functioned as an initial open investigation of the sand.

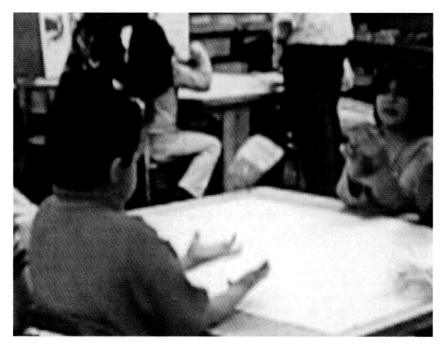

Figure 5.3 Picture of Student Throwing a Bag of Sand in the Air

In the next picture the role of the magnifying glass is addressed.

In Figure 5.4 the students are shown using their magnifying glasses to consider the visual qualities of the sand. After conducting a physical investigation of the sand the students used magnifying glasses to closely consider the visual aspects of the sand. As seen in the picture the students worked intensely on observing the sand. The following interaction occurred during this stage of observation:

> *M. Look at it, it's like sand. It's brown ... cool.*
> *(swaps sand bag with a student across the table)*
> *M. See, it's strange.*

In this brief interaction, the student directs attention to the visual investigation of the sand and expresses some surprise at the specific colour of the sand. The observation is still very open and is not focused on any of the specific questions, but consists of making an open inventory of noticed aspects and communicating these to the other students at the table.

In the next picture the process of exploring the tool itself is exemplified.

The students in Figure 5.5 are not using the magnifying glass to observe the sand but rather to look at one another. They also swapped magnifying glasses and placed them on top of one another. In all these different

Figure 5.4 Picture of Students using Magnifying Glasses

Figure 5.5 Picture of Students Exploring the Magnifying Glass

activities they essentially explored what the magnifying glass does and its specific qualities. In the present example, one of the findings was that the two magnifying glasses did not have the same magnifying power. One of the magnifying glasses was stronger and allowed more detail to emerge.

Directed, tool-based noticing

AD + NA + NM + NO

This stage is characterized by a process of directed noticing. This process consists of directing attention to a specific set of physical attributes that are of interest in answering questions that have been posed. The result of this form of noticing is an understanding of the specific qualities of the object or phenomenon under investigation. This stage consists of a connection between an action directive (in this case, instructions from the teacher) and the use of tools to find and observe specific qualities that are of interest to the student investigator. Consider the following set of instructions from the classroom teacher:

> *Teacher 1: What I would like you to do next is work together and put the sand in order from the very lightest colour sand to the next lightest all the way to the darkest sand. So you could put them in order. So from the lightest colour to the darkest colour. And after you've finished that ... you ready? Are you ready for a hard job? Put them in order from the smallest size all the way up to the largest size. You have two jobs to do. First, colour. Then size.*
> *Teacher 2: From light to dark, small to large.*

In this example, the teacher directs the students to observe a particular aspect of sand. The direction is to observe the colour and size of the sand and place the bags of sand in a certain order. Both these tasks require the process of directed noticing to be fulfilled. The students need to pay attention to differences in shades of colour and size of grains of sand in order to make comparisons. As opposed to the process of open noticing, this stage of the task is characterized by looking for specific physical qualities. The task requires the use of tools. The size of the grains of sand cannot be seen without the use of the magnifying glass or the microscope. Only through a tool-based directed observation can the required distinctions be made.

World knowledge organization

WK + GWK + GP + APA + LC

This stage interacts with the process of directed noticing. Once distinctions in the physical qualities of the sand have been made, this information is then utilized in a knowledge organization task. The type of organization is directed by knowledge that is external to the observation task but still allows a process of categorization and grouping to take place. This grouping based on world knowledge may involve the physical grouping of the noticed objects or other forms of conceptual representation such as writing or drawing. Consider the following example:

> *Teacher 1: ... Who has the very lightest colour of sand? B, what is the lightest colour? Colour? Colour of sand? ... Hold it up. What is the name of that?*
> *Teacher 2: Does it start with a ph?*
> *S: Philippines.*
> *Teacher 1: Who agrees with that? The Philippines! How many of you know where the Philippines are on our globe? C?*
> *Teacher 2: Were you born there? Yeah, she was born in the Philippines. I'll give you a clue: the Philippines are also known as the Philippine Islands. T, magnifiers are down.*
> *Teacher 1: Anybody know where the Philippine Islands are? You think? ...*
> *[Student pointing to globe as Teacher 1 holds it.]*
> *Teacher 2: Near Asia.*
> *Teacher 1: Good, L! So here's China and here are the Philippines. That's a long ways away! Here are the United States. Right here. You'd have to travel all the way across the United States, across the Pacific to get to the Philippine Islands. OK, what's the next colour? What's the next lightest? A? You can read it.*
> *Teacher 2: You can read Spanish. La—'Puerto Rico.'*

In this example, students have directed their attention to the degrees of colour observed for particular examples of sand. This information is then organized by finding the specific geographical sites in which these sands are found. The task is to a certain extent external to the knowledge attained from the observation of the sand, but it still functions as a way of organizing the different types of sand and creates a relationship between the observations and the students' wider knowledge base.

Scientific organization

NA + I(ICR, IC, ICC) + CC

This stage interacts with the process of directed noticing. The stage of scientific organization consists of utilizing information obtained through directed noticing in a process of scientific thinking. The forms of scientific organization consist of patterns of relationships such as comparison and contrast. The noticed information is integrated by applying wider patterns of organization that allow scientific information to emerge. This process of integration may involve some degree of discussion and subsequent directed noticing. The result of this process is the organization of a wider set of observations in a scientific construct. Consider the following picture addressing this task.

In Figure 5.6, a group of students combined resources and used their magnifying glasses to order the bags according to size of grains. Each bag was examined and placed in order. As can be seen in the picture, this process included changes in the order of the bags and additional re-examination of the sand with magnifying glasses. The bags were physically placed on the table according to the observed order of size. The process resulted in a rank ordering of the bags of sand according to the observed size of the sand.

Scientific argumentation

NA + AC + ADE

The stage of scientific argumentation interacts with the stage of directed noticing. The stage of scientific argumentation consists of utilizing information obtained through directed noticing in a process of scientific thinking. The form of a scientific argument consists of basing claims upon empirical evidence. The noticed information is used to support a claim relating to the phenomenon under investigation. The scientific argument

Figure 5.6 Picture of Students Reordering Bags of Sand According to Size of Grains

is a form of inference that results from an observation. Consider the following example:

> *T1: Go ahead and use your magnifying lens to look at the sand now*
> *S. Cool! … Remains of an animal … an animal, ah!*
> *(Student passes the card to another student)*
> *M. I see just the white*
> *T1. Do you still think it's made out of bone?*

In this example, one student has observed that there are white pieces within the sand sample. She reaches the conclusion that these are the remains of an animal. Presumably, the white grains are considered to be bone. The second student looking at the same card makes the same observation of the white coloured grains within the sand but is not sure that it is bone. The teacher refers back to the original inference that white particles are bone. The claim made by the first student is empirical in that it was generated by an observation of the sand and has evidence to support it. This of course does not make the inference accurate but it is an example of a very rudimentary form of scientific argumentation (although the warrant as formulated here was not explicitly stated by the student).

Summary – observing sand: understanding tools of measurement

This task is characterized by a movement towards a more scientific basis for the organization of knowledge. This transition consists of moving away from open noticing to a process of directed noticing in which students utilize tools to observe specific qualities. This directed tool-based form of noticing produces specific distinctions that can be integrated into wider organizational structures. These organizational structures can be based upon world knowledge or scientific thinking. In particular observations can be integrated into larger patterns of organization such as comparison and contrast or utilized in the structure of a rudimentary scientific argument.

5.3 Understanding Process through Shared Reading

Scientific knowledge frequently consists of understanding a process. An understanding of a scientific process in the sense used here refers to the understanding of the chronological and procedural development that results in a specific and defined outcome. This involves an understanding of a chain of cause and result, chronological and/or procedural relationships. This understanding is significant in that it provides a more systematic understanding of the physical world allowing the student to understand how the world functions.

The analysis presented below relates to the classroom activity of a shared reading of a specially prepared reader entitled 'Sandy's Journey to the Sea' and the associated production of a summary chart based on the reader. The aim of these activities was the development of the understanding of how sand is formed. The method employed to develop this understanding consisted of the literacy activity of shared classroom reading and teacher-led visual representation of this process. Figure 5.7 summarizes the main stages defined for this task.

As can be seen in Figure 5.7, the understanding process through the shared reading task consists of four main stages. The first two stages are introductory and aim to generate knowledge that is helpful for the understanding of process. The shared reading and process summarization stages are repeated several times through the reading and consist of the major aspect of this task. The summarization process is the moment that the shared reading is transformed into a more general template of a physical process and the point at which the specific process of sand formation is described. In the following sections a detailed discourse analysis is provided for each stage.

Introduction: Scientific thinking – process

ICR/+ACP + QP + QWK + WK + GGT

This stage is characterized by development of a rudimentary conceptual understanding of the nature of a specific process. This stage consists of the presentation of a claim about a specific process. This claim might be based on a prior experience, world knowledge, a prior observation or the integration of prior statements in a more inclusive presentation of a process. This statement of process may be preceded or followed by further questions relating to the concept of process or the specific process under discussion. There is also an attempt to activate prior knowledge through the questions of world knowledge and personal experience. The statements of world

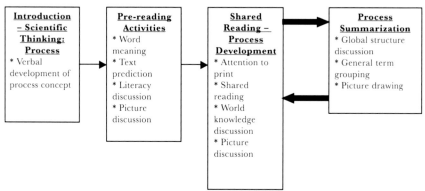

Figure 5.7 Stages of Development – Understanding Process through Shared Reading

knowledge that are elicited are utilized within more inclusive statements summarizing the process being addressed. In order to make the understanding of process move beyond a specific observation or phenomenon, there is a tendency to move to more general categories, thus allowing the generalization of the discussion. Consider the following brief interaction between the teacher and a class of children preceding a shared reading:

> *Teacher:* ... *So that was a model of how sand could be made from things on the beach. Right? They get crushed with the waves, right?*
> *M: We were pretending to be the waves.*
> *Teacher: You were pretending to be the waves, that's right. Can you think of another way besides waves that sand could be made? Think of some other kinds of forces that could happen that maybe could break things on the beach, or things other places, that maybe could break things into sand.*
> *Teacher: Ooh, some ideas out there already. F?*
> *F: Shells.*
> *Teacher: That's something that could be broken into sand. What could break a shell? What force could work on a shell to make it turn into sand?*
> *S: A wave.*
> *Teacher: What besides a wave? Is there any other force you can think of? A?*
> *A: People?*
> *Teacher: How could people do that? I agree with you. How might people do that?*
> *A: Step on it.*
> *Teacher: They might step on it, stomp it, crush it. That's a good way.*

In this example, the teacher starts the discussion by presenting an integration of a previous classroom activity and explaining it in the form of a process claim. Through questioning about world knowledge this process claim is generalized to include additional options. The shift from 'waves' to 'other kinds of forces' is significant in that the wave has now become part of a series of factors termed 'forces' that can make sand. The question elicits a series of world knowledge statements from the students. As can be seen in the final statement, these individual statements of world knowledge by the students are reformulated as process statements in order to reinforce the understanding of how the process being described works. The teacher's verbal integration plays a crucial role in the development of the concept of a process.

Pre-reading activities: Discussion of word meaning

WM + LC/ + E/ + GRA/ + P/ +APA/

Learning or refining the meaning of a word is an important part of the pre-reading activities that function as an introduction to the shared reading and discussion of science. The process of word learning in the current data set is characterized by its multimodal nature. Learning a word can involve verbal discussion, reference to pictures, extensive elaboration and acting out. All these activities are conducted in conjunction with the verbal explanation of the word being learnt. Accordingly, to learn the meaning of a word might mean physically acting out the meaning, observing some physical activity, looking at pictures, comparing an object with a picture and its title and discussing a variety of ways a word is used and exploring the current usage of the word within the science programme. This discussion around the meaning of a word may also include a discussion of the spelling or morphology of the word. Consider the following example:

Teacher 1: Beach wrack.
Teacher 2: And look at the spelling of the 'w' and the 'r' together. It's different than the 'rack' that you hang something on. It's different than your shoe rack or your clothes rack.
Teacher 1: If you can remember what a beach wrack is and ask your parents. Say, 'I learned a new word today. Wonder if you know what this means?' You can say, 'Beach wrack.'
Teacher 2: Beach wrack is a synonym for something that we've already talked about. We never gave you this term before.
Teacher 1: When we had those—the beach buckets? And there was all that stuff piled on top, all the loose materials. Not the sand, but what were the other things that we had?
C: Shells—
Teacher 1: Shells, feathers—
S: Plastic
Teacher 1: — Seaweed
S: sea urchin—
Teacher 1: OK, you guys know a beach, that's for sure. OK, so all those things that get washed up—Ch, are you listening?—All those things that get washed up on the beach and end up in a big pile there? That's the beach wrack.

In this example, the teacher introduces the term 'beach wrack'. Initially, the spelling of the word is introduced and the word is differentiated from its homonym. To explain the meaning of the word a previous activity that the children had conducted is referred to and used as a basis for the explanation. Essentially, the word is introduced as a general term referring to a series of specific items that were collected and known to the children. In the next example, physical example is used as the way of explaining the meaning of a word.

Teacher 2: And another word that I want to mention is the word 'widen'. Take your two hands like this and pull them apart a little bit. This is the beginning of a little creek. It's skinny. And as the creek flows downhill it gets more wide and it starts to widen and widen and widen [demonstrates with hands.] You have just widened, OK?
It means grow—it's like getting longer, but it's the other dimension. Longer, wider.

In this example, the teacher uses a physical demonstration to explain the word she is teaching and at the same time to explain a physical process. The children follow the teacher's example and by physically acting out the word are learning the meaning of the vocabulary item.

Pre-reading activities: Predicting text

QWK + WK + WM + TDPC

The process of predicting aspects of a written text is an important component of any comprehension exercise and may be a precursor to the construction of scientific hypotheses. In the current data set, the activity of predicting meaning consisted of activating world knowledge through questioning and exploring word meanings in order to predict the development of a chronological progression that had not yet been explicitly presented. In this sense, prediction consists of the proposal of new information based on the existence of world knowledge and the associative extension of word meanings. Consider the following example:

> *Teacher 1: What's the journey to the sea about? What does journey mean? A?*
> *A: An adventure?*
> *Teacher 1: An adventure! Sometimes journeys are adventures. T?*
> *T: Does it mean travelling?*
> *Teacher 1: Travelling, yeah. So maybe Sandy is going to take a trip. Sandy's gonna be travelling and have some adventures along the way that we will be able to read about. Ch?*
> *Ch: Or look for something?*
> *Teacher 1: Or look for something. Will Sandy be looking for something on her journey? I don't know, we haven't read it yet! Any other ideas? Where is she going? She or he – I don't know.*
> *Ch: I think it's going to go to the sea and find something.*

In this example, predictions about the text are generated through the discussion of word meanings and world knowledge. The teacher fulfils the role of asking prompting questions about word meaning or world knowledge. The answers essentially consist of predictions relating to how the text will develop. At the same time, in this example, the nature of the specific story being addressed allows an initial introduction into the way sand is formed and the nature of the chronological and procedural process that is involved in finding something on the beach.

Pre-reading activities: Literacy discussion

LDG + LDAI + LC

This pre-reading activity is characterized by an explicit discussion of the nature of the written material that is being used in the classroom. This discussion can relate to the genre aspects of the written material such as its aim, structure and special characteristics. The discussion may also include a discussion of the author and/or illustrator who produced the written material. In many cases literacy comments are added which allow discussion of the way this type of writing is conducted. Consider the following example:

> *Teacher 2: Now, there's something else very special about that cover that I want everybody to see ... Below the picture, you see in capital letters D-R-A-F-T? Draft. That means someone has written this book, but it's not finished being written. It will be changed a little bit or a lot. This is like the first writing, like your draft writing, OK?*
> *Teacher 1: Part of that is, you guys are gonna help us make it better. You're going to read it and help us decide how can we make this better for second graders to read?*
> *Teacher 2: And I want you to notice that it's not bound. It's not a paperback book, it's not a hardback book. See how it's held together by staples? See that? So we have to be a little bit careful with these draft books to make the pages stay together.*
> *Teacher 1: The other things I want to tell you is this book—this draft—was written by someone that both teacher and I—we both know this person who wrote it.*

In this brief example, comments made by both teachers generate an understanding of the written material being used in the classroom. This material consists of a draft of a book that is in the development stage. The comments make use of this aspect of the written material to explain the aim of the reading and connection between this and their own writing. This type of discussion makes the genre of the text explicit and thus may allow a metacognitive understanding of writing and literacy to develop. Within this brief discussion the author as a person is also related to. The comments made about the author should allow the children to make the written text more personal (as a text written by someone well known to both teachers).

Pre-reading activities: Picture discussion

P + TDPC + Q (QS, QWK, QP) + WK

This activity is characterized by a discussion that is focused on visual material that is present within the classroom setting. Learning about science may involve a wide range of visual materials; therefore, this type of discussion can be very significant. In the current data set, this activity involved directing attention to a picture and then through the processes of questioning, world knowledge elicitation and text prediction constructing an understanding of the development of the scientific process that is being taught. The questioning process is the means through which world knowledge and understanding is generated. This is not a formal analysis of the pictures but rather a process of meaning construction for the aim of content learning. Consider the following example:

> *Teacher 2: Excuse me, we're on the cover right now. We're looking at this picture and we're travelling down that picture.*
> *Teacher 1: Everybody put your finger on that first picture.*
> *Teacher 2: Starting place. Good. OK, M, try that one again. Where's Sandy starting?*
> *M: In the mountains.*
> *Teacher 1: In the mountains. And then where does Sandy go? It's hard to tell in that picture.*
> *Ch: Waterfall?*
> *Teacher 1: Yes! Ch, we were so happy that this story had a waterfall in it because we knew you would like that.*
> *Teacher 2: C. predicted that.*
> *Teacher 1: Yes, so something happens in the mountain. Sandy goes over a waterfall, and then where does Sandy go? Oh, you're getting the hang of it. L?*
> *Whole Class: Forest.*
> *Teacher 1: Goes to the forest. And then where does Sandy end up? Oh, look at all these hands! [xxx]? At the sea. Ends up at the sea.*

In this brief example the teacher is trying to reinforce the idea that objects and sand found on the beach have travelled a great distance to arrive on the beach. The teacher uses the pictures found in the reader to enhance this idea. First, she focuses the children's attention on the pictures and makes them place their fingers on the pictures. She then, through a process of questioning, makes them follow the journey of the rock through the different pictures by making them identify the places in the pictures. This is used as a way of creating a verbal description of the journey taken and the places that will be visited.

Shared reading – Process development

LP + APRA + Q (QS, QWK, QP) + P + TD (TDL, TDG, TDPC) + WK

This stage is characterized by the reading aloud of a section of the text followed by an exploration of the local meaning of a text. The process starts by directing the children's attention to the print in the written material. This is followed by a shared choral reading of the text in which all the children participate. One of the pitfalls of reading out loud is the option that all the children's cognitive resources are focused on the sounding out of the words and that no resources are left over for meaning construction. In the current data set, this danger is overcome by combining the choral reading with a discussion process. This discussion consists of teacher-directed questions and a focused discussion on the local meaning of the text. In order to enhance this process, the use of pictures and world knowledge is encouraged. The whole process focuses the children on both the decoding and meaning construction aspects of reading. Scientific knowledge is generated through the detailed discussion of local content. Essentially the process described in this stage is a literacy process but since the material being read and discussed presents scientific knowledge a basic understanding of this scientific knowledge is generated as well. Consider the following example:

Teacher 2: OK. J, can you find the first word? J, let's fold this back so you can actually see the words. There you go. What's that first word? High. [Class joins her.]
[Entire class reading along]: 'High in the mountains fall was turning to winter. Gold and red leaves drifted down from the trees. Rivers and creeks became covered in ice and snow covered the rocky mountaintops.'
Teacher 2: OK, have you got a picture? Which season is it?
S: Winter.
Teacher 2: Fall is turning into … winter.
Teacher 1: It's probably like now, I think.
Teacher 2: Yeah, it's just about now. Let's go on to the next paragraph.
[Entire class]: 'Beside the tall pine tree on one of these mountaintops a small stone called Sandy was [xxx] in the rocks [xxx] broken off during the mountain long, long ago. She'd been caught in this crack for hundreds of years.'
Teacher 2: OK, let's pause here a little minute … What is Sandy, right this second, in the story? What is Sandy right now? If you're not sure, go back to the text and look in the first paragraph. 'Beside a tall pine tree on one of these mountains a small … I'll take a quiet hand please. A small …
S: Stone.
Teacher 2: A small stone. And where is she, this Sandy, this Sandy stone. Yes? … Look in the text. It's written right here. Lots of clues. Read, B. Right here. Find where it says 'A small stone called Sandy,' everybody … We really can't go on until we establish where she is. I'll take a quiet hand. B? Where is she?
B: Stuck in a crack?
Teacher 2: Stuck in a crack, and who remembers how long she's been there? T?
T: For hundreds of years?
Teacher 2: For hundreds of years, she's been—so here's this crack.

In this section, the teacher starts the shared reading process by directing the attention of the children to the written material. This is then followed by making the children focus on the picture that accompanies the written text. Through a process of questioning the season being discussed is established. This ensures that the chronological development of the journey is being followed by the children. The teacher then continues with the shared reading process. The reading is paused to make sure that the local information relating to the setting of the story is understood. The teacher questions the children and focuses them on the actual text in order to utilize the explicit information in the text. The questioning process and the focus on the text make sure that the local information in the text is comprehended.

Process summarization

$$P + LC + Q\,(QS, QWK, QP) + TDG + PD + I\,(ICR, IC, IN) + GGT$$

Process summarization is a stage that comes in conjunction with the shared reading stage. The importance of this stage is that it attempts to ensure that the global level of the text is understood and that this global understanding can be further abstracted as a more general scientific understanding. In other words, the process of summarization is crucial for the creation of scientific knowledge. The summarization process documented in this data set was conducted by the teacher and consisted of the production of two types of representation – pictorial and written. The process of summarization started through the production of a drawing depicting the information presented in the text. This information consisted of the journey of a rock and accordingly the pictures summarized the actual physical journey. The second form of summary consisted of note-taking of the main points of the narrative. Essentially the global information structure of the narrative is summarized. In order to produce these notes and/or the pictorial representation previous comments and statements made may need to be integrated according to more inclusive discourse patterns such as cause and result or chronological development. The summarization processes address the content of the text that has been read and ensure that a global understanding is established. In order to make this a more abstract understanding of a scientific process a process of generalizing the terms used is enacted. This upgrading of the terms to more general categories allows the drawing and summary notes to address a wider set of cases than might be understood from just comprehending the story in itself. Consider the following section that exemplifies the process of pictorial summary:

> Teacher 1: — Look at that.
> Teacher 2: [Drawing] Here's the mountain with the snow on top of it. And here's a crack and this little circle right here? It's Sandy. Remember it said she was—I don't know if it's she or he, I keep saying she. In the book, it's 'she.'
> Teacher 1: OK. She's stuck in a crack near a pine tree.
> Teacher 2: And it said she started off as part of the mountain and she got broken off and fell in this crack and got stuck there. So she was originally part of the mountain, and she broke off from the mountain, and got stuck in a crack on the mountain. Let's go in the last paragraph and see what happens to her.

In this brief example, the teacher generates a pictorial image that is used to summarize the events described in the story. As the picture is drawn it is explained to the children and they are directed to focus their attention on the new picture summary. The picture summary is combined with a verbal integration of the information from the narrative. This integration is chronological and offers a global understanding of the events of the story. In this example, pictorial and verbal modes of representation are used to generate a global understanding. In the next section, the same information is covered but this time written notes are used to summarize the textual information:

Teacher 1: ... We need a couple of notes so we can remember what happens in this chapter because we're gonna use this later. Remember how we've been taking some notes? So, how about if we get like three things down here about this Chapter 1, 'The High Mountains in Winter.' What's one thing that you think is important to remember about this chapter? What do you think is the important part of what we just read?

Teacher 2: I'll give you a clue. Is it important that it's a pine tree? Is that key? Is it critical? No. Is it important that she—right now, Sandy is a small stone?

Class: Yeah.

Teacher 2: That's important.

Teacher 1: I'm gonna write that down. [Writing] So Sandy is a small stone. I need two more ideas for this chapter. Maybe where she is might be important—

Teacher 2: — All these sleeping sea lions ... thank you. A, would you get up, too? I know I stretched out, too, because it was easier to get close to the print and—

Teacher 1: Ch, how about you giving me one? ... We know that Sandy is a small stone. We haven't written down where she is, though.

Ch: She's stuck on the mountain in the crack?

Teacher 1: She's stuck on the mountain—

Teacher 2: Where? Where on the mountain is she?

Teacher 1: —in the cracks.

Teacher 2: Can you sit up, too? We're all gonna make an effort to sit up.

Teacher 1: [Writing notes on a board] Sandy was stuck in a crack on the mountain.

Teacher 2: How about this, you guys? Is it important which season it is? Is it important that it's winter? Fall turning into winter? Could that be important? 'Cause what special things happen in winter? ... Snow. And the temperatures get very very—

Class: Cold.

Teacher 2: And the coldness changes the things that happen up in the mountains.

Teacher 1: [Writing notes on a board] So, the season is fall turning to winter. I think that describes this chapter pretty well. OK, should we turn the page? Chapter 2.

In this section, the teacher produces a series of notes that are used to provide a written summary of the text and the process described. The notes are written by the teacher on a board in clear view of the students.

The aim of the note-taking is initially explained to the students, and the relationship between the notes and future literacy activities is explained. Through a process of questioning the students are asked to focus on the global level of the information and to differentiate important information that should be used in note-taking. This process is enhanced by addressing the student's world knowledge. Information that is identified from the text is written up as a note on the board. As with the case of the pictorial representation, the information in note form is integrated into a more inclusive verbal statement that uses the discourse pattern of cause and result. Once again this reinforces the summarization of the text and provides a representation of the global structure of the information. In the next section, the transformation of these representations into more abstract scientific descriptions is addressed:

> Teacher 2: So—don't turn yet ... The trees that live up near the top, a lot of times those trees are hundreds of years old, too. Ch, we're not turning. And the roots grow and break into the rock and this time the tree root widened the crack and now Sandy is a little bit loose. Do you think she's gonna stay in that crack her whole life?
> Class: No.
> Teacher 2: Now, is there really, really, actually a small stone named Sandy?
> Class: No.
> Teacher 2: There isn't. But there are lots and lots of stones and mountains that are in this position. We're just following one stone and seeing what happens to it.

In this section, the teacher summarizes a specific section of the text and focuses on a cause and result pattern to integrate the information in the text. But having accomplished this aim, the teacher redirects the students away from the world of the text to a more general and abstract understanding. The story is about a stone called Sandy, but the process that the students are learning about is not limited to this specific stone. The stone is one of a much larger group of stones, all of whom follow a similar path. This movement to recognizing the stone as a member of a much larger and more general group is an attempt to make the information in the story useful as a more general abstract scientific description of the way sand is formed and objects appear on the beach. This shift is crucial because if it is not achieved the story will stay on the level of an imaginative narrative and will not be useful for the development of a scientific concept of a process.

Summary of the understanding process through shared reading task

In the video data collected for the current study, the task of understanding a process involved a four-stage learning cycle. The initial stage involved generating some basic knowledge about the specific process being learned and providing a more general template of what a scientific process is. The second stage consisted of activities directed at enhancing and developing the reading and learning process. These activities form an introduction into the reading itself and the meanings that will be encountered. The third stage consisted of a shared reading activity in which the text was read together and local meaning was discussed. The final stage consisted of summarizing the meanings found in the shared reading. This process of summarization was conducted through verbal interaction, pictorial representation and written note-taking.

5.4 Summarizing Sand Formation through Picture Drawing

An important aspect of scientific knowledge development is the ability to represent and store scientific knowledge. The role of multiliteracy in this framework is to allow information to be clearly organized in a format that will allow it to be remembered and understood at a later date. There is a double aim here of both representing specific scientific knowledge and learning how to represent knowledge. As such this task addresses both the development of specific scientific knowledge and the development of an epistemological tool for the development of subsequent knowledge.

The analysis presented below relates to the classroom activity of producing a pictorial account of a rock's journey to the sea and was designed to summarize the process of beach formation. This task followed the shared reading of the reader 'Sandy's Journey to the Sea.' Figure 5.8 summarizes the main stages defined for this task.

As seen in Figure 5.8, there are three main stages to the summarization through picture drawing task. The first and third stages are drawing stages in which a pictorial representation is developed. The first stage of drawing differs from the last stage in that the first stage focuses on outer contours and the last stage deals with the details of the picture and the relationship

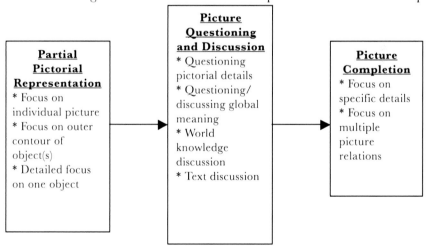

Figure 5.8 Stages of Development – Summarization through Picture Drawing

to other pictures. The middle stage is crucial in this shift in pictorial representation. Through verbal interaction the additional aspects of the process that is being represented are noticed and required to be represented. In the following sections, a detailed analysis is provided for each stage.

Partial pictorial representation

PGC/PDD

This stage is characterized by development of a partial representation of the most salient aspects of the text that has been read and the process which is being represented. In the current data set this partial representation could consist of a global contour approach or a local detailed component approach. In both cases only a partial representation is developed. For the detailed component approach a specific object is chosen and represented on the page. The object has some detail but is represented by itself. For the global contour the pictorial representation includes very few details and is in a limited set of colours. Very few objects are represented and those that do appear are represented only through an external contour of the object. Some relations among objects are represented and there may be some external symbolic marking such as an arrow to designate where the rock is situated or to emphasize a particular aspect of the drawing. Consider the following example in the picture below.

Figure 5.9 Picture of First Stages of Rock Journey Drawing

In Figure 5.9, the student has produced the first stages of a drawing of Sandy the rock travelling in a wave. The picture has the outer contours of two waves but without any detail. The rock is represented by a single big dot on the left hand of the page. This picture does represent a part of the rock's journey but does not address the process of the journey or other objects that might be in the sea. As such it is a partial representation.

Picture discussion

P (PL, PG) + TD (TDL, TDG) + WM + WK + LP

This stage is characterized by a discussion surrounding the partial pictorial representation that has been created. This discussion includes focusing on the local and global aspects of the picture. This could include questioning the student about the absence of detail or asking the student to focus on the wider process that this particular picture is a specific part of. The discussion can also refer the student back to the original text and involve a discussion of the meaning of the text that has been read. The discussion can also make use of world knowledge to provide the details for understanding the process that is being depicted. World knowledge can also be used to provide connections to the wider process that is being described. The discussion process is central to the development of the complete representation in that it makes the student pay attention to additional details that are required or makes the student consider the relations between the pictorial representation and the wider process being learnt. The discussion also makes sure that the picture is accurate in relation to the material being learnt. It is through the discussion process that the pictorial representation is developed and modified. Consider the following example:

> Teacher 2: What's Sandy doing?
> T: Got caught in the wave.
> Teacher 2: Terrific ... are there any other things travelling in her wave? Other little, um, pebbles, or bits of sand, seaweed ... any other things caught in the same wave, T?
> T: Nope.

In this example, the student has drawn a picture utilizing the global contour approach. The picture consists of a representation of the outer contour of two waves in blue and a big dot in black representing the rock. Apart from this, the picture is empty. The teacher's questions direct the student to the story that has been read, prior experience with the classroom beach bucket exploration and world knowledge. This process points out the gap between what is represented in the story as the process of beach formation and the pictorial representation produced by the student.

In the next example, the teacher focuses the student on the global relations among different aspects of the process of the rock's journey:

Teacher 1: What was carrying her down the mountain? Was she just falling?
...
Teacher 1: Maybe you could draw some water.
Teacher 2: In this picture, Sandy is ... riding in the ocean. It's a big winter storm.
Teacher 1: Do you remember where that water was coming from?
S: From the river?
Teacher 1: From the river. And remember the snow on the mountaintop? What happened to that snow? It melted—

In this example, the teacher questions the student about the process of the journey of the rock. The teacher's questions direct the student to causal relations between the change in the weather and creation of a water flow and the effect of this on the rock. The picture in itself provides a partial representation of the process which is missing a lot of information. Through a questioning process which involves reference to the text that has been read and world knowledge the teacher invites the student to construct a representation of the process.

Picture completion

PDD + PGC

This stage is characterized by the completion of the pictorial representation of the process being learnt through the addition of required details and the construction of global relations. This process follows the picture discussion process in which certain aspects of the pictorial representation were seen to be inconsistent with the process being described. This stage involves adding details to the pictures and negotiating multiple pictures and representations of the process. The final product should represent the whole process and make each of its components as accurate as possible in relation to the process being learnt. This stage is important in that it provides a rich pictorial summary of the process that is learnt and a pictorial method of recording a process. Consider the following examples in the pictures below.

In this example, a student represents the rock's journey from the mountain to the sea. This process is represented in two individual pictures that are physically connected. The connection between the pages and the use of a shared colour scheme allow the representation of a process of movement. Notice that the mountain is represented on a page that is 'higher' than the river that brings the rock to the sea. This is a visual enactment of topological relations among the physical locations that the rock travels through. In this example, as seen in the second picture, a third

Figure 5.10 Two Pictures of a Rock's Journey from the Mountain to the Sea

page is also attached to the project. This picture is connected on the same level as the second page, but the sea is drawn at the bottom of the page following the mode of presentation used in these pictures. The three pages taken together as a single entity cover the movement of the rock from the mountain to the sea. This is a pictorial representation that presents a specific process.

Summary of the summarization of process through picture drawing task

In the video data collected for the current study, the task of summarization through picture drawing involved a three-stage process. The initial stage consisted of the creation of a partial representation of the process. This partial representation could focus on a detail or provide a schematic contour without details of an aspect of the process. In the second stage, a verbal interaction directed an understanding that additional features need to be represented in the pictures in order to capture the process. This led to the completion of the pictorial representation. In this final stage, the global aspects of the process were addressed and solutions posed as to how to pictorially represent this.

5.5 Summarizing Sand Formation through Narrative Writing

As discussed briefly in relation to the task of summarization through picture drawing, an important aspect of scientific knowledge development is the ability to represent and store scientific knowledge. In task three this was achieved through a picture drawing summarization mode. The current task utilizes narrative writing to achieve the same aims of representing knowledge of a specific process and the acquisition of the epistemological tool of narrative writing to understand a process.

The analysis presented below relates to the classroom activity of producing a narrative account of a rock's journey to the sea. This narrative writing task followed the pictorial summary of the same process. The pictorial representations in the form of postcards and the original readers from the shared reading were present during the narrative writing process. Figure 5.11 summarizes the main stages defined for this task.

As can be seen in Figure 5.11, the summarization through narrative writing is an integrative multiliteracy task that includes written text discussion as well as picture discussion as a way of generating written text. As represented in this figure, the two modes of analysis develop the actual writing of the narrative. It is important to notice that the narrative integration is enacted in the writing itself. The two preceding stages of analysis are crucial for this final process of integration to happen. In the following sections a detailed analysis is provided for each stage.

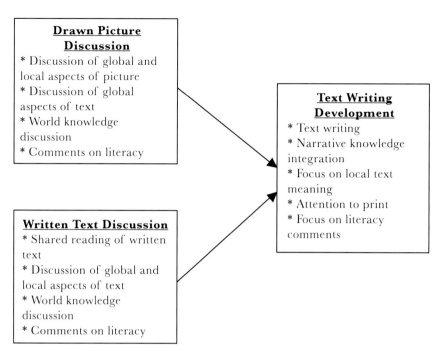

Figure 5.11 Stages of Development – Summarization through Narrative Writing

Drawn picture discussion

P (PL, PG) + TDG (global narrative structure) + TDL + QWK + WK + LC

This stage is characterized by the close analysis of the pictorial representation of the postcard as a method of generating written text or developing text that has already been written. The analysis of the pictorial representation may relate to the local or global information in the picture. By questioning the picture, the teacher directs the student to consider new information either on the local or global narrative levels. This may include the usage of world knowledge or a discussion of the original text in the classroom reader. The use of the pictorial information in this way enriches the potential content for the next stage of writing. This discussion of the pictorial representation also allows the raising of a series of literacy comments relating to the appropriate way of spelling or pronouncing a word. Consider the following example:

> *Teacher 2: I want a sentence that starts with Sandy. So tell me where Sandy is in the picture. Let's look at your picture again. Where's Sandy. What are you trying to do. Where's Sandy? OK? Where is she in the picture? Is she in the mountain? The*

river? She's on a beach? What's happening to her? I can't hear you. Oh, is this at the end? OK, and she's—this is at the end, when she's on the sandy beach? OK, 'Sandy . . .
[student writes]

In this example the student is having difficulty in starting the writing task. The teacher makes her look at the picture she has produced and enters into a process of questioning the student about the information presented in the picture. The questions relate to both the local information and to the more global aspects of the relationship between this picture and the wider narrative that has been told. The teacher provides some literacy instruction through her comment as how to start the sentence. The discussion has the desired effect in that immediately following this discussion the student starts to write.

In the next example, an analysis of the pictorial representation was used to develop a written text:

Teacher 2: Okey-doke. Listen. Shov-el. Eh. Eh. She fell from the shovel into . . . into . . . a picture might help you. Into a bucket . . . uuuu . . . et. And what happened? . . . So now she's in the bucket, then what? . . . Is she in the bucket here? Nope, she's already on the . . . So tell how she got from the bucket to the sandcastle. What did that girl do? . . .
OK, go ahead. You've got another minute to write.

In this example, the teacher directs the student to reconsider her painting. This redirection of attention to the painting and subsequent analysis of the pictorial information makes the student formulate a richer narrative summary of the events that are being described. The questioning process directs the creation of connections of what is being described to previous events. As in the previous example, following this interaction the student continued to write.

Written text discussion

APRA + LP + TDG + TDL + QWK + WK + LC

This stage is characterized by the shared reading and close discussion of the student's written text or the classroom reader. This process consists of reading and discussing a piece of writing and using this as a way of developing the student's writing. At the beginning of the writing process this could involve analysing and discussing the classroom reader as a mode of generating information for the student's own writing project. This process also involves the teacher reading the student's own work with the student and discussing its content. In the process of this discussion, issues of literacy like spelling or usage of the correct form may arise and will be presented by the teacher. These moments are cases of individualized literacy instruction addressing specific needs of students. The discussion of the text could address local or global issues in relation to the developing piece of writing and can activate world knowledge. Consider the following example:

Teacher 2: She's on a beach. She became part of the … uh huh. You can find the word 'castle' right there. Castle. Now, here's what I want you to tell. I want you tell how she got from being on the beach to being part of the sandcastle. How did she get moved from the beach? She …

She fell from the shovel into the bucket. The 'ir' comes right before the 'l'. So the r has to be right next to the l. Ch, I'd like you to stay and finish the writing. Read it to me. I'm sorry, I need to know how Sandy got to the castle. You haven't done the job yet. Sandy's in the castle now. Tell me how she got there. Write it. Who picked her up? Who made the castle? OK, the girl picked her up with what? …

…

The girl tossed the bucket … tossed the bucket and made the castle with her … Yeah, how about—made the castle … with … OK, I want you to slow down. Wi—i— l—just a little shift of letters and you'll have the word. Look at it again. Wi—OK I'd like you to stop with what you have and we'll see if it makes sense.

In this example, the teacher closely considers the text written by her student. The teacher poses questions that make the student consider the global narrative connections in the story she is writing. The student needs to answer the teacher's question as to what happened before in the narrative to result in the current description. The teacher directs the student's attention to the written text and addresses issues of spelling. The text is read aloud with the student and stylistic corrections proposed. The reading process also consists of a case of individualized instruction in which a reading and spelling lesson is involved. In this example, issues of meaning construction and written form are both discussed in relation to the student's writing. Following this discussion the student continued writing.

Written text development

TW + IN/ + TDG + TDL + WK

This stage consists of the student writing and developing their written text. An important aspect of this process is that statements made in the analysis of the picture or the classroom reader appear in the written text as an integration of prior statements. This might involve the development of the narrative or the filling in of missing details to make the text clearer or more coherent. In some cases the writer does start writing without prior discussion. In developing the writing several different sources may be used and integrated in the written text. These sources may include the analysis of the classroom reader, the discussion of the pictorial representation, and reference to classroom notes on the board. However, the analysis of the picture presented seems to have been the main resource addressed for the written text. As an example consider the following series of pictures.

The three pictures in Figure 5.12 were taken in sequence. In the first picture at the beginning of the integration task, the student considers the postcard she has drawn. She still does not start writing. She then opens the reader and leafs through a few pages till she finds a page which is relevant to the picture she has drawn on the postcard. She reads a short section and then starts writing. During her writing she refers mainly to the picture but also utilizes the classroom reader. Both are used to inform and develop her writing.

Summary: Summarizing sand formation through narrative writing

In the video data collected for the current study, the task of the summarization of scientific process through narrative writing is characterized by the process of cross-modal integration. As seen in the analysis the stages of written text discussion and drawn picture discussion provide knowledge that is then utilized in the text production process of written text. The text produced is a limited narrative mainly based on a pictorial analysis but informed by other sources of information as well.

Figure 5.12 Three Pictures of a Student Using Pictorial and Written Material for Written Summary

5.6 Erosion and Weathering: Developing a Scientific Vocabulary

Scientific knowledge is characterized by the understanding of scientific processes and an understanding of the meaning of specific vocabulary items utilized in scientific discourse. In this sense, vocabulary learning is an understanding of the specific scientific meaning of a term functional in explaining a phenomenon. Development of a scientific vocabulary can be seen as a step towards a conventionalized understanding of scientific phenomena and a personal conceptual development in understanding and describing the world.

The analysis below relates to the learning of the concepts of weathering and erosion. The learning of these concepts was a specific aim of this science education programme. The activity consists of a classroom discussion of the meaning of the scientific concepts and an acted out demonstration of the weathering and erosion process. Figure 5.13 summarizes the main stages defined for this task.

As can be seen in Figure 5.13, the development of knowledge of scientific vocabulary was found to consist of four stages. The first stage is an

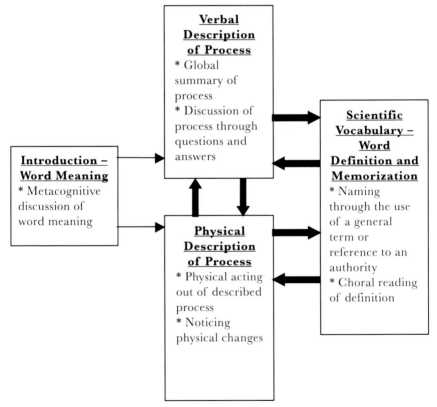

Figure 5.13 Stages of Development – Scientific Vocabulary Task

introductory stage in which the idea of learning a new scientific concept is presented. As designated in the two directional arrows among the stages of the verbal description of a process, the physical description of a process and the stage of scientific vocabulary word definition, these three stages are interconnected. Essentially, the new word definition is described three times: once as a verbal summary of a learnt process, once through physical action and once explicitly through a definition process. This is a word-learning process that is multimodal and multifaceted. In the following section a detailed discourse analysis is provided for each stage.

Introduction – Word meaning

LC

This stage is characterized by the metacognitive discussion of the process of learning a new vocabulary item. This metacognitive discussion is a form of literacy comment that addresses what a new vocabulary item is. The aim of this discussion is to provide an introduction to the idea that vocabulary is a naming process and that it can be conducted at various different levels of specificity. This introductory discussion provides a conceptual space for the introduction of new names for known processes and phenomena. Consider the following example:

> *Teacher 1: We're gonna add to our knowledge today. We're gonna add some new concepts. Are you getting kind of tired of looking at those? (points to board of scientific concepts) B. said he was tired of looking at them. OK, I've got some new ones here. And it's things that we've been working on but we're just gonna give it a new name. Remember when Sandy was on the mountain top and Sandy wasn't quite as tight in her crack, anymore. Something was happening. There are some words that we're gonna introduce to you today. They're not hard ... You've even heard them before. But Sandy—*
> *Teacher 2: These are sort of like scientific words to describe what you know.*

In this example the teacher refers to a board of previously learnt concepts and explains that new concepts are about to be introduced. The learning process for these new vocabulary items is one of renaming. The students are informed that the new concept is really a new way of defining knowledge that they already possess. In this sense they will learn to call a process they already know by a new name. This renamed concept will come in the form of a new vocabulary item used by scientists.

Verbal description of process

Q (QWK, QP) + I (IN, ICR, IC) + ACP + WK

This stage is characterized by the verbal description and discussion of a process. Through a process of questions and answers a process that has already been learnt is discussed and summarized. The summary has the form of a global text organizer such as the integration of a narrative, the construction of a cause and result pattern or the presentation of a processing claim. The questions are designed to elicit the required information in order to allow a global text organizer to be used. The result of this interaction between question–answer sequence and summary is the description of process. Consider the following example of a question and answer session:

> *Teacher: What is it that broke Sandy into smaller pieces? And what made it so her crack wasn't so tight anymore? Remember she was getting smaller so it wasn't quite so tight?*
> *B: The tree roots.*
> *Teacher 1: The tree roots, OK, so they were spreading the crack. A? ...*
> *Teacher 2: There's more than one answer. A whole bunch of forces.*
> *Teacher 2: So what was breaking her?*
> *Teacher 1: What part of that that you just described was what actually broke her into smaller pieces? What was the force? Remember jolly ranchers? What was the force?*
> *S: Waves.*
> *Teacher 1: Yes, very good. Was there another force that you can think of that was working on Sandy up there? M?*
> *M: When she fell down the waterfall?*
> *Teacher 1: So, what was the force that was making her smaller?*
> *M: Water?*
> *Teacher 2: Force of the water? Huge volume of water could break off some pieces.*
> *Teacher 1: A, you had your hand up. No?*
> *S: Rocks.*
> *Teacher 1: Other rocks.*

In this example the teacher questions the class about the forces that break rocks into smaller pieces. The aim of the discussion is to elicit information about the way rocks are fractured and the forces in nature that act upon rocks. The emphasis is on obtaining a wide range of forces that fulfil the same role of splitting the rocks. In this brief example, tree roots, waves, waterfalls and rocks are all mentioned as forces that can break rocks.

In the next example the process of summarization is presented:

> *Teacher 1: OK to freeze and to warm up, to freeze and then warm up. That's really hard on rocks. That causes cracks in rocks to be frozen and then unfrozen and get warm and then freeze again. It causes those cracks to happen. And if a crack happens in a rock, maybe it ends up falling off. And so that rock ends up being a little bit smaller.*

In this example, the teacher summarizes a process of a rock being broken through changes in temperature. The summary has the form of a cause and result process in which changes in temperature cause cracks to form in the rock that then result in pieces of the rock breaking off. The teacher fulfils the role of summarizing the whole process using a global text organizer.

Physical description of process

AD + APA + NA

This stage is characterized by the description and understanding of a process through physical action. The students' active participation exemplifies the process that is being defined using scientific vocabulary. This process of physically acting out is combined with cognitive noticing so that the results of the process being learnt will be clear to the students. The students act out an approximation of the process under discussion and then this is used in conjunction with the verbal description to provide a verbal and non-verbal representation of the scientific process. Consider the following example:

> Teacher: This rock is called pumice. But I have a smaller one that's exactly the same material. I'm asking you ... everyone ... you get to touch and you get to grind. If you keep putting your hands there then we have to stop and you don't get to do it before recess. So I need you to follow directions because I want you to get to do it. Now, this one is not quite as rough, B, but it is still pumice out of the volcano. Here goes another rock. Do you hear that sound? Here goes a hiker walking. Here goes a sudden stream of water. Look what's happening. Look. Can you see in the sunlight?
> [Responses from students. 'Look at [xxx]']
> Teacher ... OK. Now, it's going from a big hunk of pumice into many little ... tiny bits. And you have a chance to do it. I'd like you to do it over this. So this is becoming like a little pumice beach. And after you try it you can pass it to the next person.
> [Students practise grinding.]

In this example the teacher exemplifies the process that is being defined. The teacher presents a rock to the children and then grinds it in front of them. As she grinds she reminds the students of the forces of nature that may perform a similar task so that the demonstration is connected directly to the phenomenon being studied. The grinding of the stone produces a powder-like residue on the carpet. Students respond to the teacher's demonstration with cognitive noticing. They call out to look at different aspects of the demonstration and the residue that has been produced. The teacher summarizes the process verbally to enhance the understanding of the phenomena. Following the teacher demonstration the students are directed to perform the same task, so that every student gets the chance to grind the pumice and produce a pumice beach.

Scientific vocabulary – Word definition and memorization

GGT + GRA + WM + LC

This stage is characterized by the process of defining the word that is being learnt and enhancing the memorization of the word. The process of definition consists of providing a meaning for the word and the naming of the phenomena through the use of a general term or by reference to an authority. The general term groups series of descriptions or experiences that the students are aware of and provides a specific name for this set of phenomena. This is an important moment in that the students move from an everyday vocabulary to the renaming and redefining of the world around them. In order to enhance the memorability of the word, choral reading and repetition are used. Both of these make the student say the word being learnt out loud and offer multiple opportunities for exposure to the word. Consider the following example:

> *Teacher 2: Well, we call those kinds of things 'weathering'. We'll just put them up here now …*
> *Teacher 1: Have you heard that word 'weather' before? Every morning you hear the weather?*
> *S: Yeah.*
> *Teacher 2: That's where this word comes from. Weathering just means like the forces of nature causing things to break up the surface.*

In this example, the teacher takes all the examples that have been provided by the students of forces of nature that break rocks and provides the more general term of weathering as more accurate and inclusive. Whereas before, in the introduction of this term, the process of water breaking rocks and changes in temperature breaking rocks were examples of two different processes that reached the same result (sand formation), through the term weathering there is a common basis for both of these processes. In this sense the scientific term is a general term that groups seemingly diverse phenomena together. Having provided the scientific term, and demonstrated its grouping potential, an explicit explanation of the term is provided. This description of the word allows the students to use the new term in other situations beyond those already discussed.

In the next example, the process of memorization is exemplified:

> *Teacher 1: This is about travelling! Everybody look up here! I have a new word. It's called 'erosion'.*
> *Teacher 2: Is it e-rosion or ah-rosion? I never know.*
> *Teacher 1: Ah-rosion. What is erosion?*
> *Class and Teacher 1 [reading together]: 'Erosion moves the small pieces from one place to another by streams, rivers and ocean currents.' So first weathering is the force*

that breaks the rocks into smaller little bits. And then erosion takes over and moves the small pieces and there might be some more weathering that happens on the way, too. So all these little pieces got picked up by big waves—woosh—then it would be eroding away. Erosion. OK? That's the movement. So, tomorrow we'll come back to these words. So, think you can remember them until tomorrow?
Teacher 2: You know what? The way to get to the line is to tell me one of the words. You have to say 'weathering' or you have to say 'erosion'. Weathering, bye.
Teacher 1: What is small pieces? What is travelling?
Teacher 2: Erosion, erosion, erosion. Oh, come on, somebody. Weathering! Now I'm ready for some erosion. OK. And what's that travelling called?

In this example, a new word 'erosion' is introduced to the students. Following a brief discussion of pronunciation, the definition of the word is presented through a choral reading. The choral reading provides reference to an authority and information as to the meaning of the term. This is followed by a verbal description of the process. In this case the verbal description covers both the scientific terms that are being taught in this lesson (weathering and erosion). The vocabulary development task ends with the students repeating one or another of the words that are being learnt.

Summary: Erosion and weathering: Developing a scientific vocabulary

In the current video data, the process of learning a scientific vocabulary involved three different stages of description. These three stages work together to provide a multi-representational description of the word meaning. The scientific term is described through a verbal description of the process being described. This verbal description involves the use of students' prior knowledge and a global text organizer such as a narrative or cause and result pattern. The scientific term is also described through the physical acting out of the process being described. This physical process is combined with a process of noticing so that the stages and results of the process can be internalized. In the word definition stage, the scientific term is shown to group together different observations and phenomena under a common heading. Within this context, the explicit definition of the term is provided. These three ways of developing a scientific vocabulary work together with quick shifts among the three stages. Together they should produce a strong representation for the new term.

Chapter 6: The Genre of Scientific Inquiry

The aim of the analysis of the written and pictorial products was to provide data relating to outcomes of the science inquiry and literacy tasks conducted by children in the class studying the Sandy Shoreline science unit. As with the previous chapter, the analyses in this chapter provide a detailed, qualitative account of the multiliteracy tasks and activities of science education. As described in the methodology section, the materials collected consisted of both pictorial and written products that were produced by the whole class throughout the study of the science unit. These products can be seen as snapshots of the student's knowledge at different points in the course and thus provide some insight into the development of knowledge through this science unit. These products also provide some insights into specific outcomes of the science-literacy tasks described in the previous chapter.

In broad terms, three different levels of analysis were conducted on these products. The three levels were:

1. *Content analysis*: This level of analysis addressed the content of the multiliteracy products. The analysis of the content provides evidence of the structure of knowledge of the students. This is particularly useful for defining what the student is aware of in relation to a particular phenomenon being studied.
2. *Genre analysis*: This level of analysis addressed the representational forms that were used by the students while conducting the tasks of this science unit. The analysis of genre provides information on the representational resources of the students, the representational requirements of the science unit and the way these representational resources were manifested by the students.
3. *Cognitive processes analysis*: This level of analysis addresses the cognitive processes involved in the production of the written products. This analysis is inferential based on the analysis of the final product. This level of analysis provides information that is supplemental to the in-depth video analysis conducted in the last chapter.

In the sections that follow the analysis of each of the multiliteracy products is presented

6.1 Beach Folder Pictures

The analysis presented below relates to one of the first activities conducted by the students. This activity consisted of producing a drawing of a beach. This drawing was used as a cover for a folder that was designed to include vocabulary items and scientific concepts. This activity was part of a process of early knowledge activation relating to the students' understandings of what a beach is. The analysis of the contents and representational genre of this multiliteracy product represent an analysis of initial understandings of what constitutes a beach and what its components are.

The results of the content analysis of the beach folder pictures are presented in Table 6.1.

The analysis in Table 6.1 presents the list of objects depicted in the beach folder pictures. For purposes of our analysis of the participants' initial understandings of the nature of a beach, the pictures can be divided into three spaces – a beach area, a sea area and a sky area. Each of these areas had designated objects that occurred within them. The beach area had within it people, trees, rocks, grass, shells, sandcastles, turtles, crabs and balls. People and trees were the most frequently represented objects. Only five students represented rocks and four students represented shells. The sea area had within it fish, sharks, turtles, octopuses and shells. Sharks and fish were the most frequently represented objects. The sky area had within it clouds, sun, birds and rainbows. The sun and clouds were the most frequently represented objects. Overall the content analysis of these three areas reveals an experiential understanding of the beach. This understanding includes expected objects at the beach, in the sea and in the sky. The understanding is at this early stage in the course undifferentiated as to the contents of the sand, the sea or the shoreline.

An analysis of the genre of artistic representation found in these pictures revealed two main genres of visual representation:

1. *Narrative action picture*: A narrative action picture uses artistic visual methods to foreground a central action that is portrayed in the picture. The action portrayed can be verbally restated as a scene from a narrative.
2. *Descriptive picture*: A descriptive picture uses artistic visual methods to portray a static description of a physical situation. The physical situation can be verbally restated as a physical setting.

These two main types of genre were further differentiated in relation to the form of visual presentation. The two issues of form addressed in the current analysis consisted of the level of artistic representation and the density of information presentation. Each of these categories is described below on p. 98.

Table 6.1 Summary of Content Analysis for Beach Picture Folders for Whole Class (n=20)

Represented Object	Frequency of Occurrence	Mode of Representation
Sea	19	Coloured blue area (square or wavy) Thin black, blue or green line
Sun	16	Small yellow, pink, brown or orange coloured area in upper corner of page with extended lines (rays) Half circle centre of page with extended rays
Beach area	20	Thin black, gray, yellow or brown line White space Yellow, brown coloured area marked with a clear straight or wavy line
Sky	18	White space Thin blue lines across the top of the page Blue space
Clouds	15	Pencil contour of bulbous cloud shape Coloured line contour of bulbous cloud shape (blue, orange) Coloured bulbous cloud shape (small or big)
Birds	8	Pencil or coloured line soft M shape (blue or black) Pencil or coloured line soft V shape (blue or brown) Pencil or coloured line soft W shape (black or brown) Drawn bird with beak, wings and legs (black, purple or brown)
Rainbow	3	Coloured lines in half circle across top of page
Fish	10	Coloured or pencil line contour of oblong and triangle (orange, black) Drawn coloured fish shape including tail, fins and eye (blue, brown, yellow or multicoloured)
Shark	7	Drawn coloured shark with mouth full of teeth, fins, tail and eye (blue, black, orange, brown or green) Pencil or coloured line contour of shark with a mouth full of teeth and fin (black or blue)

Represented Object	Frequency of Occurrence	Mode of Representation
Crabs	6	Drawn and coloured circle with protruding lines and claws (orange, red, brown) Pencil drawn contour of circle with protruding lines and claws
Turtle	4	Coloured oval shape with legs and head (green) Pencil outline of oval shape with legs and head
Octopus	3	Drawn and coloured circle with protruding square-shaped legs (blue, purple, green) Pencil contour of circle with protruding square legs
Trees	8	Drawn and coloured tree shape including tree trunk, branches, foliage and coconuts (brown and green) Drawn and coloured tree shape (brown, green, orange)
Grass	3	Green coloured area differentiated with a line Green curvy line Green pointed lines
Rocks	5	Coloured circular shapes (purple, orange, yellow, pink, blue) Pencil contour of circular shape
Shells	4	Pencil or coloured rounded triangular shapes (purple, orange)
People	11	Coloured or pencil contour of human figure with a head, eyes, mouth, hands and legs (brown, blue) Pencil or coloured stick figure
Sandcastle	3	Pencil or coloured drawing of castle shape with turrets and windows
Beach balls	3	Coloured circle with diagonal lines (red, white) Pencil contour of circle with diagonal lines

- *Level of artistic development*: The category of level of artistic representation as used in the current analysis addresses the form through which
  objects in the world are visually represented. The development of
  artistic representation at the ages of 7–9 covers a period in which there
  is transition from the representation of objects through schematic,
  symbolic representations to early realistic representation. The major
  difference between these two modes of representation is the degree to
  which the visual representation is an attempt to present an object as it
  appears in the world. A schematic representation produces a symbolic,
  learnt representation of the object (i.e. a stick man to represent your
  father or a square with a triangle on top to represent a house), whereas
  an early realistic representation is a problem-solving task in which
  there is an attempt to represent the object itself. For the current study
  two levels of development will be addressed: schematic representation
  and early realistic representation.
- *Density of information presentation*: The category of information density
  in artistic representation used in the current analysis addresses the
  number of objects presented in the picture. A simple frequency
  count was used to define the density of information. Three objects
  or fewer in a designated sea, sky or beach area was considered
  to be a low density of information. Four objects and above was
  considered to provide a higher density of information. For the
  current study two levels of density were addressed: low and high
  information density.

The overall scheme of analysis which integrates the genre definitions
with the associated categories of form produces a 2 (genre) × 2 (level
of artistic development) × 2 (levels of information density) analytical
scheme. In Table 6.2 the frequency of occurrence of the different genre
for the current data set is presented.

As seen in Table 6.2 the analysis of the genre of the visual presentation shows that 15 of the pictures were descriptive, 12 were of
low density and 11 were schematic. The largest genre category was
descriptive, low density and schematic. Overall the analysis of genre
reinforces the content analysis of the same pictures. The pictures are
not detailed and tend to present static descriptions of expected objects.
The limited number of narrative action pictures tended to produce
narratives that included extraneous information. These narratives
consisted of either sharks attacking other fish or underwater sea
adventures.

Summary – Beach folder pictures

The beach folder picture was an early visual representation task that was
designed as a way of activating knowledge relating to the beach. This
was an open task that essentially asked for a static representation of a

Table 6.2 Summary of Genre Analysis for Beach Folder Pictures for Whole Class (n=20)

Genre Category	Frequency of Occurrence
Narrative Action – High Density – Realistic	1
Narrative Action – High Density – Schematic	2
Narrative Action – Low Density – Realistic	1
Narrative Action – Low Density – Schematic	1
Descriptive – High Density – Realistic	4
Descriptive – High Density – Schematic	1
Descriptive – Low Density – Realistic	3

beach. As analysed here this task presents an early picture of students' understandings of what beaches are and the objects that occupy them. The analysis presented here shows that at this early stage in the educational process of the science unit, the students had undifferentiated under- standings of the beach and its contents. These understandings consist of expected experiential objects in relatively low-density descriptive settings.

6.2 Coloured Map

The analysis presented below relates to another early activity in the science unit. As described by the classroom instructor the overall aim of this activity was to make students understand that most of the world is covered with water. This had been a point of discussion in an early class, and the teacher decided to introduce a visual representation as the best way of overcoming any misconceptions in relation to this geographical knowledge.

The map colouring activity was conducted on a photocopied map of the continental United States. In its original form, the map was a black and white page with the land mass presented with an outer line contour. The land mass presented consisted only of North America; Canada is not represented. Visually the map shows North America and Mexico as an island. The central aspect of this activity for the student was the colouring in of three aspects of the map – the water in blue, the land in brown and the shoreline in red.

The black and white map was accompanied by a brief key on a separate page that functioned as a set of instructions. As seen in Figure 6.1, the page consists of a checklist in which the student is required to colour the land in brown, colour the water in blue, mark the shoreline with a red pencil line, put a five point star as a marker of the Pacific Ocean and an asterisk as a marker of the Atlantic Ocean. The instructions include colour coding and symbolic representation.

As a closed colouring activity, the students' pictures are similar. However, three different variations were found. The three variations consist of the

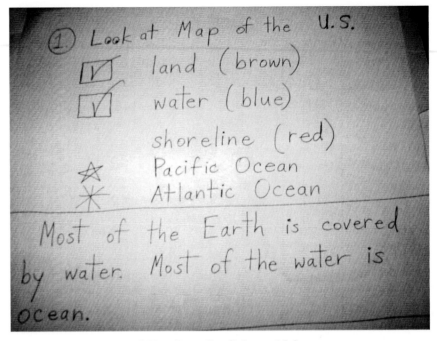

Figure 6.1 Picture of Key Page for Coloured Map

addition to the map of Canada as a small square on top of North America that is surrounded by sea, the addition to the map of Canada across the whole of the North American continent and the colouring in blue of the Great Lakes. It is important to note that those maps which represented the lakes in blue also had an accurate representation of Canada. In all, 15 coloured maps were analysed. Table 6.3 shows the frequency of occurrence for the three variations.

This activity consists of a coded colouring worksheet. From a genre perspective, the form of visual representation is of a *Schematic Visual Representation*. The objects represented in this task are water, land and shoreline. These are represented schematically through colour coding. The visual representation has a low density of represented information as it focused on only three objects. This specific manifestation of this form

Table 6.3 Summary of Coloured Map Type (n = 15)

Map Type	Frequency of Occurrence
Partial Representation of Canada	2
Full Representation of Canada	9
Full Representation of Canada and Coloured Lakes	4

of visual representation was conducted as a closed directed activity. The schematic nature of the product does not represent the students' level of artistic development but rather the restrictive nature of the directed activity.

As can be seen in the picture of the key page, this page included a stated conclusion at the end of the key. This conclusion is supposedly based on a process of logical inference and as such is a stage in the development of the epistemology of science that the unit wishes to address. The cognitive process being developed involves a visual analysis of the coloured map and the construction of an inference based on this analysis. The conclusion being proposed is that most of the world is covered with water. In terms of the present task this would consist of a visual analysis of the amount of blue as compared with the amount of brown visually present in the picture. The conclusion that there is more water in the world would be based on the visual analysis that there is more blue in the picture than brown. Unfortunately, as seen in Figure 6.2, the actual map used for colouring does not have more blue than brown and the presented inference is actually invalid in relation to the presented evidence.

Summary – Coloured map

The coloured map was introduced into the unit as a way of overcoming misconceptions as to the amounts of water and land that exist in the world.

Figure 6.2 Coloured Map

This task involved using a key, colouring and symbolically marking using the key and understanding a basic inference based on a visual analysis. As analysed here the task produced schematic visual representations with limited informational content. The inferential component of the current task was flawed and thus could not develop the required epistemological understandings.

6.3 Photograph Description

The analysis presented below relates to an early knowledge activation activity. The central aim of this activity was to generate discussion about beaches and to activate the students' knowledge of beaches. The activity is multimodal and consists of the description of a beach presented in a photograph. The analysis of this activity allows insight into the student's initial understandings of what constitutes a beach and what its components are. It also allows an early insight into the way these children use visual evidence in making claims.

The central aspect of this activity consists of the analysis of a photograph of a beach and the written presentation of those features of the photograph that represent the beach. The activity was organized as a worksheet in which the photograph is at the bottom of the page and space for the written description is left at the top of the page. There is room for six lines of writing in the form of a paragraph at the top of the page. The written description has been started by placing a sentence and a half at the beginning of the paragraph. The beginning sentences are 'Here is a photo. I can tell that a beach is there because.' The second half sentence sets up a causal relationship in which evidence for the claim that the photograph is of a beach needs to be presented. In this way the written description which follows this sentence should present a series of noticed objects that exist in the photograph and support the claim that this is a beach.

This activity consists of both a visual analysis of the picture and a written description based on this analysis. An important component of the activity would seem to be the attempt to develop the concept of using sensory evidence in supporting a claim. In this case, the objects discerned in the picture were supposed to be used as the basis for the written support of the claim that this is a beach.

Table 6.4 presents the content analysis of the written paragraphs in relation to the specific photographs that were presented to the students. The analysis differentiates between the objects and actions that actually exist in the picture and those that do not.

As can be seen in Table 6.4 the objects and actions found in the pictures present an experiential understanding of a beach. This experiential understanding describes the beach in terms of the expected objects and actions that stereotypically can be found at the beach. Specifically, the main objects presented are water, waves, land, sand, rocks, shells and

Table 6.4 Content Analysis of Written Photograph Descriptions for Each Student (n=15)

Student	Specified Object or Activity in Picture	Specified Description not in Picture
1	waves rocks	'see water meet land' 'I can walk on it'
2	walking in the water	'a place where water meets land'
3	shoreline sand water meets land	'There is a lot of sea creatures like a whales, sharks, dolphins that can live underwater'
4	waves water meets land	'I could walk on the beach there rocks on the beach' 'The beach meat has crab'
5	shoreline water meets land	'I see that it has seaweed' 'A beach have loose material' 'A beach is a nice place to walk'
6	shoreline rocks pebbles waves water meets land man	
7	rocks sand water meets land	'mud'
8	people walking	'Beaches are composed of mud, sand, pebbles and other loose material.'
9	land meets water	
10	lot of people	
11	land meets water	'I see lots of seaweed' 'beach are composed of mud, sand, pebbles and other loose material'
12	seaweed people walking mud	'I see people swimming'
13	water meets land mountains with grass sand	'Pebbles and other loose material'
14	seaweed shoreline people walking	'It has land and it has a ocean' 'And because there are a lot of anemos'
15	water meets land kids walking	'There is sand and rocks, shell, mud

seaweed. The main actions consist of people walking on the beach and the water meeting the land. As seen in previous knowledge activation exercises this is still an undifferentiated understanding of the shoreline.

An analysis of Table 6.4 also reveals an initial understanding of how visual evidence is used by these students. Of the 15 photo descriptions analysed, 12 students added information and statements about objects and actions that were not actually in the photographs that they were given. The list of objects or actions added in these statements is similar to the list of objects actually found in the whole set of pictures (but not the specific picture that each student used for the written description). This suggests that this activity was completed using background knowledge more than a visual analysis of the photographs. The students presented what they knew was on the beach more than they presented a visual analysis of what was in the picture.

Several specific statements were repeated across the written photo descriptions. Eleven of the 15 students used the statement 'Where the water meets the land' or 'Where the land meets the water.' Six of the 15 students described the beach as 'a nice place to walk.' Four of the students used the statement 'The beach has loose material.' These statements seem to come from the verbal interaction and teacher-directed discussion that preceded the writing of the passages. The written description utilized the verbal information and the students' background knowledge in addition to the visual analysis.

The genre used for this activity consisted of a *descriptive paragraph*. This paragraph consisted of a series of mentioned objects and actions related to the sea and beach. The objects and actions were presented through a single noun or verb. None of the descriptive paragraphs used descriptive language that went beyond the naming of the object or action. The paragraphs consisted of a list of items noticed in the picture, a series of items from background knowledge that were associated with the sea and beach and specific phrases that came from the teacher's directed discourse. Two different sentence forms were used to generate the lists of objects and actions that appeared in the paragraphs:

1. single sentences for each presented object or action;
2. a single sentence with a series of presented objects.

Nine of the 15 students created their paragraphs only using single sentences for a specific object or action. Three students only used sentences that presented a series of objects in a single sentence. Four students used a combination of both types. The descriptive paragraphs were made up of an average of three sentences with the range of one to seven sentences. Overall the descriptive paragraphs were short and presented lists of individual objects and actions.

The cognitive process of utilizing a visual analysis in supporting a stated claim seems to have been only partially successful. The students produced paragraphs that presented information from background knowledge and teacher discourse in addition to the visual analysis. Only three students based their descriptions solely on the visual analysis. The other students deferred to the authority of the teacher's discourse or to their own background knowledge. Although this is not problematic in relation to the overall aim of the task that consisted of activating prior knowledge, this does show a limited understanding of the importance of the use of sensory information in supporting a claim.

Summary – Photograph description

The aim of this activity was to generate discussion and activate knowledge relating to the shoreline. The activity also had a component of developing an understanding of the role of visual analysis in supporting a claim. The analysis of the descriptive paragraphs supports previous analyses about the experiential nature of knowledge of the shoreline at this early stage in the science unit. The students have an undifferentiated understanding of the sea and beach. In producing the paragraphs the students used three sources of information, the visual analysis, background knowledge and stock statements from the teacher's discourse. This suggests an early and limited understanding of the use of visual information in supporting a claim.

6.3 Beach Bucket Exploration and Categorization

The analyses below relate to the written products that resulted from the beach bucket exploration. This analysis complements the analysis of the video data of the beach bucket exploration task. The three products to be analysed are a beach bucket findings list, an evidence categorization activity and an alive/never alive categorization activity. The aim of this task and the associated written activities was to develop an understanding of how systematic observations could be made and recorded and to acquire an understanding of the process of categorization. There was also the epistemological aim of developing an understanding of using existing evidence to construct an inference. This task and the associated written product activities constituted the first stage in the development of a scientific thinking process.

The central aspect of the beach bucket findings list consisted of the recording of the objects found by the students in the form of a list. A dedicated lined page was provided for the list. In the attempt to make an explicit connection between the beach bucket and the beach, the list page started with the sentences 'My full beach bucket is a *model* of a real sandy beach. In my bucket I found:' The list was written on the lines below and consisted of all the objects taken out of the beach bucket and placed on the table. As seen in the video data, a process of early categorization had already taken place in that types of objects had been grouped together. However, these were early categories that addressed natural categories such as rocks and shells. An analysis of the content of the findings list provides an insight into the content of the students' developing understanding of the beach and its composition. Table 6.5 presents the content analysis of the findings list.

As can be seen in Table 6.5 the list of noticed items found in the beach bucket shows evidence of the extension of the students' knowledge of what can be found on the beach. The list reflects the students' classroom work in exploring the beach buckets and the actual contents of the beach buckets that were organized by the instructional team. When compared with the contents of their beach pictures (Table 6.1), the current list of 21 items consists of 19 new components that were not considered beach contents at the beginning of this science unit. The major change consists of the addition of human and animal debris such as soda cans, paper, feathers, crab shell and sea urchin spines. This reflects a much greater diversity in relation to the potential objects found on a beach.

The genre of this activity consisted of the construction of a *list of found objects*. The list was conducted on a worksheet that contained 11 empty lines to be filled in. Of the 19 beach exploration lists that were studied, 12

Table 6.5 Content Analysis of the Beach Bucket Findings Lists (n=19)

Specified Object	Frequency of Occurrence
Shells	19
Feathers	18
Rocks	17
Sand	16
Soda Can	15
Paper	15
Plastic	14
Wood	13
Crab Shell	13
Sea Urchin Spine	13
Metal	12
Seaweed	11
Tennis Ball	10
Pebbles	9
Bones	7
Old Tyres	6
Candy/Ice Cream Wrapper	3
Toy	3
Glass	1
Golf Ball	1
Starfish	1
Pencil	1

consisted of 11 items written one to a line. Students who did not write one word to a line tended to identify more objects in the beach bucket (2×19, 2×16, 1×15). The average number of objects discerned by the students was 12.4 with a range of 9–19. The form of the worksheet seemed to limit the number of observations recorded. However, the recognition of even nine items is an important development from the early stages of the science unit.

The creation of a list can be seen as a cognitive process of the widening of a conceptual schema through a visual and tactile recognition activity. As seen in the analysis of the video data the process of creating this list of observed objects includes a process of noticing and grouping. The written lists represent the results of this process of observation and grouping.

The second product of the beach exploration and categorization activity consisted of an evidence categorization activity. This writing and thinking activity is based upon the recorded observations presented in the list of found objects but also extends work that has been done so far. This categorization activity consists of organizing the lists of observed items into four different categories: evidence of humans; evidence of non-human animals; evidence of plants and seaweed and evidence of non-living things. In order to complete this task, a worksheet format was presented to the students. The worksheet started with the sentence: 'One way that objects found on beaches can be sorted is in terms of *evidence.*' The rest of the worksheet consisted of four circles with the titles of the different types of evidence. The central role of students in this process was to consider their list of found objects and to categorize them as one of the four types of evidence. This was a process of reorganization into categories using inferential information. Table 6.6 presents the list of categorized objects, the objects that were wrongly categorized and the erased words. Table 6.6 is organized according to the four categories of information (evidence of humans; evidence of non-human animals; evidence of plants and seaweed and evidence of non-living things).

As can be seen in Table 6.6, the students were generally successful in categorizing the different objects found in the beach bucket exploration into the different potential categories. Thirty-seven objects were chosen and correctly categorized according to the categories of information. There were 11 cases of mistaken categorization. Sand, shells and wood seemed to be difficult objects to categorize. Shells were mistakenly seen as evidence of non-livings things and evidence of plants and seaweed. Wood was not seen as evidence of a plant but rather as a non-living thing, non-human animals and evidence of humans. Sand was categorized as evidence of plants and seaweed three times. The words that were erased demonstrate the process of questioning the category. The category of evidence of non-living things seemed to generate the most changes as seen in the number of

Table 6.6 Content Analysis of the Evidence Categorization Activity According to the Four Categories of Information (n = 19)

Evidence of Humans

Specified Object	Frequency	Mistaken Categorization	Frequency	Erased Object	Frequency
Soda Cans	13	Wood	1	Sand	1
Plastic	10				
Paper	10				
Tennis Balls	7				
Rope	6				
Metal	4				
Trash	3				
Toys	2				
Firewood	2				
Candy Paper	1				
Old Tyres	1				
Fan	1				
Comb	1				
Hat	1				
Footprints	1				

Evidence of Non-Human Animals

Specified Object	Frequency	Mistaken Categorization	Frequency	Erased Object	Frequency
Shells	11	Wood	1	Crab	1
Crab Shells	10	Rock	1		
Sea Urchin Spines	10	Metal	1		
Feathers	9				
Bones	2				
Shrimp	1				
Seaweed	1				

Evidence of Plants and Seaweed

Specified Objects	Frequency	Mistaken Categorization	Frequency	Erased Object	Frequency
Wood	11	Sand	3	Rocks	1
Seaweed	10	Shell	1	Sea Urchin	2
Stick	2	Sea Urchin	1		
Plants	1	Crab	1		
Paper	1				

Evidence of Non-Living Things

Specified Objects	Frequency	Mistaken Categorization	Frequency	Erased Object	Frequency
Rocks	13	Shells	4	Shells	5
Sand	7	Crab	2	Crab Shell	3
Metal	6	Wood	3	Sticks	1
Soda Cans	3			Bones	1
Tennis Balls	2				
Rope	1				
Plastic	1				
Rope	1				
Paper	1				
Trash	1				

erased items. Five students erased the word shells from the category. These results with the data of mistaken categorization suggest that there was a tendency to see shells as non-living things rather than evidence of non-human animals.

The genre of this task consists of a *graphic organization of word lists*. The worksheet was designed so as to have four independent circles, each representing a different category of information. Thus information was presented as four independent categories. Completion of the activity consisted of conceptual categorizing through the placement of the word in the right space. The activity of erasing included replacing and changing the assignment of an object to a different category. In some ways, this written activity parallels the physical placing of the objects found in the beach bucket on the table and then circling and naming them. But the categories here are more abstract and include inferential information.

The construction of lists of objects organized according to an abstract category system can be seen as a development of scientific thinking. This development includes the use of inferential information for categorization and the reorganization of information according to categories. In the initial stages of the beach bucket exploration task, the understanding of objects on the beach was extended and diversified as seen in Table 6.5. In the evidence categorization task, this extended list was reorganized and placed under abstract headings requiring inferential analysis. This process of categorization seems to include questioning of the nature of an object and its relevance to a category. Some objects seemed more difficult than others to categorize and this addresses the specific knowledge that students have of the various objects. A shell can be seen as an object in its own right that just exists at the beach but from the point of view of the categorization activity, this is evidence of non-human animal life. This activity provides experience of the process of categorization and a visual graphic method of organization. The process of categorization can be seen as a deepening of the developing schema of the beach's properties, including a wider set of objects and a series of conceptual distinctions for organizing this list of objects.

The third product of the beach bucket exploration and categorization task was a once alive/never alive categorization activity. This activity utilized the same basic list of objects found in the first product of the beach bucket exploration and is similar to the second product which is also a categorization activity. However, this task was different in that it required a more complex graphic and conceptual categorization process. Rather than four independent circles representing four different categories, the once alive/never alive categorization task was organized around a Venn diagram consisting of two interconnecting circles with an overlapping area. This activity was presented on a worksheet. The top of the page was titled 'A Sort of the Beach Bucket into Once Alive Objects/Never Alive Objects'. Underneath the title were two big circles with an overlapping area. Next to each circle and the overlapping area was a lined area for writing in the name of the specific category (never alive; once alive; overlapping never alive – once alive). The name of the third overlapping category was not specified anywhere on the worksheet. This directed the students to propose their understanding of this overlapping category. Table 6.7 presents the list of objects according to the three categories.

As can be seen in Table 6.7 most students were able to categorize found objects according to the three categories. However this task is to be seen as more difficult than the last task. While all students used the once alive/never alive categories, only 9 students actually used the overlapping category. Completing the overlap categories seemed to pose a specific problem of conceptual understanding. Table 6.8 summarizes the different titles given to the overlapping category. Not all students who provided a title for the overlapping category actually wrote a list of objects in the overlapping space.

These different titles designate different understandings of the meaning of the interlocking circles of the Venn diagram. For titles 1 to 4 no lists of objects were listed in the overlapping area. Both options 1 and 2 consisted of not providing a title for the overlapping category, perhaps suggesting that the students did manage to conceptualize what this space represents. Titles 3 and 4 consisted of repeating the clearer categories of once alive/ never alive. Once again this space was not used because essentially it was redundant (the list of objects appeared within the bigger circles with these titles). Title 5 consisted of a simple combination of both categories once alive and not (never) alive. Three of the five students who created this category did write the names of objects in the overlapping space. Title 6 offers a more sophisticated conceptualization by proposing that the object can be seen as a collection of parts, some of which are alive and some

Table 6.7 Content Analysis of the Once Alive/Never Alive Categorization Task (n=20)

Objects Categorized as Alive	Frequency	Objects Categorized as Never Alive	Frequency	Objects that Overlap the Categories of Alive/ Never Alive	Frequency
Shells	11	Plastic	10	A shell with a rock inside	7
Wood	10	Rock	10	Paper	5
Feathers	9	Soda Can	10	Drawing on paper	3
Seaweed	7	Rope	7	Shell	2
Bone	5	Trash	2		
Sea Urchin Spines	5	Metal	2		
Paper	3	Sand	2		
Stick	2	Bottle Cap	1		
		Juice Tab	1		

of which were never alive. Finally title 7 presents the conceptualization that two objects can be connected with one encompassing the other. All of these titles propose a response to the difficulty in conceptualizing the overlapping space of the Venn diagram. But only titles 5, 6 and 7 produced a category definition in which written lists of words could be assigned.

The genre of this activity consisted of the *graphic organization of lists* according to the format of a Venn diagram. This activity was conducted on

Table 6.8 Frequency of Titles for Overlap Category in Venn Diagram

Proposed Titles	Frequency of Occurrence
1. No titles on any category	1
2. No title for overlap category (but titles for once alive/never alive)	5
3. Use of circle title twice – once alive	1
4. Use of circle title twice – never alive	1
5. Once alive and not (never) alive	5
6. One part alive and one part never alive	4
7. Objects that were never alive with something alive inside	2

a worksheet that presented two interconnected circles with an overlapping area. For each of the circles, the process of categorization was similar to the evidence categorization task that preceded the Venn diagram categorization. As analysed above the overlapping area posed specific conceptual problems. Essentially the students had to make meaning of this category by providing a title and adding objects. This posed a conceptual problem-solving activity in that the students needed to find a title designating a concept that bridges the opposites of alive/never alive. Once this problem was resolved, objects could be added to the list.

The use of a Venn diagram can be seen as an attempt to develop the scientific thinking of the students. This activity went beyond the evidence categorization activity in that the students needed to provide an understanding of the overlapping area. This proved difficult for half of the students. However, nine students came up with innovative solutions to this problem. This activity reinforces the process of categorization on the basis of inferential evidence that was used in the previous categorization task. The problems encountered by the new graphic format highlight the connection between graphic forms and conceptual understanding. At the very least students were exposed to this graphic format although 11 students did not use all of the Venn diagram options for representation.

Summary – Beach bucket exploration and categorization

The aim of the beach bucket exploration and categorization activity was to develop an understanding of how systematic observations can be made and recorded and to acquire an understanding of categorization using an inferential process. The data shows a widening of the knowledge the students have relating to the contents of the beach. The beach exploration list includes a much wider set of objects that has been recorded than in the early knowledge activation tasks. In the categorization tasks this wider list was reorganized into a series of categories based on inferential information. In both of the categorization activities students demonstrated the ability to use inferential information in the assignment of objects to the different categories. The exploration and categorization activities involved the generation of word lists. There is a progression in the graphic format among the three activities. The first one used a simple line format, the second one used the graphic organization of four separate areas on the page and the third utilized a Venn diagram with two interconnected circles and an overlapping area. Students easily negotiated the first two formats but had difficulty with the overlapping area of the Venn diagram. These activities show a development in scientific knowledge, procedure and thinking. The knowledge of the beach has more differentiation than in the early knowledge activation activities. Students have learnt and practised methods of data observation and data recording using word lists and graphic organization. In order to generate the lists according to categories, an inferential process was involved, and for the Venn diagram an additional problem-solving component in relation to the overlapping area was included. Students were involved in the reorganization of the same data for two different categorization exercises. Although there were difficulties for some students in relation to the graphic organization of the Venn diagram, the current set of activities show a rudimentary development in scientific knowledge and thinking.

6.5 Rock and Shell Description

The analysis below relates to the activity of describing a shell and a rock. The activity consisted of providing both a written and a pictorial description of a shell and a rock. This activity had several related aims. First, it was designed to direct the students to conduct a detailed observation of objects found at the beach. It also had the aim of providing experience with methods of recording the observation. Finally the activity had the aim of enhancing the epistemological understanding of a basic argument structure of a claim supported by specific evidence. This activity provides some insight into the observational and representational abilities of the students at this stage of the science unit.

This activity was conducted in several stages. First students were offered an array of shells and rocks to choose from. They were directed to choose their favourite shell and rock. Having chosen a shell, they were provided with some criteria to observe the shell. They were then provided with a worksheet with lines that had the following sentence at the beginning of the page: 'This shell from the beach is my favourite for many reasons.' They then wrote a first draft and produced a drawing of the shell. The draft was corrected and a second, final draft was produced. The students then addressed the rock. They were provided with similar criteria for the observation of the rock as those of the shell. They were given a worksheet with lines for the description of the rock as well. The worksheet was lined, and at the top of the page the following sentence appeared: 'This rock from the beach is my favourite beach rock because.' Only one draft of the rock description was produced. After finishing writing the students were directed to draw a picture of the rock.

Table 6.9 provides a summary of the observations and statements made in the final version of the written shell description. The table is organized according to the observational categories used in the descriptive paragraphs.

As can be seen in Table 6.9, the descriptive paragraphs followed a clear, recognizable pattern of information based on the criteria provided for the observation of the shell. This pattern addressed the qualities of colour, size, weight, pattern, texture and shape of the shell and utilized this information to create a description of the shell. In addition, the students produced statements about their associations as to what the shell is 'like' and a wish statement about the shell. Colour and texture were the most frequently used categories of information perhaps showing their salience as categories for these students. But all the categories were used by the

Table 6.9 Content Analysis of Final Descriptive Paragraphs of Shells (n = 16)

Observational Category	Frequency of Occurrence	Specific Descriptors Used
Colour	16	Colour name (i.e. brown, pink) Colour name series (i.e. orange, red, pink and white)
Texture	14	Rough, bumps (bumpy), smooth
Weight	12	Light, medium, light weight, very light
Size	10	Medium, small, feels little, large, a little bit long
Shape	11	Shape according to geometric definition: oval, triangle, rhombus, circle Shape according to adjective: pointy, skinny, curly, spiked, twisty Shape by analogy: like the horn of a rhino, like a tornado, like a fan, like a crab
Pattern	8	No pattern Pattern by colour name (i.e white, red, pink and orange) Pattern by geometric form: spiral, round and round, stripes, spots, dots
Descriptive associations	10	Like a crab holding a shell in its hands; like a mountain; reminds me of a toy dinosaur; reminds me of a drilling, digging toy; reminds me of a tornado; reminds me of people's heads; reminds me of a turtle shell; like a carrot; reminds me of a house of a snail
Statement of wishes	12	I wish I could keep (have) it; I wish it would start growing; I wish I could slide inside; I wish I could see the snail alive; I wish the shell would have a rainbow

Table 6.10 Categories of Change between the Draft and Final Version of the Written Shell Description

Category of Change	Frequency of Occurrence
Neater presentation	10
Spelling correction	9
Sentence division change	5
Change in specific vocabulary use	5
Reduction of repeated information	3
Change in phrasing	2
Tense change	1

majority of the students. The quantity of categories used and the types of descriptions seen in Table 6.9 show the richness of both the original observations and the descriptive paragraphs derived from them.

The genre of this section of the activity consisted of a *descriptive paragraph*. The paragraph was written on a lined worksheet once as a draft and once as a final product. The writing of the descriptive paragraph seems to have been closely directed by the categories of observation. As seen in Table 6.9, the content of the paragraphs consists of statements based on the categories of observation. This information structured the paragraph and provided clear scaffolding for the development of the written paragraphs. Coherence in the paragraph was achieved through the usage the pronoun 'it' and the connectors 'and' and 'because'. All the students' paragraphs were coherent and consisted of connected sentences developing the description of the shell. The final paragraphs were on average 7.85 sentences long and consisted of an average of 51 words with a range of 30 to 58 words.

The draft and the final paragraph were similar. However, specific changes were made to the paragraphs. Table 6.10 summarizes the changes between the two versions.

As can be seen in Table 6.10, the changes relate to the linguistic form issues of the paragraph and not to content. The option of a first draft and final version allowed the students the ability to produce a neater and more accurate written description.

In the original design of this activity all the students were supposed to draw the shell and produce a written description. Nine students produced a pictorial representation of the shells they had chosen. All the pictures were descriptive visual representations without narrative components. Five of the descriptive pictures were schematic and presented only an outer contour of the shell. These pictures did not include any specific details of the shells themselves. Four of the descriptive pictures were realistic and high density addressing the colour, size and pattern of the specific shell. High-density descriptive information included use of multiple colours, attempts at representing the texture and specific characteristics of the shell. These four pictures were attempts to realistically represent in visual form the shells themselves.

The written descriptive paragraph of the rock followed a similar structure to that of the written description of the shell. As with the shell description, the descriptive paragraphs were constructed from the categories of observation provided to the students. Table 6.11 summarizes the observations and statements made in the descriptions of the rocks. The table is organized according to the observational categories used in the descriptive paragraphs.

As with the shell descriptions, the descriptive paragraphs of the rocks utilized the categories of observation to structure the information in the paragraph. As can be seen in Table 6.11 the descriptions were multilayered utilizing several categories of information to produce the descriptions of

Table 6.11 Content Analysis of Final Descriptive Paragraphs of Rocks (n=17)

Observational Category	Frequency of Occurrence	Specific Descriptors Used
Colour	17	Colour name (i.e. grey, black) Colour name series (i.e. green and brown)
Shape	15	Shape according to geometric definition: circle, round, triangle, oval Shape according to adjective: long and thin Shape by analogy: like a hammerhead shark, like a bowling ball
Texture	13	Bumpy, smooth, pretty smooth, very smooth, has holes in it, very rough
Size	12	Long, medium size, small, huge, big, little
Pattern	12	No pattern Pattern by colour name (i.e black and grey) Pattern by geometric form: stripes Pattern by analogy: has a belt
Weight	11	Heavy, kind of heavy, very light, light, medium
Descriptive associations	14	Like a hammerhead shark; like a fish with a long tail; like a little egg; like a ducky head; like a bar of soap; like green eggs; like a bowling ball; like a mask; like an eye; like a sock; like a big egg; like Eggo waffles; like a bench; like a line
Statement of wishes	15	I wish it would glow in the dark; I wish I had 200 (100) (1,000,000) of them; I wish it would be gold; I wish it was mine (had one); I wish I had found it; I wish I could keep it for a secret; I wish I could play with it forever; I wish it was a magic rock

Table 6.12 Summary of Genre Analysis for Rock Picture Description (n=17)

Genre Category	Frequency of Occurrence
Narrative Action – Low Density – Realistic	1
Narrative Action – Low Density – Schematic	2
Descriptive – High Density – Realistic	12

the specific rocks. In both the shell and rock descriptions, the students showed both detailed and creative use of language that provided a clear description of the rock or shell being examined. Associative comparisons as well as detailed observation allowed a verbal picture of the object to emerge. The statement of wishes revealed a personal aspect to this activity. Obviously, many of the students wished to own the object that they were describing and ascribed personal value to it.

The written paragraphs belong to the genre of *descriptive paragraphs*. The paragraphs were written on a lined worksheet. On average they were 6.6 sentences long and 39.94 words long with a range of 30 to 58 words. The paragraphs were coherent, utilizing the pronoun 'it' and the connector 'and' to create coherence in the paragraph. The paragraphs provided a variety of information structured according to the observational categories. This allowed this writing activity to be directed by the information provided by the observation itself, thus easing the writing process and producing successful descriptions of the rock and shell characteristics.

In addition to writing a descriptive paragraph about the rocks, the students were also encouraged to produce visual descriptions as well. Fifteen of the students produced pictures of the rocks they had chosen. Table 6.12 presents the genre of pictures used for this description.

As can be seen in Table 6.12, 12 students produced descriptive high-density, realistic representations of the rocks they had chosen. These pictures included detailed information addressing the size, shape, colour, pattern and texture of the rocks. The detail in the pictures is impressive, showing a detailed visual analysis of the rocks and the ability to represent this in a drawing. This is a development in relation to the number of realistic pictures produced in previous activities.

From a cognitive perspective, the descriptive activities outlined here are an extension of the students' visual and categorical analysis of objects found at the beach. The descriptions, whether visual or written, demonstrate an ability for a controlled and detailed observation of a specific object and the ability to record this in a written and visual mode. This is an extension of the previous activity. Whereas in the beach bucket explorations and categorization the students knowledge of the beach and its contents was widened through an observation exercise, in the shell and rock descriptive activity students experienced an in-depth observation of a single object and successfully described this object. In the design of the activity, these observations were to be used as a way of enhancing the students' understanding of the argument structure. The observations were to provide evidence explaining why the students liked the rock and shell they had chosen. The paragraphs did not directly address this issue. Instead, they provided detailed descriptions of the object of observation. Indirectly, this can be seen as providing evidence for a statement of liking and choice. But there were no direct connections of this kind made by the students themselves in the paragraphs.

Summary – My favourite rock and shell description

The aim of the rock and shell description activity was to provide students with the experience of a directed observation of an object found at the beach and the experience of describing this object in both a written and visual format. The written paragraphs and majority of the rock pictures were rich with content and demonstrated that the directed observation was successfully conducted. The paragraphs were coherent, organized around the categories of information used for the object observation. As a writing activity, the analysis above shows that the students produced well-organized, detailed written descriptions. This activity widens the knowledge and ability-base of the students by providing them with general categories that can be used for the description and comparison of objects that are of interest. The epistemological aim of enhancing the students' understanding of argument structure does not seem to have been achieved in this activity.

6.6 Chapter Beach Books

The analysis below relates to the activity of writing a beach book consisting of four chapters relating to different aspects of the beach. In its design this activity had the aim of summarizing previously learnt material and experiences relating to the beach and a component of individual research in which the children were supposed to read and summarize their own knowledge of different beach creatures. In order to facilitate the book writing process, each student was provided with a schematic outline of the book and its chapter headings, a page with a summary of key concepts that have been learnt and sources to conduct individual research. These materials in conjunction with brainstorming and outlining activities, were intended to provide a scaffolded book writing and knowledge summarization activity.

The schematic outline of the book consisted of a central oval in which the student was to write her/his name and four adjacent boxes with the chapter titles. The chapter titles were Chapter One: Where the Water Meets the Land; Chapter Two: Beaches and Sand; Chapter Three: Evidence Found at a Beach; and Chapter Four: (Whatever you have researched). This outline was designed to serve as a way of organizing the knowledge the students had acquired up until this point in the course and allow them to summarize this in a writing activity. To help with this process, a printed handout summarizing the material learnt was also provided. The handout addressed scientific knowledge such as the composition of beaches and sand and types of shoreline, as well as scientific modes of thinking and procedures such as the explanation of what a scientific model is and how evidence is to be used in scientific thinking. In addition to these aids and in order to facilitate the book development, the writing process was conducted in the classroom.

Although support was provided to the students, analysis of the written data reveals that this task was difficult to complete for the children in this classroom. The difficulty seems to be situated in the literacy activity of actually writing the chapters for the books. None of the students wrote all four chapters. Four students wrote only one chapter, nine students wrote two chapters and five students wrote three chapters. Each chapter consisted of loosely connected or unconnected sentences in a paragraph format. These chapters were brief, consisting of between one and six sentences. Chapter One entitled 'Where the Water Meets the Land' had an average of 3.94 sentences and 38.8 words. Chapter Two entitled 'Beach and Sand' had an average of 3.15 sentences and 31.7 words. Chapter Three entitled 'Evidence Found at the Beach' had an average of 1.6 sentences and 15.3 words. Chapter Four entitled 'Whatever You Researched' had an average of 3.6 sentences and 40.6 words. All 18 students did Chapter One, 13 students did Chapter Two and only three students did either Chapter Three or Chapter Four. Table 6.13 presents a content analysis of the statements made by the students in each of the chapters and is organized according to the chapter headings.

As can be seen in Table 6.13, in relation to the content analysis of Chapters One and Two, students demonstrated some understanding of the phenomena of sand and beaches. The highest frequency statements related to the definition of a shoreline as a place where the water meets land and that sand is made up of tiny bits of rocks, shells and other materials found at the beach. These basic understandings went past the experiential understanding presented at the beginning of this science unit. However, it is important to note that these understandings were drawn directly from the worksheet summarizing key scientific concepts that was presented to the students as an aid. All the statements made in relation to Chapter One came from the summarizing worksheet. The three highest frequency statements of Chapter Two also came from the same worksheet. This suggests that this exercise was directed through the worksheet with the teachers' explicit summary of key concepts being used to produce the brief written paragraphs. This also explains some of the difficulties seen in relation to Chapters Three and Four. By design these include more independent work but were only done by six of the students (three for Chapter Three and three for Chapter Four). This suggests that at this stage and for these students, independent writing and research in literacy was a difficult task.

Table 6.13 Content Analysis of the Chapter Beach Book Writing Activity (n=18)

Chapter One: Where the Water Meets the Land (n=18)

Thematic Statements Identified	Frequency of Occurrence
Where the water meets the land is shoreline	14
The shoreline can be found on a map or globe	9
The beach is a special kind of shoreline	8
Most of earth is covered in water	8
A shoreline can be by a lake, river or cliffs	6
Beaches are composed of mud, sand, pebbles and other loose material	6
Most of the water on earth is ocean	4
The force of the waves breaks anything on the beach to make sand	3

Chapter Two: Beach and Sand (n=13)

Thematic Statements Identified	Frequency of Occurrence
Sand is composed of tiny bits of everything found at the beach	13
The force of waves breaks rocks, shells and cans to make sand	5
Beaches are a special kind of shoreline	4
Sand is on the bottom of lakes, rivers and oceans	3
On beaches you can find shells and feathers	2
Sand can be yellow and white	2
Sand comes from many places	1
Sand can be all colours and shapes	1
Some rocks are hard to break and some are easy	1
Water is salty	1
We can walk on the shoreline	1

Chapter Three: Evidence Found at the Beach

Thematic Statements Identified	Frequency of Occurrence
Sand is made of rocks, plastic and shells	1
A snail lived in a shell	1
Feather is evidence of a bird	1
Crab shell is evidence of a crab	1
Plastic is evidence of humans	1

Chapter Four: Whatever You Researched

Thematic Statements Identified	Frequency of Occurrence
Fish and animals can live in harmony	1
Some fish help others	1
Dolphins swim in groups	1
Dolphins swim fast	1
Dolphins are mammals	1
Dolphins eat fish, squib and crabs	1
Hyanodon was larger than other carnivores	1
Hyanodon lived 30 million years ago	1
Hyanodon liven in North American and Eurasia	1
Hyanodon ate hoofed animals called ungulates	1
The Hyanodon got its name because of its big jaws and head	1
The Hyanodon is not an ancestor of the hyena	1

Three different genres were connected to the chapter beach book activity. These genres consist of note-taking, outlining and informational paragraph writing. For all the students and for all the individual chapters of the beach books, the genre of the *informational paragraph* was used. Organizational structures such as taxonomy, chronological structure, cause-effect, comparison-contrast, direction sequences and expository-explanatory are generally utilized in the construction of informational paragraphs. The informational paragraphs presented in the beach book chapters lacked clear organizational structure. Of the 37 paragraph chapters analysed (the complete data set of written paragraph chapters), only four had an identifiable organizational pattern of taxonomy. The other 33 paragraphs consisted of a collection of individual sentences that were graphically organized in the form of a paragraph. The only linguistic markers of paragraph organization consisted of connecters of addition (i.e. and, also). The method used for constructing these loosely organized paragraphs seemed to consist of finding facts on the handout of key concepts and then placing them under the chapter headings. Some students did provide and add their own information, but this was mainly in the third and fourth chapters, which was limited to six students. The overall picture that emerges of the usage of the informational paragraphs is that of an early stage of writing development in which there is only limited usage of informational paragraph organization.

The students showed an understanding of the idea of a book structured into chapters. As seen in the content analysis there was a differentiation of the information presented in the different chapters. This demonstrates the idea of categorizing information according to chapter title. The construction of differentiated chapters was enhanced through a scaffolded process of note-taking and chapter outlining. Of the 18 students who created beach chapter books, 17 used note-taking and chapter outlining. The note-taking seemed to involve a general activation of ideas without any attempt at chapter organization. The note-taking consisted of lists of objects, copied sentences from the key concepts worksheet and questions the students asked themselves. In three cases the note-taking also included the use of symbolic notation. In all three cases, symbolic notation was used to express the same idea that sand was made up of everything from the beach that the waves had crushed. Figure 6.3 presents one example of the type of symbolic notation used.

For the chapter outlining, the students divided a page into four equal rectangles with a number designating the chapter heading in each square. In each rectangle information to be used in the chapters was written down. Three ways of representing knowledge were used to outline the content of the chapters – lists, sentences and symbolic notation. The chapter outlines were created using lists of objects and concepts; sentences taken directly from the key concepts worksheet, sentences paraphrasing the students' understanding and the development of symbolic notations. The chapter outlines divided the students' knowledge according to the

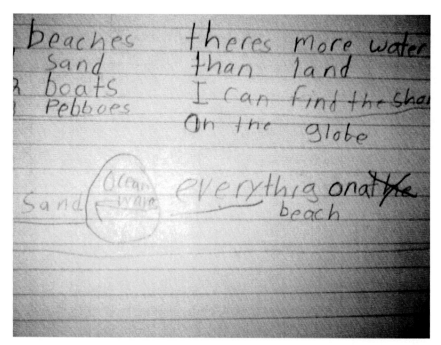

Figure 6.3 Picture of Symbolic Notation of Sand Formation

chapter headings. For Chapters One and Two lists and written sentences were used to outline the students' ideas for chapter content. In Chapter Three, which is entitled 'Evidence at the Beach', 11 students used symbolic notation to describe their ideas in relation to this chapter. The specific notation used was common to all the students and consisted of the use of an arrow shape to state a relation of a part and whole inferential relationship. For example, to express the idea that a feather found on the beach is evidence of a bird, the following notation was used:

Feather ◄——— birds

Table 6.14 summarizes the conceptual relationships expressed through the symbolic notation system of an arrow and two referents.

The symbolic notation was used as a form of shorthand to designate specific relations. However, it is interesting to note that only three students actually went on to write the third chapter. In this sense the chapter outlining process was potentially richer than the written beach chapter books.

From a cognitive view point, the chapter book writing process is based on the concept of writing as a way of crystallizing, summarizing and explicitly formulating one's ideas and knowledge. As seen in the note-taking, chapter outlining and chapter writing, a certain amount of key ideas, relationships and knowledge was expressed. However, this utilized a multiliteracy format and simple textual structures such as lists and single sentences. The structurally organized informational paragraph was not used to organize the students' thoughts. It is interesting to note the use of symbolic notation as a way of stating relationships reflects the use of such notation systems within the classroom and is the beginning of scientific symbolic methods of representation.

Table 6.14 Conceptual Relationships Expressed through Symbolic Notation

Conceptual Relationship	Frequency of Occurrence
Shell evidence of animal life	4
Feather evidence of a bird (gull/seagull)	4
Rocks evidence of non-living things	2
Wood evidence of burning	2
Can evidence of humans	1
Feather evidence of living things	1

Summary – Chapter beach book writing

The beach chapter was an attempt to use literacy to summarize knowledge acquired from the science unit activities and discussions. As seen in the analysis above, the ability to write informational paragraphs seemed to limit the writing of the specific chapters of the book. No student wrote all four chapters with most students writing only two chapters. The content of the chapters does reflect some of the key ideas developed in the science unit and in this sense demonstrates recognition of the core knowledge being developed. But the writing of the chapters seems to have relied heavily upon the summary of key ideas provided on the handout. These were expressed in brief paragraphs consisting of collections of individual sentences rather than organized informational paragraphs. The content of the chapters and the process of note-taking and chapter outlining do show an understanding of differentiated chapter content. The use of symbolic notation is an interesting development showing a movement towards the type of notation that is often used within descriptions of scientific processes. Overall, this activity did not result in the students clearly conceptualizing their understandings of the work conducted within the science unit. Nevertheless, this activity can be seen as a literacy learning process in which the students were exposed to the process of chapter book writing. The outlining and note taking activities do seem to have organized the students' thoughts into differentiated chapter headings and the students were exposed to an extended writing activity.

6.7 Directed Observation of Sand

The analysis which appears below addresses the literacy activities of 'Sand on Stage' and the 'Unknown Sand' worksheet. This analysis complements the video analysis of 'Observing Sand: Understanding Tools of Measurement' presented in the previous chapter. Both of these multiliteracy products functioned as a method of both recording and directing the process of scientific description of sand and the role of tools of measurement in this process. Both of these multiliteracy activities consisted of worksheets with a series of questions and activities that needed to be addressed. The aim of these activities was to develop the students' understanding of measurement, directed observation and the multiliteracy representation of observational findings.

The 'Unknown Sand' worksheet was part of an exercise in which students were presented with a bag of sand and were directed to observe the sand using a magnifying glass and a magnet and infer its source based on the recorded observation. The worksheet consisted of seven questions to be answered. These questions can be divided into questions directing observation, questions of comparison and identification and questions of inference. The questions of directed observation consisted of questions relating to the colour, size, shapes and magnetic qualities of the sand. The question of comparison and identification consisted of finding rocks that have similar colours to the sand being observed. The question of inference addressed the issue of the source of the sand that was observed. Table 6.15 summarizes the answers provided to the worksheet questions:

Table 6.15 Content Analysis of the Unknown Sand Worksheet (n = 18)

Worksheet Question	Response Type
Colours	Name of colour: white, black, blue, yellow, red, pink, pinkish, peach, brown, green, grey, orange, gold, silver Colours written with appropriate coloured pencil Use of coloured dots representing the observed colours
Size of the grains	Size according to single adjective: tiny, small, flat, little Size according to series of adjectives: small-medium-big; small – big; small up to large; little and big
Shapes of grains	Shape according to geometric definition: not rounded, rounded, not round, round, square, circle, triangle, cube, hexagon, circlish, squarish Shape according to adjective: irregular Shape described by drawing of shape
Magnetic	Yes, no
All grains the same size	Yes, no, it is different, different
Name of rocks with same colour as sand	Gypson, coal, marble, chalk, basalt, pink granite, grey granite, quartzite, ironstone, siltstone, sandstone, obsidian, limestone, slate, dunite, serpentine
Where do you think the sand originated?	Name of geographical feature: mountains, cliffs, volcanoes, beaches Name of object: rocks, shells, rock crystal, animals, shell animals Name of geographical location: California, Aliva Beach, Hutchinson Island, Florida, South Africa, Port Townsend

The worksheet was completed by all 18 students and every question was answered. As can be seen in the content analysis in Table 6.15, the worksheet functioned as a recording and organizational device for the observation made by the students of the sand samples. The observations are based on the use of both a magnifying glass and a magnet. The observations show a level of visual differentiation that goes beyond schematic presentation. This is most clearly seen in the definition of shape in which the geometric forms are not seen to be perfectly suited in describing the shapes. Adjectives such as circlish, squarish and not rounded suggest a process of trying to really describe the shape as it is seen and not as it appears in some abstract concept of what sand is. This deeper visual analysis can also be felt in the usage of a series of adjectives to describe the size of the grains and in choices, such as the use of the term pinkish in the description of the colour. The use of the magnifying glass allowed distinctions to be made that would not have been possible without this tool. The magnet functioned in the same way. A visual analysis cannot differentiate magnetic from non-magnetic. However, a simple test of the sand using the magnet provides a clear answer to the question of magnetism on the worksheet. The name of the rocks mentioned on the worksheet demonstrates exposure to a wide variety of potential rocks and thus to potential sources for the sand. The comparison question directs the students to compare their observation with a wider set of samples and to make comparisons based on the quality of colour.

The genre of the unknown sand activity consisted of a *directed observation worksheet*. The worksheet both provided the instructions for the observation of the sand sample and the means to record and organize observations made. Completion of the worksheet consisted of conducting a series of specific observations and then directly recording these on the worksheet. As such this genre connects literacy directly to the scientific inquiry conducted by the students. All the students successfully negotiated the observation and the recording components of this exercise. An important component of this activity consisted of the multiliteracy responses students provided, although these were not explicitly elicited. These consisted of the use of colours and drawings presented in the students' observations. The worksheet did not require the use of visual information but some students used this option as the mode of representation that expressed their understandings.

The sand on stage extended the work conducted in the unknown sand activity. This activity utilized a directed worksheet and the tools of a magnifying glass and a magnet. The worksheet was divided into two sections. The first section elicited tool-based observation of the sand samples and the second section required the comparison of the sand sample to other samples. This worksheet had a clear multiliteracy component to it which was different from the 'Unknown Sand' worksheet. Observations of colour, shape and size required a visual representation of the observation. For the colour of the sand a series of boxes were provided in which the colours observed were to be recorded. For the shape of the sand grains students were asked to draw the grains of sand and to choose among three pictures of sand grain types the picture that most closely resembled the shape of the sand they were observing. For size a graded line of dots that gradually grows larger in size was provided and students were required to choose and mark the dot that was closest in size to the grains they were observing. As part of the directed observation, students were asked to mark off those components which they thought they observed in their sand samples. Rock, plants, glass, shells, wood and plastic were all provided as options that could be marked.

In the second section of the 'Sand on Stage' worksheet, students utilized their observations to make comparisons to other sand samples and to other rocks. The comparisons were organized around the observations that had been made during the first section of the activity. The comparisons requested consisted of finding similarities between the sand sample and the pieces of rock in a selection of labelled rocks provided by the teacher. The observation of similarity was recorded on the worksheet by naming the closest rocks to the sand sample. Comparisons were also conducted among sand samples from different locations in relation to the lightness/darkness of the colours of the sand and size of the sand grains. As with the 'Unknown Sand' worksheet all 18 students successfully completed the directed questions on the worksheet.

From a cognitive perspective, the 'Unknown Sand' worksheet and the 'Sand on Stage' worksheet extended and deepened the students' scientific understanding of the components and source of sand and beaches. This extension of understanding was tied to the use of tools of observation and the directed nature of the observation. Students were not left within the context of an open observation of the sand. The worksheets directed close observation of specific qualities of the sand and required the use of specific tools to be able to actually make the observations. This process of directed observation was then used to make comparisons and inferences based on the observations collected. This observation-based comparison consisted of a rudimentary stage of tool-based measurement. The size and colour of the grains required a magnifying glass, recorded observation and direct comparison among different samples. As a result of the directed tool-based observation that students have a more in-depth understanding of the shape, size, colour and magnetism of different sand samples. This means that the students had much greater diversification in their concept of what sand is and the differences to be found in various sand samples.

Summary – Directed observation of sand

The 'Unknown Sand' and the 'Sand on Stage' worksheets consist of worksheets that direct, record and organize an observation process. This directed, tool-based observation and the use of the worksheet extend the students' understanding of the components of sand and the way scientific observation is conducted. The recording of detailed and rich observations of the sand demonstrated the students' understanding that science involves the attempt to represent what is observed and not just schematic responses. The students' responses to the worksheets show an ability to use the tools provided to them and to work in a systematic and guided format. The specific knowledge acquired during this observational process consists of a more in-depth and detailed understanding of the qualities of sand, the connection between the sands observed and rocks, and some understanding of the potential sources of this sand. In recording their observations the students used both written and visual forms of representation. This activity can be seen as providing an experience of scientific observation and the tool-based comparison exercises as developing a rudimentary understanding of scientific measurement.

6.8 Sand Summary

The analysis which appears below relates to the activity 'My Sand Summary'. This activity is a continuation and intensification of the activities described in the analysis of the directed observation of sand activities described in the previous section and the video analysis of the task of observing sand. The activity of My Sand Summary consisted of the observation of a small sand sample under a microscope and in two drafts' writing of a descriptive paragraph summarizing the observation. The aim of this activity was to widen the students' experience with different scientific tools and to provide additional experience of using literacy to record observations made.

The use of a microscope required the development of a specific set of procedures suitable for the use of this tool. Before any observation was conducted rules of appropriate behaviour surrounding the microscope were explained to the students. These included leaving the microscope on the table at all times, working cleanly around the microscope and ways of adjusting the lens for better viewing. In addition to rules relating to the microscope, the sand to be observed also had to be prepared for observation under the microscope. Students were carefully instructed as to the method most appropriate for correct viewing of the sand. A small circle of sand was stuck to a small card and this was placed under the microscope for observation.

The observation itself was recorded using the literacy aid of a worksheet. This worksheet consisted of two different sections. The first section, under the heading of ideas, listed different options for observation and description. These consisted of size, colour, shape, origin, forces, texture, similar to, comparison and different from. Next to this list was an open space for the writing out of ideas. In the open space students listed different observations and ideas that they had while observing the sand. The second section of the worksheet consisted of a lined space in which to write a first draft paragraph of the sand observation. This first draft was corrected by the teacher and returned to the students. A final draft was carefully prepared. This final draft included the original sand card created for observation and the carefully written final draft of the sand summary. Table 6.16 summarizes the content of the final my sand summaries. The table is organized according to the categories of information found in the analysis.

As can be seen in Table 6.16, the final sand summaries are based on a detailed visual analysis using the tool of a microscope. Overall, the content analysis reveals that the students have greater differentiation in relation to the characteristics of sand. The sand summaries use the terminology of describing the grains of sand and not just sand. This distinction is also apparent in the different categories of description that are used. Rather than the use of a single descriptor for colour, shape, size or texture, a variety of options was presented by the majority of students. Sand is seen as comprised of sand grains that differ from one another and do not have the same characteristics. This type of observation is possible because of the increased visual distinctions enabled by the microscope. It suggests a diversified concept of sand. This aspect of the current task is clearly present with the descriptions of the sand composition in which sand is seen as a collection of little rocks or pebbles collected together but not necessarily of the same type. As with the previous magnifying glass observation, there is a real attempt to describe the sand grains that are observed and not just present schematic definitions. This can be seen in the use of terms such as blackish, whitish, the use of analogy to describe the specific nature of the grains observed (i.e. like a hat, like a cup, like an egg) and the attempt to modify geometric shapes to match the observed grains (i.e. a little bit rounded but not very rounded). Overall, the contents of the sand summary suggest that the components of the directed observation worksheet used in conjunction with the magnifying glass have been internalized by the students. Many of the same categories are utilized in the sand summary description.

From a genre perspective the sand summary was a *descriptive paragraph*. The paragraphs were written out on a carefully prepared and designed page. The central section of the page consisted of a series of lines for writing the descriptive paragraph and a space to stick the card with the sand sample used in the microscope observation. Around both of these, sand was sprinkled and glued to the page. This design did not leave a lot of room for the writing of the descriptive paragraph but did create a very special multiliteracy space describing and presenting the sand sample. On average 5.6 sentences (with a range of 4 to 8 sentences) and 41.9 words (with a range of 26 to 63 words). The paragraphs were coherent using the phrases 'My sand', The sand' or third person pronouns to create connections across the descriptive paragraphs.

As described above, the writing of the final sand summary paragraphs was preceded by an idea generation and first draft writing activity. Table 6.17 summarizes the changes found between the first and second drafts of the sand summary.

As can be seen in Table 6.17, there were changes to the draft versions of the sand summaries. These changes were both to the content and to the form of the written paragraphs. Changes to the content consisted of specification of vocabulary items, erasure of repeated information changes to phrasing and the addition of new sentences. These changes tended to shorten and focus the written paragraphs. Changes in form consisted of making sure that the writing fulfilled the grammatical requirements of standard English writing.

Table 6.16 Content Analysis of My Sand Summary (n = 19)

Observational Category	Frequency of Occurrence	Specific Descriptors Used
Colour of Sand Grains	19	Colour name: (i.e. black, blackish, pink, whitish, kind of golden) Colour name series: (i.e. red, white and yellow, blue, green, brown, black and grey) Statement: It is colourful, lots of different colours
Geographical Source of Sand	17	Name of geographical feature: volcano, cliff, mountain, coral reef. Name of geographical location: Baja California, Mexico, Phillipines, Puerto Rico, Reno Nevada, Australia
Shape of Sand Grains	15	Shape according to geometric definition: octagon, round, triangular, square, a little bit rounded, mostly rounded, not round, kind of rounded but not very rounded, hexagons Shape according to a list of geometric shapes: triangles, hexagons, circles and squares Shape according to adjective: small, little Shape by analogy: like a hat, like a cup, like small rocks, looks like little pebbles, like an egg, like small little beans
Magnetic	10	Black grains are magnetic, some grains are magnetic, lots of magnetic grains, a few grains are magnetic, found only one magnetic grain, no magnetic grains
Size of grains	10	Small, small grains, tiny and puny all way up to large grains, sand grains are a little bit big, some little and some big, small to big
Sand Composition	9	Sand is made up of coral, is made of little rocks, sand looks like little black rocks with clear glass, sand is comprised a little pieces of coral
Texture	3	Soft, smooth and rough, very smooth
Reference to Rock Sources	2	Colours of grains is similar to chalk, grains match the colour of coal, gypsum and marble
Weight	1	Light weight

Table 6.17 Categories of Change between the Draft and Final Version of the Sand Summary (n = 19)

Category of Change	Frequency of Occurrence
Neater presentation	19
Change in specific vocabulary use	16
Reduction of repeated information	10
Change in phrasing	10
Tense change	12
Sentence division change	7
Change of pronoun	4
Add new sentence	4
Spelling correction	3
Capitalization	3
Change order of sentences	2
Sentence syntax change	1

From a cognitive perspective, the sand summary activity extends previous work on scientific observational processes. The microscope extends the visual analysis that the students can conduct on the sand grain samples. This magnification fulfils the role of clearly showing sand as a collection of 'little rocks' which can be differentiated according to their different colours, size, shape and source. Thus, the students' schema of the composition and nature of sand was deepened through the use of the microscope. This activity can also be seen as additional experience in working with scientific tools to observe and conduct measurements of natural phenomena.

Summary – My sand summary

The 'My Sand Summary' continued the process of tool-based observation and using literacy to record the observations made. The aim of this particular activity was to provide students with the experience of using a microscope and recording and organizing their thoughts in a descriptive paragraph. This activity extended previous observational tool-based activities conducted by the students. In the descriptive paragraphs, the students discussed the grains of sand and saw the sand in a diversified manner differentiating among differences in colour, size, shape and source. The use of the microscope changed the mental representation of the sand grains. The specific knowledge gained by the students addressed the composition of the sand and the individual characteristics of the sand grains.

6.9 Making Inferences

The analysis below relates to a pedagogical activity designed to teach students how to make evidence-based inferences. This activity consisted of two worksheets that required students to make an inference and then explicitly state the evidence that was used to make this particular inference. This activity had the epistemological aim of making the structure of a scientific argument explicit. The argument structure that this activity addressed was the evidence-based inference. An analysis of this activity provides evidence of the students understanding of scientific argument structure.

The two worksheets had a similar, three-part structure. Both worksheets consisted of the presentation of some initial information under the heading 'What I know' or 'You know'; the call for an inference under the heading 'My inference is' or 'inference' and a final section with the request to explicitly state the nature of the evidence used to support the inference that has been made. In all, there were four requests for evidence supported inferences on the two worksheets. The stimuli used as initial information were as follows: 'At the beach the dog saw a crab moving fast'; 'We bought tickets and some popcorn'; 'My tongue turned blue' and 'Anna played piano every day'. The written answers to the worksheet under the categories of 'inference' and 'evidence' were analysed according to the type of response found. Table 6.18 summarizes the type of response and frequency of occurrence for both these categories.

As can be seen in Table 6.18, 70 of the 76 student responses to the request for an inference were world knowledge inferences. These inferences consisted of adding additional information to the source stimulus in order to explain what is happening. For example, in response to the stimulus 'At the beach a dog saw a crab moving fast', the inference 'the dog is going to chase the crab' was made. The inferences made by the students were based on a schema of world knowledge and consisted of a logical development of the described scene. The majority of the inferences related to the actions of the animate actors in the scene.

Sixty-four of the 76 responses to the request for evidence to support the inference referred to personal experience or knowledge. The request for evidence supporting the made inference was understood by these students as the request to explain the source of the knowledge that allowed them to generate the specific inference made. In other words, the concept of evidence was not understood as supporting evidence relating to the specific inference but rather as an answer to the epistemological question 'How do YOU know this?' In answer to this question the vast majority of responses referred back to personal experience and this was utilized as the major source of information for providing and supporting the inferences. Five students also used personal knowledge in the same way. In answering the request for evidence they pointed out that they already knew this and therefore they could make the inference. Twelve of the responses did not provide any sort of evidence either for the inference or explaining the source of the inference. Eight of these responses provided an additional inference instead of evidence. This may show some difficulty in understanding what the evidence category signified. Two responses just repeated the stimuli of given information. Two of the responses provided information that was not within the context of this inference exercise. This additional information was not part of the developed schema in which an inference could have been made. Thus, in this context the information was irrelevant.

The tri-part structure of the two worksheets was designed to make students understand the relationship between inference and evidence. When both the inference and evidence categories are taken together a concept of the form of scientific argument understood by the students can emerge. In the current data set, six forms of argument relating to the categories of inference and evidence were found. Table 6.19 summarizes the argument types and the frequency of occurrence for each type.

As can be seen in Table 6.19, 55 of the 76 responses showed the same pattern of an argument structure in which a world knowledge inference which was generated through knowledge acquired out of personal experience. For this argument type, personal experience plays a very important role in that this is the source and the justification of the proposed inference. A similar situation exists for the argument structure of a world knowledge inference supported by reference to personal knowledge. Personal knowledge functions as both the source and the justification of the inference that has been made. Sixteen of the 76 responses did not have the designed argument structure of an evidence supported inference. Eight students just added an additional inference when asked to provide evidence. They did provide new information and these were logical extensions of the schema presented in the stimuli and original inference. But this did not fulfil the epistemological aim of either supporting the original inference or providing information as to the source of this inference. Two of the responses provide an inference but did not provide any evidence to support the inference and two responses did not move beyond a paraphrase and repetition of the original stimuli.

The genre of this activity consists of a *directed worksheet*. The outline of the exercise was directed by the design of the worksheet itself. All 19 students completed all the components of both worksheets. The requests for inference and evidence were answered using complete single sentences with an average of 4.2 words. The literacy requirements of this worksheet were well within the capabilities of the students. Twenty-three of the responses to the request for an inference were accompanied by a drawing of the situation being described. For example, in addition to the inference 'They are at the movies', a small drawing of chairs with people sitting might be added.

From a cognitive perspective, the making inferences worksheet provides an insight into the way students understand the structure of an argument. The majority of the students generated an inference through a process of schema activation. In this process the inference was a logical extension of the information provided in the stimuli. The request for evidence was

Table 6.18 Summary of Types of Response for the Categories of Inference and Evidence in the Making Inferences Worksheets (n=19)

Category – Inference		
Types of Response	**Frequency of Occurrence**	**Example Utterance**
World Knowledge Inference 1. Action of animate object (dog, crab, person)	35	'The dog is barking at the crab' 'She drank something blue'
World Knowledge Inference 2. Thought of animate object (dog, crab, person)	2	'The crab thought the dog would chase her'
World Knowledge Inference 3. Feeling of animate object (dog, crab, person)	15	'She liked playing the piano' 'The crab was scared'
World Knowledge Inference 4. Physical location of animate object (dog, crab, person)	18	'They are at the movies'
Non-Inference 1. Paraphrase	6	'The dog is looking at the crab' 'The crab ran'

Category – Evidence		
Types of Response	**Frequency of Occurrence**	**Example Utterance**
Reference to Personal Experience	59	'I did this' 'I saw this' 'Happened with my cousin's dog'
Reference to Personal Knowledge	5	'I saw a picture' 'I know crabs'
Additional Inference Instead of Evidence Response	8	'She is a good piano player'
Repetition of Stimuli	2	'The dog saw the crab'
Irrelevant Information	2	'I practice soccer with Chirtan and with my friend'

understood as the request for the source and validation of the information. In most cases this involved the reference to personal experience as the major source of information and justification. Some of the responses showed that the argument structure of evidence-supported inferences was not well understood. Providing evidence was replaced by the addition of an extra world knowledge inference or just irrelevant information.

Summary – Making inferences

The aim of this activity was to raise the students' awareness and understanding of the structure of a scientific argument. The specific form

Table 6.19 Summary of Inference Argument Types and Frequency of Occurrence

Argument Type	Frequency of Occurrence	Example
World knowledge inference – reference to personal experience as source of inference	55	Stimulus: At the beach the dog saw a crab moving fast: 'The dog is barking at the crab' – 'I have seen this one time' Stimulus: My tongue turned blue: 'She sucked or licked something blue' – 'I have done this myself'
World knowledge inference – reference to personal knowledge	5	Stimulus: At the beach the dog saw a crab moving fast: 'I think that the dog is gonna chase the crab' – 'I know that dogs like to chase people and sea creatures'
World knowledge inference – additional world knowledge inference	8	Stimulus: Anna played the piano every day: 'She likes playing the piano' – 'She is a good piano player'
Paraphrase of original stimulus – reference to personal experience	4	Stimulus: At the beach the dog saw a crab moving fast: 'The dog saw the crab and the crab ran away' – 'I've did this'
Paraphrase of original stimulus – repetition of original stimulus	2	Stimulus: At the beach the dog saw a crab moving fast: 'The dog saw the crab moving fast' – 'The dog sees the crab'
World knowledge inference – irrelevant information	2	Stimulus: Anna played the piano every day: 'She likes playing the piano' – 'I practice soccer with Chirtan and with my friend'

that was addressed consisted of an evidence-supported inference. The analysis of this activity showed that the students did produce inferences. These inferences were extensions of activated schematic knowledge. The request for evidence within the argument structu e was understood by the students as a request for the source of the info mation used to generate the inference. This was an epistemological position dealing with the validation of the inference. However, this was not a scientific, evidence-based argument structure. Thus the task did raise awareness for the need for evidence but does not seem to have contributed to the wider aim of utilizing evidence in supporting one's claims.

6.10 Postcard Story

The analysis which appears below relates to the activity of creating postcard stories. This analysis complements the analysis of the video data of the task of summarizing sand formation through picture drawing and the task of summarizing sand formation through narrative writing. The postcard story activity followed the shared reading of the classroom reader 'Sandy's Journey to the Sea'. The aim of this activity was to direct the students to summarize their understandings of the process of sand creation. This summarization was conducted in both pictorial and written modes.

The activity of creating pictorial and written narratives of the process of sand creation was preceded by a shared reading of a book which person-ified one rock's journey to the shoreline. This shared reading created a forum in which knowledge relating to the process of sand formation could be both presented and exemplified. The shared reading built knowledge of this process. The activity of postcard story drawing and writing was designed as an activity that would allow the students to present the process of sand formation themselves. It summarized their understandings of how sand was formed. As a product the postcard stories provide evidence of the knowledge the students have acquired of this process.

The process of postcard creation was conducted in two stages. First, the pictorial representations were drawn and then on the back of the cards with the drawings the narratives were written. As a scaffolding process, the students produced pictorial sketches of the proposed postcards before drawing the final versions of the postcards. This scaffolding process was conducted on a handout divided into four panels. The first panel of the handout specified that the student should 'Draw a picture of where your sand came from (a clam, a mountain, a coral reef, or ...?) before it arrived on the beach'. The next two panels had the more general instruction 'Here's what happened next'. The final panel stated 'My grain of sand now looks like this'. The handout directed the students to describe the process of sand formation in four stages each represented on a single card. The specific instructions on the first and last panels direct the students to tell a narrative of a journey parallel to the journey described in the shared

Table 6.20 Content Analysis of the Pictorial Sketches of the Postcard Stories (n=16)

Narrative Type	Frequency of Occurrence
Mountain Narrative:	8
1. A rock is on a mountain	
2. Water on the mountain moves the rock down the side of the mountain	
3. Waves push the rock in the sea	
4. Rock/sand reaches the shoreline and is next to the sea	
Volcano Narrative:	3
1. Volcano blows pieces of rock into the sky	
2. Waves move rock in the sea	
3. Rocks are on the seabed	
4. Rocks reach the shoreline	
Bottle Narrative:	2
1. Bottles are on the beach	
2. The bottles are smashed into small pieces by the force of the waves and by other rocks	
3. A tsunami carries the pieces of smashed glass	
4. Individual pieces of glass are on the shoreline	
Coral Narrative:	2
1. Coral is in the sea	
2. Water and waves move the coral in the sea	
3. Water reaches the beach	
4. Some coral stays on the seabed and some is on the beach	
Cliff Narrative:	1
1. Rocks are on the edge of a cliff	
2. The water rises next to the cliff	
3. A wave rises above the cliff	
4. The rocks are knocked into the sea by the wave	

reading. Table 6.20 summarizes the different types of narrative journey presented by the students in the pictorial sketches of the postcard stories.

As can be seen in Table 6.20, the students produced five narratives representing different understandings of the process of sand formation. Eight of the students followed the narrative presented in the classroom reader. The other students created narratives using different sources of information from the class discussion and science unit. All the narratives were set out in the four stage format directed by the design of the summarization activity. The presence of five different narratives of the process of sand formation suggests that in the class there was a diversified understanding of the potential ways in which sand is formed. The content of the narratives demonstrates an understanding of how natural forces erode, and move rocks and other materials so that sand can be formed.

The pictorial genre of the pictorial sketch of the postcard stories was a *graphic narrative*. The graphic narrative consisted of a series of four pictures that are connected and together describe the process of sand formation. All the pictures were schematic, utilizing symbolic learnt representations for the objects described (for example a triangle representing a mountain). All the pictures had low densities of information and represented only those elements that were central to the narrative development of the journey of sand formation. Of the 64 picture panels (16 students × 4 panels each), 57 were narrative-low density- schematic and 7 were descriptive-low density-schematic. These seven descriptive pictures were all pictures of the first or last panel. They did not represent an action (and thus were not narrative pictures) because they represented static beginning or end states. The use of a low-density and schematic format can be explained in relation to the fact that these pictures were designed as an initial pictorial sketch that was supposed to help with the production of the full postcard story.

In the design of the activity, the development of the postcards in their final format was a continuation of the pictorial sketch process. As designed, a sketch was conducted first, then a pictorial version of the postcards was produced and finally a written version was added to the back of the same postcard. However, the production of the final postcards was less intensive than the pictorial sketches. Only 32 cards were actually produced. Only one student produced a narrative story covering four cards (this student used five cards to tell the story). Two students used three cards; eight students used two cards, and five students used only one card. Of the 16 postcard sets, 13 utilized the mountain narrative and the other three partially addressed the sea or waterfalls. For these three card sets, it was difficult to tell what the full narrative of the sand's journey consisted of because these three were only partial representations and seemed to have been stopped before completion. The extensive use of the mountain narrative for the final versions of the postcards was a shift away from the diversity of five different narratives found in the pictorial sketches. This also suggests that the students did not refer back to their pictorial sketches while producing the postcards (as seen in the video data).

The genre of pictorial representation is still the *graphic narrative* with the pictures starting a process of describing the journey of sand formation. Of the 32 cards produced, 25 were low density – schematic. Seven of the cards were high-density and schematic. Twenty-nine of the cards were narrative action and three were descriptive. As with the pictorial sketches, the descriptive cards represented initial states. As opposed to the pictorial sketches, the pictures of the final postcards utilized more colour and slightly more detail. The seven high-density postcards provided much more detail and information.

The writing on the back of the postcards was on the whole brief. On average only 1.78 sentences were written with a range of 1 to 5 sentences. Eighteen cards had only one sentence on the back. On average 15.5 words were on each card with a range of 6 to 36 words. The sentences tended to provide basic descriptions of the pictures on the front of the card. The writing on the back of the cards was designed as a summarization process in the form of a narrative. Four students used connectors relating to chronological development such as 'next'. But the majority of students (12 students) did not connect their writing across cards but rather described the card itself and left the narrative connections implicit or pictorial.

Overall, from a cognitive perspective the aim of this activity was to direct students to summarize knowledge they had acquired about the process of sand formation. Of the three representations (pictorial sketch, drawn postcard and written postcard), the pictorial sketches provide the best evidence of a summarization process. These graphic narratives presented different options of explaining how the beach was formed and the processes involved.

Summary – The postcard story

This activity was designed as a summarization process in which the students would use their newly acquired knowledge of the process of sand formation to produce new narratives addressing the sand's journey to the beach. The pictorial sketches did show the development of this knowledge and the ability to pictorially express it. The diversity of the narratives in the pictorial sketch showed the presence of knowledge about different ways in which sand was formed and the forces of nature that help in this process. The analysis of the final postcards in both their pictorial and written formats demonstrated a certain difficulty in completing this task within the time restrictions provided for it. The postcard stories were not completed by the majority of the students and the written component was limited, lacking explicit connections across cards. The disparity between the knowledge expressed in the pictorial sketches and the knowledge shown in the postcards would suggest that this was a representational rather than a knowledge problem. The sketches show that the knowledge did exist. But in the postcards, either because of time or writing difficulties, this knowledge was not fully presented.

6.11 Beach Animal and Plant Report

The analysis that appears below relates to the writing activity of producing a written report about animals and plants which live on the beach. This activity followed a process of conducting literacy research on the topic for the report. The reports were written utilizing the information that had been acquired from reading encyclopedic descriptions of the different animals and plants that were chosen by the students. As a literacy activity,

Table 6.21 Categories of Content for Topic-chapters in the Beach Animal and Plant Reports (n = 13)

Topic One – Description

Categories of Content	Frequency of Occurrence	Example
1. Colour	10	'green with a stripe'; 'light pink or sandy brown'
2. Size	10	'six inches'
3. Weight	2	'250 pounds'
4. Shape	2	'round'
5. Physical characteristics	12	'has black sharp jaws'; 'has six legs'; 'eyes on the end of each arm'
6. Comparison to other animal	6	'looks like a lobster or a shrimp'; 'like an armoured sea star'
7. Scientific descriptor	4	'isopod'; 'marine mammal'
8. By analogy	3	'like a stuffed pillow'; 'like a balloon on top of the water'

Topic Two – Habitat

Categories of Content	Frequency of Occurrence	Example
Physical location	10	'live on the beach'; 'on the coast by the bay'; 'on the ocean floor'
Description of habitat	9	'live under sand'; 'in rotting seaweed'; 'bury edge of shell in sand'
Aims of habitat	2	'hide from predators'; 'keep warm'
Creation of habitat	3	'tube feet help them burrow'; 'dig fast'; 'burrow in sand'
Time spent in habitat	2	'rest on beach at high tide'
Description of animal	6	'jumps with black legs'; 'excellent swimmer'; 'is not a good swimmer'

Topic Three – Prey and Predators

Categories of Content	Frequency of Occurrence	Example
Type of prey or food source	10	'eat bloodworms'; kelp'; 'eat fish and squid'; 'They eat plankton'
Type of predator	9	'can be eaten by a bird'; 'crabs eat beach hoppers'; 'sharks and whales'

Method of hunting	2	'shoots a tube to catch prey'; 'catch plankton in antennae'
Method of defence	1	'may hide'
Amount/time of eating	2	'eat little'; 'eat every day'
Description of habitat	1	'live in water'
Physical description of animal	2	'silver grey with black spots'

Topic Four – Miscellaneous Facts

Categories of Content	Frequency of Occurrence	Example
Physical description of animal	4	'the exoskeleton is like a shell'; 'many spines on arms'
Description of young and breeding	2	'lay eggs on warm sand'; 'seal pups need to stay warm'
Method of hunting	2	'feels for prey with arms'; 'fly over cement and drop clam to break it open'
Size of animal	1	'one inch long'
Description of habitat	1	'burrow in sand with antennae sticking out'
Life span	1	'kelp flies live only 2 weeks'
Dangers	1	'can't survive high waves'

this analysis provides some insight into the report writing and summary abilities of these students towards the end of this science unit.

This activity was conducted in three stages. The initial stage consisted of finding a plant or animal of interest and then reading appropriate encyclopedic material relating to the animal or plant that had been chosen. This involved a comprehension and internalization process of the material that had been read and some note-taking. The second stage consisted of writing a draft of the report. The report was to be written as a four-chapter mini-book. Each chapter was termed a 'Topic'. The idea behind this design seems to have been the development of a taxonomic structure for an informative text. The information found in the first stage would be reorganized around four specific topics that together describe and explicate the plant or animal of the beach that had been chosen. The last stage consisted of writing a final report. The final report followed editing suggestions by the teacher.

In all, 13 students produced written reports on animals of the beach. Ten of these students wrote four-chapter reports; one student wrote two chapters and two students wrote only one chapter. The average length of topic-chapter one was 4.2 sentences (with a range of 2–6 sentences) with an average word length of 30.38 words (with a range of 11–48 words). The average length of topic-chapter two was 3.6 sentences (with a range of 1–7 sentences) and an average word length of 30.5 words (with a range of 11–53 words). The average length of topic-chapter three was 3.3 sentences (with a range of 1–5 sentences) and an average word length of 22.3 words (with a range of 11–57 words). The average length of topic-chapter four was 3 sentences (with a range of 1–5 sentences) and an average word length of 18.6 words (with a range of 7–45 words).

These reports addressed the following list of beach animals: bristle worm, beach hoppers, harbour seals, burrowing sea star, elephant seals, turtles, sand crabs, kelp flies, herring gulls, sand dollars, jellyfish, rove beetles and Pismo clams. The information reports were divided into four topic-chapters. The topics were: Topic 1 – Description; Topic 2 – Habitat; Topic 3 – Prey and Predators; and Topic 4 – Miscellaneous Facts. Table 6.21 summarizes the categories of content found for the four topic-chapters.

As can be seen in Table 6.21, the students present a range of information clearly organized under the topic headings. The information for each topic chapter was relevant to the topic heading and the chapters presented a logical construction of information. The information used came from the encyclopedic items read by the students. However, the division of information was conducted by the students and showed a level of control of the structure of an informational report. The animals chosen for these reports went beyond the original list of animals found in the students' work at the beginning of the science unit. This demonstrated a certain widening of specific knowledge in relation to the beach as a living ecosystem. The content of the reports and each of the specific topic-chapters showed a certain depth of knowledge. The students presented the pertinent facts relating to each of the topics and together the topic-chapters presented a range and depth of information relating to the specific animals chosen.

The genre of this activity was the *informational report*. In the case of the beach animal and plant report, this informational text was made up of four individual sections each one the length of a paragraph. As seen in Table 6.21, the information concerning the chosen beach animals was divided into topic-paragraphs with relevant information present within the specific chapters. Ten students wrote all four chapters in their reports, one student wrote two chapters and one student wrote two chapters. All of the 44 topic chapters of the 13 students were coherent and organized. The structure used for these paragraphs consisted of pronoun or proper name repetition which constructed paragraphs organized as coherent taxonomies of information. This is a development when compared with previous informational chapter writing. In the case of this report, the students managed to control both overall chapter organization as well as the paragraph structure, creating well-organized, informational reports.

From a cognitive perspective, the informational report consists of comprehending, synthesizing and organizing information acquired from reading other sources. For the beach animal and plant report, this process seems to have worked smoothly with students clearly utilizing and organizing the information that they found. The ability to comprehend, synthesize and organize expert descriptions such as encyclopedic items are important science-literacy abilities as they allow access to acquired scientific knowledge.

Summary – Beach animal and plant report

The aim of the beach animal and plant report was to allow students to experience the process of acquiring knowledge from encyclopedic sources and to deepen their specific knowledge of the animals and plants that live on or close to the beach. In the 13 reports analysed, on the whole, these aims seem to have been achieved. The reports provided a depth of information that was clearly organized on the chapter book and paragraph levels. Relevant information was comprehended and synthesized from the encyclopedic sources and organized into topic headings. The overall reports provided clear information allowing a description of the animals described on a variety of parameters to emerge.

6.12 Observation and Prediction Worksheet

The analysis which appears below relates to a worksheet that was utilized to direct, organize and summarize an experiment on the appropriateness of different materials for cleaning up oil spilt in the sea. This worksheet was preceded by a discussion of oil spills, a teacher-led demonstration of how tides direct oil spills and a brief demonstration of the effect of oil on feathers. The final stage of learning about oil spills consisted of small group experiments in which students investigated the roles of different materials in cleaning up oil spills. The worksheet was part of this final stage of small group experiments and aimed to direct a process of scientific thinking. Specifically, the worksheet directed the students to make predictions, check these in an observational setting and consider their conclusions from the observed data.

Table 6.22 Summary of Prediction and Observation of Absorption Abilities of Different Materials on the Oil on the Beach Worksheet (n=18)

	Prediction	Observation
Clean a Little	40	10
Clean a Lot	66	96

The small-group experiment that was directed by the 'Oil on the Beach' worksheet consisted of observing the absorption qualities of different materials. The specific materials were nylon, cotton balls, sand or cat litter, hay, feathers and fake fur. In each case, the group placed these materials in oil and water to observe the materials' ability to absorb the oil effectively. The worksheet was designed to have three sections that worked in conjunction with the conducted experiment. The three sections of the worksheet were a prediction section, an observation recording section and a conclusion section. Completion of these sections was related to the stages of the small-group experiment with students first offering predictions, then recording the results observed in the experiment and finally reaching conclusions as to the best materials to use for oil spill clean-ups. The format limited the answer on both the prediction and observational components of the worksheet. Under the heading of prediction, students could only answer, 'Will clean up a little' or 'Will clean up a lot' next to the name of a specific material to be observed. Under the heading of observation, students could only answer, 'Cleaned up a little oil' or 'Cleaned up a lot of oil' next to the name of the observed material. These answers were signified through the schematic drawing of a smiling or frowning face. The columns of prediction and observation directed the students to propose a hypothesis and then write out an observed empirical outcome through which the prediction could be evaluated.

The worksheet was completed by 18 students. For 17 of the 18 students there were differences between the predictions and observations. Table 6.22 summarizes the predictions and observations in relation to the absorption abilities of different materials.

As can be seen in Table 6.22, the overall direction of the change is towards viewing materials as having greater absorption abilities than originally predicted. The students predicted that more of the materials would have lower absorption abilities than was actually observed. For the whole group 50 specific ratings were changed from the prediction to the observation columns. This suggests a role for the experiment in directing the students' understanding. However, the data shows that in the experiment ten of the students marked all the materials as being able to clean up a lot. This suggests that the observations made by these students did not differentiate among the materials and thus they all ended up with the positive designation of 'clean up a lot'.

The last stage of the worksheet consisted of reaching a conclusion as to which materials should be used to clean up oil spills. The students were asked to rank three materials that they had chosen and to provide evidence supporting their position. All 18 students did choose three materials that they thought were most suitable. All the choices were made from the list of materials that had been observed and categorized as 'cleaned up a lot'. However, none of the students wrote out any evidence in support of their choices. Thus the basis for choosing these particular materials was not provided by the students on the oil on the beach worksheet.

The genre of this activity was a *directed observation worksheet*. The 'Oil on the Beach' worksheet directed the students to make predictions, record observations and reach conclusions. In this sense the worksheet directed and organized the students' experimental observations. The current genre went beyond previous worksheets because it allowed the predictions and observations to be directly compared and thus enacted the type of thinking characteristic of empirical hypothesis testing.

From a cognitive perspective, the change between the prediction and observation stages of the worksheet shows an early form of scientific thinking. Sensory data organized in the form of an empirical observation that was recorded was used to change intuitive predictions. Beyond widening the students' understanding of the role of oil in the sea and ways of dealing with this phenomenon, the worksheet also directed an initial process of hypothesis testing, raising the role of empirical evidence in reaching conclusions.

Summary – Observation and prediction worksheet

The 'Oil on the Beach' worksheet was designed to direct, organize and summarize an experiment. The worksheet had the additional aim of directing a process of hypothesis testing. The students utilized the worksheet to organize their observations and the changes between the prediction and the recorded observation demonstrate the role of evidence in hypothesis testing. The worksheet did not allow a range of responses to degrees of absorption for different materials to emerge. The students did rank the materials for their ability to absorb oil; however, the basis for this decision was not provided on the worksheet.

Chapter 7: The Development of Scientific Knowledge

7.1 An Overview: The Progression of Scientific Knowledge

A central aspect of the research project presented in this book is the question of how scientific and literacy knowledge of second-grade students develops while studying in a science inquiry classroom. In order to address this question, the current chapter needs first to answer the question of whether there is evidence that scientific and literacy knowledge is developed in the specific second-grade classroom, studying the science unit 'The Sandy Shoreline', investigated in this study. As specified in the description of the science unit, the designers of this science unit, in line with current standards for science education, considered the science unit to cover the areas of factual and procedural knowledge in science as well as developing literacy and multiliteracy knowledge. Accordingly, the current analysis will address the issue of substantive factual knowledge development, procedural scientific knowledge development and the development of written and visual representational resources. Specifically this chapter attempts to answer the following questions:

1. What characterizes the process of substantive scientific knowledge development in this science inquiry classroom?
2. What characterizes the process of procedural scientific knowledge development in this science inquiry classroom?
3. What characterizes the process of written literacy scientific knowledge development in this science inquiry classroom?
4. What characterizes the process of visual literacy scientific knowledge development in this science inquiry classroom?

The data used for this analysis consisted of the analyses of the multiliteracy tasks and genres presented in the previous chapters. In order to ease the discussion of knowledge development, Table 7.1 presents an overview of the whole science unit from the perspective of the scientific knowledge demonstrated and representational resources used.

Table 7.1: Summary of the 'The Sandy Shoreline' Science Inquiry Unit from the Perspective of Conducted Analyses of Demonstrated Scientific Knowledge and Use of Representational Resources

Place in Science Unit	Analysed Task or Activity	Knowledge Demonstrated	Representational Resources
Beach Bucket Scavenger Hunt: Planet Ocean Brainstorm	Beach Folder Picture	Experiential understanding of the nature of a beach consisting of three areas: beach, sea and sky with expected objects such as sea, sun, sky, clouds, etc.	Visual representation mainly descriptive, schematic with a low density of information. Pictures are not detailed and tend to present static depictions of expected objects. Genre: *Descriptive or Narrative Picture*
Beach Bucket Scavenger Hunt: Planet Ocean Brainstorm	Coloured Map	Limited geographical knowledge of the US mainland, its lakes and its relationship to Canada. Ability to follow instructions from a coded colouring worksheet. Flawed inferential process with contradicting visual analysis and authorized statement on worksheet.	Visual representation consisting of a closed colouring activity on a worksheet. Low density of representated objects: water, land and shoreline. Reading and following instructional worksheet with colour coding instructions. Genre: *Schematic Visual Representation*

Place in Science Unit	Analysed Task or Activity	Knowledge Demonstrated	Representational Resources
Beach Bucket Scavenger Hunt: My Buddy Says – descriptions of the beach	Photograph Description	Experiential understanding of the beach consisting of presenting expected objects and actions. Reliance on background knowledge and provided statements from the teachers' discourse. Limited understanding of the role of visual analysis and information in supporting a claim or a description; preference for authority or prior knowledge.	Written representation designed to describe the content of the pictures. Students presented lists of written objects without connecting among them Genre: *Descriptive Paragraph* (performed as a list of objects)
Beach Bucket Scavenger Hunt: Beach Bucket Exploration	Beach Bucket Explorations: Categorizing Objects (Video Data)	Ability to notice physical attributes, material and type of object. Ability to group objects according to perceived relations based on noticed features. Categorization according to group membership. Final categorization decision based on reliance on teacher's authority. Demonstrated skills of oral discussion and verbal reflection for grouping decisions.	Use of pencils to physically demarcate grouping of noticed objects. Pencil used to write the name of the group. Science book read in order to find scientific description and term for specific objects.

Place in Science Unit	Analysed Task or Activity	Knowledge Demonstrated	Representational Resources
Beach Bucket Scavenger Hunt: Beach Bucket Exploration	Beach Bucket Exploration and Categorization: Beach Bucket Findings List	Observational understanding of beach bucket contents. List of 21 objects, 19 of which did not appear in prior experiential descriptions of the beach. Widening of beach content knowledge. Evidence of ability to notice and record found objects.	Written record of found objects. Objects recorded in the form of a list on a lined worksheet. Genre: *List* (of found objects)
Beach Bucket Scavenger Hunt: Beach Bucket Exploration	Beach Bucket Exploration and Categorization: Evidence Categorization Activity	Evidence of the ability to categorize found objects into the general categories of human, non-human, plant and seaweed and non-living things. Use of inferential processing to create categorizations. Categorization accompanied by a process of questioning the category. Demonstrated understanding of graphic format of worksheet.	Written and visual representation of categorization process. Use of worksheet with predefined independent circles for each category. Genre: *Graphic Organization of Word Lists*

Place in Science Unit	Analysed Task or Activity	Knowledge Demonstrated	Representational Resources
Beach Bucket Scavenger Hunt: Beach Bucket Exploration	Beach Bucket Exploration and Categorization: Alive/Never Alive Categorization Activity	Evidence of the ability to categorize objects according to the general categories of alive and never alive. Use of inferential processing in order to categorize found objects according to proposed categories. Conceptual difficulty in working with Venn diagram overlapping category. Some students demonstrated creative responses to the problem of the overlapping category.	Written and visual representation of categorization process using a Venn diagram. Use of worksheet with predefined Venn diagram representing the different categories. Overlapping area of Venn diagram posed a conceptual problem-solving task for the students through its graphic form and lack of title. Genre: *Graphic Organization of Word List* (Venn diagram)

Place in Science Unit	Analysed Task or Activity	Knowledge Demonstrated	Representational Resources
Beach Bucket Scavenger Hunt: Beach Bucket Exploration	Shell Description: My Favourite Shell	Evidence of directed noticing and description. Shell described according to specified criteria of observation: colour, texture, weight, shape, pattern, analogy and personal wishes. Process of directed observation with demonstrated ability of visual analysis.	Written and visual representation of shell. Developed, relevant and coherent written paragraphs. Coherence achieved through the pronoun 'it' and connectors 'and' and 'because'. Average paragraph length 7.85 sentences; average sentence length 51 words. Draft and final version of written paragraph produced; changes between versions relating to linguistic form. Visual representation produced by only half the students. All visual representations were descriptive. 5 were schematic with a low density of information. 4 students attempted realistic representations of the shell with high densities of information. Genre: *Descriptive Paragraph; Descriptive Picture*

Place in Science Unit	Analysed Task or Activity	Knowledge Demonstrated	Representational Resources
Beach Bucket Scavenger Hunt: Beach Bucket Exploration	Rock Description: My Favourite Rock	Evidence of directed noticing and description. Rock described according to specified criteria of observation: colour, texture, weight, shape, pattern, association and personal wishes. Process of directed observation with demonstrated ability of visual analysis and representation.	Written and visual representation of rock. Developed, relevant and coherently written paragraphs. Coherence achieved through the pronoun 'it' and the connector 'and'. Average paragraph length 6.6 sentences; average sentence length 39.94 words. Significant development in visual representation. 12 students produced descriptive, realistic pictures of the rock with high densities of information. Genre: *Descriptive Paragraph; Descriptive Picture*

Place in Science Unit	Analysed Task or Activity	Knowledge Demonstrated	Representational Resources
Beach Bucket Scavenger Hunt: Mini Books	Chapter Beach Books	Demonstrated limited factual knowledge of beaches beyond experiential knowledge. Beaches understood as consisting of tiny bits of rock, shells and other materials found at beach. Shoreline defined as meeting place of water and land.	Extended written representation in chapter book form. Summarization of previously learnt material. Process supported by note-taking, schematic chapter outline and information summary worksheet. Students demonstrated difficulty in completing task. No student completed 4 chapters; four students wrote 1 chapter; nine students wrote 2 chapters and five students wrote 3 chapters. The paragraph chapters lacked coherence or a clear organizational pattern. The paragraphs consisted of collections of unconnected sentences mainly copied from the worksheet. The average paragraph length (in sentences) and sentence length (in words) of chapters was: Chapter 1 – 3.94 sentences, 38.8 words; Chapter 2 – 3.15 sentences, 31.7 words; Chapter 3 – 1.6 sentences, 15.3 words; and Chapter 4 – 3.6 sentences, 40.6 words. Evidence of symbolic, multimodal notation in the note-taking process as a way of defining an inferential relationship. Demonstrated understanding of chapter book structure in schematic book outlines. Genre: *Informational Paragraph* (collected into informational chapter books)

Place in Science Unit	Analysed Task or Activity	Knowledge Demonstrated	Representational Resources
Sand on Stage: Science Inquiry of Sand	Observing Sand: Understanding Tools of Measurement (Video Data)	Evidence of procedural knowledge of tool-based observation. Physical observation of sand, noticing physical, tactile and visual characteristics. Tool-based observation using magnifying glass and microscope. Demonstrated ability to follow instructions relating to tool-based observation. Directed noticing of sand qualities according to specified criteria for observation and comparison. Demonstrated evidence of information organization according to world knowledge, scientific patterns of organization and evidence-based argument.	Use of worksheets to direct process of tool-based observation. Use of worksheets to record observations made and allow comparisons to emerge.

Place in Science Unit	Analysed Task or Activity	Knowledge Demonstrated	Representational Resources
Sand on Stage: Science Inquiry of Sand	Directed Observation of Sand: The Unknown Sand	Demonstrated ability to follow directions and record empirical tool-based observations on a specified worksheet. Demonstrated ability for visual analysis extending beyond schematic presentations based on prior knowledge. Categories of observation included colour, size, shape, magnetism, difference in grain size, name and source. Demonstrated ability to compare sand according to colour and infer source. Deepening of understanding of qualities of sand.	Written presentation of empirical observations on a specified worksheet. Worksheet directed process of conducting empirical observations and was used to record these observations. Successfully completed by all students. Some use of visual representation in addition to the written representation. Genre: *Directed (Written) Observation Worksheet*

Place in Science Unit	Analysed Task or Activity	Knowledge Demonstrated	Representational Resources
Sand on Stage: Science Inquiry of Sand	Directed Observation of Sand: Sand on Stage	Demonstrated ability to follow directions and record empirical observations in written and visual form on specified worksheet. Evidence of tool-based visual analysis of grains of sand. Categories of observation included colour, size, shape, magnetism, difference in grain size, name and source. Demonstrated ability to compare observations based on visual analysis of observed qualities with authorized scientific descriptions and to categorize according to scientific name. Evidence of inference from observation in relation to potential sand components. Deepening of understanding of qualities of sand.	Written and visual presentation of empirical observations using the tools of a magnifying glass and a magnet written on a specific worksheet. Colour, shape and size record using visual representation. Worksheet directed the process of conducting empirical observations and was used for recording observations. Worksheet directed a process of comparison. Successfully completed by all students. Genre: *Directed (Written and Visual) Observation Worksheet*

Place in Science Unit	Analysed Task or Activity	Knowledge Demonstrated	Representational Resources
Sand on Stage: Science Inquiry of Sand	Sand Summary	Evidence of ability to follow instructions relating to the use of a microscope. Evidence of increased differentiation of sand qualities. Evidence of internalization of categories of observations: colour, size, shape, magnetism, source, weight, texture and sand composition. Evidence of enhanced visual analysis utilizing a microscope and attempt to represent what is observed and not just categories from prior knowledge. Following the use of the microscope, sand represented as a collection of sand grains from different sources and having different observable qualities allowing inferences to be made.	Written representation of tool-based visual analysis. Written representation presented on carefully prepared multi-literacy space. Written representation consisted of a descriptive paragraph. The paragraphs were coherent. Coherence was achieved through the repetition of proper nouns or the use of pronouns. On average, the paragraphs were 5.6 sentences long and had 41.9 words. Written paragraph prepared as a draft and final version. Changes in final version involved a shorter, more focused and accurate paragraph. Genre: *Descriptive Paragraph*

Place in Science Unit	Analysed Task or Activity	Knowledge Demonstrated	Representational Resources
Sand on Stage	Making Inferences	Evidence of inference generation as an extension of unstated background knowledge. World knowledge inferences relating to the actions, thoughts, feelings and locations of animate objects. The concept of support is understood as a request for the validation of the source of the information and not as evidence supporting the claim. The prevalent argument structure consisted of a world knowledge inference validated by a reference to personal experience.	Designed worksheet directed a thinking process of generating evidence-based inferences. Written responses were given under the categories of an inference (in response to stimuli information) and evidence supporting the inference. Some responses included visual representation. Genre: *Directed Worksheet*
The Sights Sand has Seen: Reader: Sandy's Journey to the Sea	Understanding Process through Shared Reading (Video Data)	Development of understanding of process of sand formation. Description, personification and visualization of the process that changes a rock to sand.	Written representation (classroom reader) read in a shared classroom reading. Evidence of attention directed at meaning and orthographic form of words, issues of written genre and picture analysis. Text prediction and discussion of local and global text meaning. Choral and shared reading. Process summarization in written and visual form. Genre: *Narrative Classroom Reader*

Place in Science Unit	Analysed Task or Activity	Knowledge Demonstrated	Representational Resources
The Sights Sand has Seen: Postcard Stories	Summarizing Sand Formation through Picture Drawing (Video Data)	Development of understanding of process of sand formation.	Extended visual representation of knowledge of a process acquired from a shared reading. Visual representation moves from outer contours to details. Verbal discussion enhanced visual representation through the activation of world knowledge. Process represented as a series of stages across several pictures. Genre: *Extended Graphic Narrative*
The Sights Sand has Seen: Postcard Stories	Summarization of a Scientific Process through Narrative Writing (Video Data)	Development of understanding of process of sand formation.	Extended written representation of knowledge of a process acquired through shared reading and picture summarization. Evidence of picture analysis as a way of generating ideas and understanding for written text. Discussion of global and local aspect of text as well as issues of orthography, text organization and syntax. Cross-modal integration of written text, pictorial representation in elicited writing. Genre: *Extended Written Narrative*

Place in Science Unit	Analysed Task or Activity	Knowledge Demonstrated	Representational Resources
The Sights Sand has Seen: Postcard Stories	Postcard Story	Evidence of internalization of the process of sand formation. Process represented in narrative form and covered 5 specific sand formation processes: rock from a mountain, volcano eruption, smashed bottle, coral erosion and rocks at the edge of cliffs.	Visual and written representation of a process. Visual representations of process set out the process in four stages covering four pictures. Visual representation produced in sketch and final postcard form. Majority of pictures were narrative, schematic with low densities of information. Limited written representation of process. Average length of writing on card – 1.78 sentences with 15.5 words. Descriptions not connected across cards but rather descriptions of the card itself. Narrative connections implicit or visual. Genre: *Extended Graphic Narrative* (with limited written description)
The Sights Sand has Seen: Teacher-Led Discussion of Sand as Material	Erosion and Weathering: Developing a Scientific Vocabulary (Video Data)	Evidence of development of knowledge of scientific terminology used to understand the process of sand formation. Knowledge of the terms erosion and weathering.	Oral and physical representation of specific scientific terms. Verbal description of process followed by the naming of the described process through a scientific term. Enhancement of term through physical acting out of meaning of term. Memorization through repetition and choral reading.

Place in Science Unit	Analysed Task or Activity	Knowledge Demonstrated	Representational Resources
Build a Sandy Beach: Report Writing	Beach Animal and Plant Report	Evidence of knowledge of a variety of beach animals. Information addressed included description of animal, habitat, prey and predators and miscellaneous facts. Range of information relating to different animals. Extension of understanding of the ecosystem of the beach and the animals that inhabit that system. Development of specific knowledge pertaining to particular animals.	Extended written representation in the form of a written informational report divided into chapters. Demonstrated reading comprehension of encyclopedic text and synthesis of information for report content. Evidence of improved understanding of informative report writing. Ten students produced 4 chapters; two students wrote 2 chapters and one student wrote 1 chapter. Chapters clearly organized dealing with different informational topics. Reports presenting a logical, relevant structure of information in chapters and whole report. Average length of Chapter One: 4.2 sentences – 30.38 words; Chapter Two: 3.6 sentences – 30.5 words; Chapter Three: 3.3 sentences – 22.3 words; and Chapter Four: 3 sentences and 18.6 words. Chapters coherently organized using proper noun or pronoun repetition. Information presented in form of taxonomy of information. Genre: *Extended Informational Report*

Place in Science Unit	Analysed Task or Activity	Knowledge Demonstrated	Representational Resources
Oil on the Beach: Cleaning Up an Oil Spill	Observation and Prediction Worksheet: Oil on the Beach	Demonstrated ability to follow instructions and record predictions and observations on worksheet. Evidence of observation-based conclusions. Changes in predictions following observation of conducted experiment. Evidence of development of scientific argument-based thinking.	Written recording of predictions and empirical observations of an experiment. Summarization of empirical findings. Worksheet-directed process of scientific thinking in which predictions were compared to observations and conclusions were reached. Designed worksheet limited abilities to compare among observation among materials. Genre: *Directed Observation Worksheet*

7.2 Differentiating Experience: Substantive Knowledge Development

As seen in Table 7.1, in broad terms the analysis of the specific tasks conducted by the students in this science inquiry classroom and the multiliteracy genres produced by these students provides evidence of meaningful scientific knowledge development. This development is to be seen on the level of substantive factual information and on the level of procedural scientific knowledge.

The overall movement of substantive knowledge development is from the experiential understanding of the phenomenon of a beach and sand to a deepened understanding of the composition of sand, the process of sand formation and understanding of the beach as an ecosystem inhabited by a range of different beach animals. In the initial multiliteracy products produced at the beginning of the course (beach picture folder, coloured map and the photograph description), the description of the beach consists of a series of expected objects and actions. These include the sun, sky, clouds, fish and people. There is limited understanding of the relationship between water and land and the students defer to the teachers' presentation that the beach is 'where the water meets the land'. In the photograph description activity there is some extension of the students' understanding that the shoreline includes a variety of different settings coming under the heading of places where the water meets land. However, at this early stage of the science unit understanding is essentially experiential and based on stereotypical activities and contents of beaches.

Through the activity of the beach bucket exploration there is a deepening of the understanding of the components of the beach. As seen in the beach bucket finding list, the components of a beach are now seen to include 19 new objects which did not appear in the experiential description of the beach. These include objects such as sea urchin spines, metal, paper, feathers, rocks, wood and plastic. The lists produced by the students demonstrate a widened schema of the potential contents of a beach.

This process is further extended by the process of describing a rock and a shell. As seen in multiliteracy products of 'My Favourite Shell' and 'My Favourite Rock', specific objects found at the beach are considered in relation to their specific properties such as colour, texture, weight and pattern. One interesting aspect of these specific descriptions is the attempt to actually represent the object that is being observed and described. This suggests a movement beyond the basic experiential understanding of the objects at the beach to an observation-based appreciation of the specific qualities of these objects.

Through the tasks of tool-based observation of sand, the concept of sand is changed. As seen in the chapter beach books, the directed observation: the unknown sand, the directed observation of sand: sand on stage and my sand summary, the concept of a beach consists of a collection of 'tiny bits of rock, shell and other material'. The directed observation worksheets show evidence of the process of close observation where sand is addressed not as a holistic entity but rather as a collection of grains of materials that each has specific properties such as colour, size, weight and magnetism and comes from a variety of different sources. The completion of the worksheets and the specific attempts to reproduce the grains as they were visually analysed using different tools of observation demonstrates a new understanding of sand. From the perspective of substantive knowledge, this is an important shift in perception of the nature of the sandy shoreline.

The next modification in substantive knowledge is the development of a concept of the process by which sand on the beaches is formed. Through a shared reading of a classroom reader students were introduced to a story which personified and narrativized the scientific process of sand formation as a journey of a single rock to the beach. As seen in the visual representations in the postcard stories, the students internalized and then reproduced five different narratives of the process of sand formation. These narratives covered the movements of different materials from different sources on their way to becoming materials that are found in the composition of a beach. The teaching of this process included the development of specific scientific vocabulary to cover this type of development. There is no evidence of the use of this vocabulary independently by the students.

The final development in substantive knowledge that can be documented consists of the extended understanding of a range of beach animals that live on the ecosystem of the sandy shoreline. The Beach Animal and Plant Reports provide evidence of student understandings of specific beach animals. These understandings developed as a result of using encyclopedic reading sources and consisted of an analysis of the animal's characteristics, habitat and its prey and predators. The assortment of animals analysed across the class shows an extended understanding of the types of animal that live in this ecosystem and a much more systematic and scientifically informed description of these animals.

Overall, the process of substantive knowledge development documented in this science unit can be seen as the development of a more scientific understanding of the nature of the beach. The facts that were learnt consisted of seeing the shoreline as a collection of eroded materials of different sources and types, the idea that each of these grains travelled long distances to reach its destination on the beach, the concept that the grains of sand have specific observable and measurable properties, and that the beach is a complex ecosystem inhabited by a variety of animals and plants. This development of these substantive understandings transforms the students' understandings from an experiential, stereotypical and holistic understanding of the beach to a differentiated, scientifically informed and observation-based understanding of the sandy shoreline.

7.3 Recognizing Observation: Procedural Knowledge Development

Procedural scientific knowledge, for the purposes of the current analysis, is considered to consist of the development of modes of scientific thinking associated with science and the development of specific skills associated with the tools and methods of empirical investigation and measurement. Both of these types of procedural knowledge were addressed within the science unit investigated in this study.

In broad terms, the development of scientific thinking can be seen as the movement from a holistic and authority-based approach to natural phenomena to a rudimentary form of observation-based conclusion. This process involved the development of cognitive concepts of property-based observation, categorization and grouping and simple hypothesis testing.

At the beginning of the science unit, as seen in the analyses of the activities of the coloured map and the photograph description, the students present experiential knowledge of their understandings of the beach. The beach is presented as a space with a series of expected objects and activities that can be found there. Each of these multiliteracy activities required a level of inferential processing. For the coloured map activity, students were faced with a contradiction between the stated conclusion that the world had more water than land and with a visual representation that did not support this conclusion. In the picture description activity, specific pictures were supposed to be analysed for what they revealed about the beach, but students preferred to present prior experiential knowledge and to use statements provided by the teachers. In both cases the students deferred to the teachers' (or written worksheets') explicit statements rather than base their conclusions on any personal inferential or observational evidence.

In the first scientific inquiry task, the beach bucket exploration, students utilized cognitive abilities designed to develop observation and categorization skills. The analysis of the video data of this task shows students deeply involved in a process of noticing and grouping different objects found in the beach bucket. The process of noticing addressed named objects, materials and physical properties. This is a movement beyond a holistic undifferentiated understanding of the beach and its components. From the perspective of scientific thinking this is the most basic skill – the ability to notice specific properties of an observed object. This development of scientific thinking is further enhanced through the process of categorization and grouping. The grouping of noticed objects according to kind and physical attributes is a reorganization task and is crucial for any scientific investigation. The breaking down of the observed phenomena into components and the reorganization into new structures allows scientifically meaningful descriptions to emerge. The categorization process in the current data set was not an automatic process. Groupings evolved over a period of time with students arguing and contesting different ways of grouping the noticed objects. Oral discussion, argumentation and verbal reflection were all part of the categorization process. However, there was still a reliance on the teacher's authority in final decisions as to category grouping and definition. But the video data clearly demonstrates the development of the cognitive abilities of noticing and categorization.

The process of reorganization through categorization was further enhanced in the multiliteracy activities of the evidence categorization activity and the alive/never alive categorization activity. Both these activities involved inferential processing based on world knowledge utilizing information gathered in the beach bucket exploration task. In the evidence categorization activity, students were required to relate to the noticed objects found in the beach bucket exploration as evidence of types of things found in the beach ecosystem. Thus the objects were recategorized and reorganized into the new categories. The literacy component of the activity involved graphically representing the categorized objects in both independent circles. The erasing and rewritings present on the worksheet show that categorization was a thoughtful process involving consideration, deliberation and discussion. The alive/never alive categorization task was based on the conceptual and graphic organization of a Venn diagram. As a categorization task, the Venn diagram went beyond previous categorization processes as it poses an overlapping area of dual categorization. This difficulty was further enhanced in the present case as no title was given to the overlapping category. Half the students could not complete this aspect of the categorization task. However, the evidence of both categorization activities is that students demonstrated the ability to use inferential processing to recategorize the found objects into new categories of information and to graphically represent this category system.

Further evidence of the development of the noticing and observation process can be found in the multiliteracy tasks of my favourite shell and my favorite rock. The descriptions of both the rock and the shell provide evidence of specific criteria of observation. The descriptions were organized around the criteria of colour, texture, weight, shape, pattern, analogy and personal wishes. From a conceptual viewpoint, these are directed observations of the specific qualities of the shell and the rock. In the descriptions, whether visual of written, there was for some students an attempt to represent the observed object in a realistic manner which took into account the unique observable characteristics of the object. This is evidence of the development and internalization of noticing abilities.

The concept of criteria for observation was utilized in the tool-based directed observation recorded in the video data of the science inquiry of sand. This process was conducted on a worksheet that directed the observation of sand using open noticing, the tools of a magnifying glass, a microscope and a magnet. All of the observations were recorded using a set of multiliteracy worksheets. Information gained from these directed observations was organized according to world knowledge, patterns of comparison and evidence-based inferences. From a conceptual viewpoint, the ability to notice specific qualities of sand and to categorize the sand accordingly had already been demonstrated in previous observation tasks. But the use of magnifying tools does enhance the ability to see and observe different qualities, providing the experience of enhanced recognition tools. Thus, the idea of observation is widened to include tools that go beyond the basic human senses. The use of these tool-based observations in this task consisted of another development in scientific thinking. Information that was acquired from the observation was utilized in two patterns that can be related to scientific thinking – the comparison of samples and the use of world knowledge inference to extend understanding of the observed objects. Students compared samples of sand and also offered understandings of the sand based on observed qualities. These are examples of basic patterns of scientific thinking.

The most direct evaluation of the students' abilities to conduct an evidence-based inference was found in the making inferences worksheets. In these worksheets, students were required to generate inferences extending knowledge provided for them and then to state the evidence used in their conclusions. The students did produce inferences in most cases. However, a very specific structure of inferential argument was used. The students based their inferences on prior knowledge and did not provide evidence supporting the actual inference made; rather they understood the concept of evidence as the request to state 'how they knew what they knew'. In other words, the majority of students provided a world knowledge inference and then said that they knew this because they had directly experienced it. This exercise does direct the students to make explicit some of the assumptions about knowledge and the need to explain the source of this knowledge. But it also demonstrates the specific structure of scientific argument that is understood by these students in this second-grade classroom.

A development in scientific thinking in a slightly different direction was the development of the concept of a process. Specifically, the process discussed and then reproduced by the students was the process of sand formation. The video data of the shared reading and the analysis of the multiliteracy product 'The Postcard Story' show evidence of the development of the understanding of process. The postcard stories produced by the students provide evidence that process is represented as narrative involving stages of development across a series of visual representations. But the narrative is not a literary narrative and the rocks (or coral, or bottles) are not personified. The students' understanding of process, as seen in the different stages of the visual representations, is the concept of a network of cause and result relationships. This type of structure is a component of both the scientific concept of process and the structure of a narrative. This concept of the process of sand formation needs to be combined with the development of the abilities to notice, categorize and infer the source of a sand grain. By internalizing the concept of process as a narrative the ability to explain the phenomenon of the sandy shoreline is extended and marks a stage in the students' conceptual understanding.

The final development in scientific thinking was found in the final multi-literacy product analysed in this study. The observation and prediction worksheet, 'Oil on the Beach' was a worksheet that directed a process of scientific thinking. Specifically, the process addressed was that of prediction (hypothesis generation) evaluated through empirical observation. In other words, it was a hypothesis-testing format. The worksheet directed the students to specify their predictions and then to mark their empirical observations collected through a small-group experiment. The worksheets do show a process of change from the prediction to the observations. Accordingly empirical evidence was used to overturn prior knowledge and specific hypotheses were tested.

The students were also required to reach conclusions based on the experiment and to explicitly state what evidence was used in order to support this conclusion. As with the inference-making worksheets the understanding of the relationship between evidence and conclusion proved problematic and not a single student actually presented evidence in support of their conclusions. Thus at this final stage of the course, scientific thinking is demonstrated in the use of empirical data to overturn prior predictions (a process of hypothesis testing) and allow conclusions to emerge. But this is not a fully structured scientific argument of explicitly stated observational evidence supporting a claim that is being made. It is a more rudimentary form that takes into account evidence but does not propose a clearly stated relationship between evidence and conclusion.

Overall, the process of scientific thinking development consisted of the development of several different cognitive abilities. The students learnt and utilized the conceptual components of observation – the ability to notice specific properties, the internalization of these criteria and the ability to organize and reorganize groupings and categorizations according to different observed properties. The students also learnt how to use observations in a series of scientific thinking patterns. On a basic level students were introduced to and shown the ability to reproduce the concept of a process of sand formation. Students conducted observation-based comparisons, made world knowledge inferences and were involved in a rudimentary process of hypothesis testing. Students demonstrated certain difficulties with the concept of explicitly connecting evidence to conclusions made and demonstrated a certain reliance on the teacher's authority and prior knowledge.

In addition to the development of certain patterns of scientific thinking the students also developed procedural knowledge of methods that are significant in hands-on science inquiry. On a very basic level, there is ample evidence in both the video data of the various tasks and the associated worksheets that students are fully capable of following instructions carefully both in the oral or written formats. In some cases, such as the microscope-based observation, the instructions were extensive and detailed. However, students followed the instructions and were competent in conducting the various observations and experiments. The evidence from the various worksheets that were used to direct observations demonstrated the students' abilities to follow written directions and record their observations in the appropriate manner on the worksheets. Although the ability to follow instructions is a very basic skill, it is crucial in the classroom where hands-on science is conducted.

This science unit developed specific methodological knowledge, useful for the process of observation. In the scientific inquiry of sand, students developed an understanding of how to work with three different instruments, the magnifying glass, the microscope and the magnet. As seen in the video analyses of these tasks, the students explored the nature of the tool itself and how it worked. The associated worksheets that accompanied the use of these tools made sure that observations and the use of these tools was not left to the experiential realm but rather was translated into recordable observation. The use of these tools in an appropriate manner was shown to change the way sand was represented and allowed direct comparisons to be made. Patterns of comparison and rank order according to size or colour are rudimentary forms of measurement. These were directly part of the worksheets associated with the scientific inquiry of sand. In general, the analysis of the video data and the multiliteracy genre demonstrated that students developed procedural methodological knowledge of tools of observations and measurement in conjunction with the types of scientific thinking that develop scientific understanding. For example, the ability to conduct an observation requires the internalization of specific criteria for observation and the development of procedural knowledge of the methods in which different tools can be used to enhance the observation process.

7.4 Synthesizing Description: The Written Genre of Science Inquiry

Representational knowledge, in the current analysis, was found to consist of written and visual representation. Representational development was found for both modes of representation. In both cases the development of representational abilities was seen to be a crucial tool in allowing scientific knowledge to be comprehended, internalized and reproduced. In broad terms, representational abilities were found to enhance the development of scientific knowledge.

The overall movement of written representation development found in the current data set consisted of the gradual development of the ability to handle larger units of information in a coherent fashion and to base this information on observation rather than prior knowledge. In the initial activities of this science unit, students used lists to represent knowledge that they had acquired. In the photograph description students were asked to produce a descriptive paragraph of what they observed in a picture provided to them. Rather than a descriptive paragraph the students produced a list of objects without any linguistic connections among them.

The format of a list was a genre decision that was not directly requested by the activity itself. The lack of required organization or coherence for a list makes it a relatively easy text to produce and thus reduces the cognitive load of this literacy activity. These lists do represent the students' understanding of the objects found in the pictures. However, many of the objects reproduced in the lists came from prior knowledge and the teachers discourse and not as the result of a visual analysis.

The use of a list in a more appropriate fashion was found in the beach bucket explorations: findings list. The list was used as a way of recording the objects found in the beach buckets. The list was the required genre of the activity itself and it allowed the preservation of the information attained through the simulated experience of the components of a beach. This literacy activity constituted the moment in which the experience of this scientific inquiry was transformed into retainable knowledge that widened the existing schema of the components of a beach.

A more developed use of lists was found in the beach bucket exploration: evidence categorization activity and the alive/never alive categorization activity. In these activities, written lists were used in conjunction with the visual representation of distinct categories in the form of drawn circles. The production of the specific lists in the designated places was, from a cognitive perspective, a reorganization of the information obtained through the scientific inquiry activity of the beach bucket exploration. The literacy component of this activity was crucial in directing the new categorizations of the observations. It was through the graphically organized listing activity that the process of categorization and grouping was really represented.

Evidence of the development of descriptive paragraph writing was found in the rock and shell description activities: my favourite rock and my favourite shell. In both these writing activities a specific object was to be observed and described in writing (and in a visual format). The students produced coherent paragraphs consisting of relevant information in a clear organizational structure. The informational structure conformed to a list of observational categories – colour, texture, weight, shape, pattern, descriptive associations and statement of wishes. The attempt was to clearly describe the object that had been observed and the genre format of a well-constructed descriptive paragraph went beyond the presentation of a list of observations creating coherence in relation to the object itself. Coherence was achieved on the linguistic level through the use of the pronoun 'it' and the connectors 'and' and 'because'. These paragraphs were a development on the way description was conducted at the very beginning of the course.

Further evidence for the ability to write descriptive paragraphs was found in the my sand activity. As with the previous descriptive paragraphs, the written paragraphs were coherent, informationally relevant and well organized. The information in the paragraphs consisted of observations made in relation to the sand. In this case, the observations recorded in the descriptive paragraphs included information acquired through the use of different tools. Coherence was achieved in these paragraphs through the use of pronouns or proper nouns. All three descriptive paragraph activities had a component of process writing in them. The students produced drafts before they wrote final paragraphs. The final version included the proposed revisions of the draft which mainly addressed issues of linguistic form.

The ability to represent information in literacy was further extended in the chapter beach book activity. This literacy activity produced an interesting disparity between the ability to design an informational structure for a four-chapter (paragraph) length book and the ability to write an informational paragraph. Students demonstrated difficulties in writing an informational paragraph. An informational paragraph is in some ways more complex than a descriptive paragraph. In a description, such as the my favourite shell paragraphs, you coordinate information relating to direct observations concerning a specific object or phenomenon. In an information paragraph, you need to gather information from disparate sources and clearly coordinate the structure of the information you are presenting. In an informative paragraph the aim is to present an explanation of the object or phenomenon being addressed. The informational paragraphs produced by the students were very brief and lacked a clear organizational structure. In writing these paragraphs, the students seemed to rely on existing statements drawn from a worksheet that was provided for them. The students did demonstrate an understanding of chapter structure and did differentiate among different pieces of information and the chapters to which they needed to be assigned. In this sense, the students' literacy abilities in relation to the global organization of written representation were extended.

The ability to write an extended narrative was also seen to be difficult for the students in this class. The written component of the postcard stories was not well developed. The students did produce visual narratives to represent the process of sand formation, but when it came to producing a written version of the narrative, the students wrote very brief sentences providing a minimal description of the content of the picture. These written descriptions did not create linguistic connections across the picture panels. The descriptions created a narrative only in conjunction with the pictures themselves. By themselves, these descriptions would not constitute a written narrative.

Towards the end of the science unit the students' abilities to write extended informational reports were seen to improve. The beach animal and plant reports provided evidence of the students' ability to use encyclopedic information and to organize this into a four-chapter (topic) length report. The encyclopedic information was synthesized and reorganized to match the different chapter headings. Ten students managed to write all four chapters and present a diversity of information in a well organized manner. The individual paragraphs were well organized and used the structure of taxonomy to present the information gathered from the source material. The paragraphs were coherent, using proper nouns or pronouns to construct coherence. This writing activity demonstrated a more advanced understanding of how to conduct informative writing than early attempts in the science unit.

The final literacy ability that needs to be addressed in the current analysis of the written representation consists of the student's ability to negotiate the various worksheets used to direct the process of scientific inquiry. Throughout the course the students demonstrated the ability to fully utilize these literacy tools in their scientific explorations. There was a process of development in the worksheets. The earlier worksheets, such as the beach bucket findings list, were used as directing and recording devices. The later worksheets in addition to these two roles also directed a set of more complex thinking patterns. In the evidence categorization activity and the alive/never alive categorization activity the process of grouping and categorization was directed by the worksheet. In 'The Unknown Sand' worksheet and the 'Sand on Stage' observation worksheets, in addition to directing and recording the students' observations the worksheets directed a process of comparison in relation to other samples and rocks. Finally, in the observation and prediction worksheet: 'Oil on the Beach', the worksheet directed a process of hypothesis testing. In this literacy activity the worksheet itself directed this process by requiring students to record their predictions and then compare these with actual observations. Thus, students working on this worksheet simulated the basic scientific concept of using observations to qualify or change proposed hypotheses.

Overall, the process of written representation development can be characterized as the development of greater control over the genre of scientific inquiry. The students' development moved from the use of a simple list to the ability to synthesize information and produce extended informational reports based on encyclopedic sources. The students demonstrated the ability to produce descriptive paragraphs and to use a variety of worksheets at different levels of conceptual complexity. There is evidence that literacy was difficult for this group of students. On the whole the paragraphs written were short and had a series of specific linguistic difficulties that were addressed through the revision process. Students had difficulty writing the extended narrative in their first attempt at informative writing. But on the level of science–literacy activities, important literacy skills and genres developed through the science unit.

7.5 Observation-based Representation: The Visual Genre of Science Inquiry

Visual representation refers to any meaningful visual material produced or utilized within the classroom setting as part of the science unit investigated in the current study. Two major types of visual information were used in this science unit – visual representations in the form of pictures and visual representation in the form of graphic, symbolic shapes. Both these forms were used to represent scientific understandings and were seen to develop as ways of representing scientific understandings through the tasks and activities of the science unit.

In broad terms, the development of pictorial visual representation consisted of the movement from schematic representation based on learnt forms to realistic representations of specific objects. At the beginning of the course, in the beach folder pictures, the majority of the students used schematic representations for the objects presented. These schematic representations are by definition not observation-based drawings but rather consist of shapes that symbolically represent specific objects. For example, in many of the early pictures the sun is represented as a quarter or full circle with lines radiating out from it. This is a learnt form that represents the sun and not an observation based representation. In the analyses of my favourite rock, 12 of the students attempted to produce pictures which represented the specific attributes of the object being observed. In these pictures, the unique contours, colours and patterns of the specific rock were represented. The attempt in these pictures is not to provide a symbolic shape to represent the rock but rather to represent the unique aspects of the specific rock that was observed. In cognitive representational terms, this shift was parallel to the development of the cognitive ability to notice and conduct observations based on specific criteria. The production of a realistic picture was the result of a detailed observation of an object and as such was part of a process of cognitive representational development.

Development was also found in relation to the use of narrative representation. In the early beach folder pictures, narrative pictures were used to represent imaginary narratives of sea adventures involving attacking sharks or hidden treasure. The narratives represented action in a single picture. In the postcard stories, visual narratives were used to represent a process of sand formation. The narratives covered three to four visual panels and represented the movement and changes of a specific object (rock, bottle or coral) from its initial place and state to its final destination on the sandy beach. The narratives create continuity across panels and thus allow a more extended narrative to be produced. The actual narrative represents an understanding of the scientific description of how sand was formed and was not a personalized imaginary narrative. In the case of the postcard stories, the visual narrative allowed the representation of scientific knowledge in a quite direct manner.

Graphic representation also played a role in the development of scientific representational knowledge. The processes of grouping and categorization were represented through the use of graphic symbolic forms. These came in three different formats. On a most basic level, in the beach bucket exploration after having collected the objects that were to be grouped together, the students used a pencil to draw a circle around the objects on the table. This circle represented the unity of the disparate objects found within its borders. On the two worksheets associated with the beach bucket exploration, the evidence categorization activity and the alive/never alive categorization activity, this process of using graphic forms to demark grouping and categorization was further enhanced. The worksheets used drawn circles as defined spaces in order to represent specific categories. Students used the spaces to write their lists of objects. The alive/never alive categorization activity used a Venn diagram that provided an overlapping space for objects with characteristics that covered both categories. The overlapping category of the Venn diagram posed conceptual difficulties for some of the students. But the difficulties found for this graphic representation actually show that the graphic forms are understood and used as semantic markers of the categorization process.

The final development in graphic representation that needs to be addressed is the use of symbolic notation. The use of symbolic notation was found in the writing process of the chapter beach books. Symbolic notation was part of the note-taking process which supported the development of the books themselves. The specific notation used consisted of arrows and circles combined with named objects designating an inferential relationship among the objects presented. Symbolic notation was used as a short form to represent that certain objects were evidence of the presence of different people, animals and objects on the beach.

Overall, the process of visual representation development consisted of the movement towards observation-based representation and utilization of graphic symbolic forms for the notation of semantic relations among objects. The students learnt how to use graphic forms to organize and reorganize their observations and to represent different relations among the listed objects. The students also learnt how to represent a scientific process through visual narratives. There is a direct connection between the development of observational abilities and the attempt to produce realistic representations of objects.

Chapter 8: The Multiliteracy of Scientific Knowledge Development

8.1 Guiding Science through Multiliteracy

As discussed in the early theoretical chapters of this book, multiliteracy was a central perspective to be considered in relation to the investigation of the science inquiry classroom explored in the research project presented in this book. Some initial research, such as the work of Kress *et al* (2001), has suggested the centrality of multiliteracy to the science inquiry classroom. But little is actually known about how multiliteracy works within the early elementary classroom and the ramifications of this on scientific knowledge development. In the last chapter, evidence was presented of the development of substantive, procedural, written and visual literacy scientific knowledge development. Scientific knowledge was shown to develop within this classroom. The question that now needs to be addressed is the role of multiliteracy in this development. Specifically the current chapter will attempt to answer the following question:

1. What is the role of multiliteracy in the development of scientific knowledge?

As in the case of the previous chapter, the approach taken to answering this question is to ground the presented understanding within the detailed analysis of the classroom activities and genre. In very simple terms, the process of learning science as reflected in the analysis of the video data and the products created throughout this science unit was seen to be a multiliteracy process which integrated oral, written, pictorial and physical modes of communication to develop procedural and substantive scientific knowledge. The process of learning science was directly tied to the multimodal forms of communication used in the classroom. The science inquiry approach to science teaching is intrinsically connected to a multimodal approach to instruction and the centrality of multiliteracy to this endeavour is clear in the way different written, visual, oral and physical genres are utilized in conjunction. In this chapter, the way these modes of communication allow the development of scientific knowledge will be analysed. The analysis describes three multimodal progressions that were characteristic of scientific inquiry in this science classroom and were repeated at different points in the course and also describes the multiliteracy roles of the teacher in the classroom. As will be seen in the analysis, the three multimodal and multiliteracy progressions are connected to each other and to the roles of the teacher. Together they present an answer to the role of multiliteracy in the development of scientific knowledge in the science inquiry classroom.

8.2 Multimodal Direction of Hands-on Science Inquiry

One crucial aspect of any scientific inquiry classroom is the ability of the teacher, teaching materials and course designers to produce a meaningful science learning experience. The potential pitfalls of the scientific inquiry are that the science activities will regress into an unmanageable classroom experience and/or that the activities themselves will stay on the level of experiences and not enhance scientific knowledge development. In the current data, both these potential difficulties were addressed through a multimodal teaching design. The basic design consisted of an interaction between oral discourse and written worksheets. The oral discourse introduced the basic concepts and instructions for conducting the science inquiry activity, made sure students stayed on task and provided a summarizing discourse presentation. Written worksheets directed the moment-to-moment activities of scientific inquiry and provided a framework for recording observations. The oral discourse provided an envelope within which the hands-on science activities were conducted and the written worksheets made sure that the tasks were correctly paced and that the experiences were transformed into data that could be addressed and manipulated. For example, in conducting the 'Sand on Stage: Science Inquiry of Sand' task, the teacher's starting point was the presentation of an introduction to the epistemological and methodological aspect of the hands-on science activity of observing sand samples with various tools. This introduction was oral but was accompanied by physical actions demonstrating different aspects of how the task was to be performed. These included the picking up of tools and showing them to the students. The students were provided with a worksheet to accompany the observation process. Following a process of open observation, a more directed tool-based observation utilizing the worksheet was started. The students made observations directly in relation to the questions posed by the worksheets. At various intervals, the teacher would come to the various student groups and just make sure that they were involved with the observation task and to provide input to the various observations that had been made. The observations were recorded on the worksheet. At the

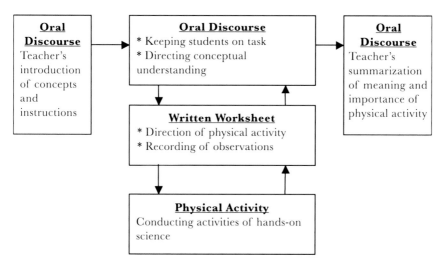

Figure 8.1 Multimodal Direction of Scientific Inquiry

end of this process the teacher collected group observations and discussed findings with the class situating different sand samples on different shorelines around the globe. Figure 8.1 presents a schematic representation of this progression.

As seen in Figure 8.1, scientific inquiry in the early elementary classroom is constituted within an oral presentation controlled by the teacher's discourse. The teacher both introduces and summarizes the scientific inquiry activities and provides specific scientifically informed understandings of the scientific content that is being taught. This oral envelope provides a conceptual, directing frame within which the students' activities are conducted. The work of scientific inquiry in this classroom was further directed by the presence of written worksheets and verbal interaction with the teacher. The worksheets provided instructions that guided the students through a variety of stages of the different activities and required written or visual responses. The written worksheets provided very close direction for the scientific inquiry. As such the physical activities that constitute the most salient aspect of scientific inquiry were directed through both the introductory teacher discourse and the instructions on the written worksheets. As an additional level of control, the teacher also visited the students at different points during the scientific inquiry activities and provided verbal input. This further directed the students' understandings. Multiliteracy used in this way essentially provided a series of levels of direction that guided the whole of the scientific inquiry process.

8.3 Multimodal and Multiliteracy Negotiation of Scientific Understanding

The attraction of scientific inquiry is its ability to engage students in scientific activities. However, as with all physical activities the conceptual implications and meanings of the activity need to be directly addressed and made explicit to the students. In the science inquiry classroom studied in this research project, this manifested itself as a process of multimodal translation from physical actions to verbal or visual symbolic conceptualizations. This process of multiliteracy translation and conceptualization was the process through which the science inquiry activities became scientific knowledge. In the current data, this process was seen to be a multimodal and directed process resulting in a multiliteracy representation. The meaning of various activities conducted by the students was gradually directed towards the meanings considered important by the teacher (and the course designers) through a multilayered negotiation. A characteristic progression of this kind was the movement from physical activity to verbal discussion to written or visual representation. This process can be schematically described as the following progression of events: students are involved in the physical activity and make some initial observations, the teacher comes over and discusses the findings and redirects or modifies verbally statements being made, these new understandings are then represented through a written or visual format. For example, in the beach bucket exploration at the early stage of initial grouping students were involved with physically setting up groups of objects. These groups may or may not have been verbally identified. The teacher came over and provided verbal input either by identifying the basis for the grouping (i.e. 'a metal group') or by providing a more general name for the group (i.e. 'you have a shell group here'). Following this interaction, the students used a pencil to demark the collected objects as a group and wrote the name provided by the teacher next to the pencil circle with the collected items.

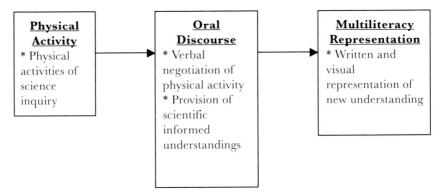

Figure 8.2 Multimodal and Multiliteracy Negotiation of the Scientific Understanding

In this example, the physical activity of grouping has taken on scientific value through the representational and conceptual process. Figure 8.2 provides a schematic representation of this progression.

As can be seen in Figure 8.2, the physical activities of scientific inquiry move through oral discourse and become written or visual multiliteracy representations. It is at the point of multiliteracy representation that they become scientific knowledge. In one sense this progression is situated within the wider progression of the multimodal direction of scientific inquiry presented in the previous section. The difference is that this progression describes the conceptual process of change. By translating the physical activities of science inquiry into multiliteracy representations, the physical activity becomes a symbolic activity that can be addressed as knowledge. The teacher and the worksheets play a major role in this symbolic activity making the students focus on specific aspects of the activity and making them represent specific aspects of what has been observed and concluded. This process is further enhanced by the next progression to be presented.

8.4 Multiliteracy Summary

An important aspect of scientific learning is the ability to retain the central scientific concepts or processes that are being taught. In the current data set, multiliteracy was seen to play a major role in scientific concept and process retention. The summary of the major understandings of the science instruction was usually handled by the teacher addressing the whole classroom and, at a later stage, by the students themselves in the production of new representations of this knowledge. The form of the summary by the teacher consisted of a verbal, oral description accompanied by a series of written notes of the main points and drawn visualizations of the major points of the process. In some cases the visualization would be the physical presentation of an object and the focusing of the students' attention on a specific component of that object. The multimodal summaries were complementary, essentially summarizing the same material in two or three formats. The relation among the formats was one of reinforcement with each mode providing the same information but using its own mode of representation. Thus, information was on the one hand repeated but on the other hand allowed access from a different modality. In the students' multiliteracy reproductions of these scientific understandings, it was observed that information may have been better represented in one mode or the other. For example, in the summary of the process of sand formation, the teacher's final summarization consisted of an oral summary accompanied by the writing of notes on the stages of the journey of a specific rock to the sandy beach and, at different points, the production of pictorial representations of where the rock was at different points in the story. The students' visual reproductions provided much more information on the process of sand formation than their written

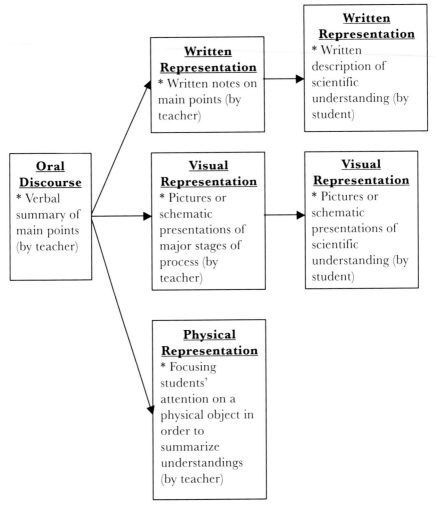

Figure 8.3 Multiliteracy Summary

descriptions of this process. The presence of a multiliteracy summary and the option for students to represent knowledge in a multiliteracy format enhanced the students' ability to both acquire and express the learnt knowledge of a scientific process. Figure 8.3 provides a schematic representation of this progression.

As can be seen in Figure 8.3, there is movement from the content of the teacher's multiliteracy summary to the content of the student's multiliteracy summary. As was seen in relation to procedural and substantive knowledge development, the teacher is considered the authority within the classroom and her notes and understandings need to be directly addressed by the students. The students' deference to the authority of the teacher and the teacher's use of a summarizing component for each science inquiry activity create a situation in which the understandings and concepts that are being taught to the students can be directed by the teacher's discourse. This progression is situated within the wider progression of the multimodal direction of scientific inquiry presented in section 8.2 of this chapter, but can also be seen as an extension of the teacher's oral summary. Within the context of the specific scientific inquiry activity that is conducted, the teacher provides an oral and multiliteracy summary. What the current progression represents is the longer-lasting ramifications of this summary on the understandings of the students. They take this summary as a major source of information for their own understandings of the science inquiry activities. As such, the multiliteracy summary provided by the teacher once again directs and guides the students' understandings of scientific inquiry as a symbolic activity. Ultimately through the multiliteracy summary the scientific inquiry activities are understood in relation to the concepts and positions summarized by the teacher.

8.5 The Multiliteracy Roles of the Science Inquiry Teacher

The description of the role of multiliteracy in the development of scientific knowledge is to a certain extent intertwined with the role of the science teacher. In this section the nature of this relationship will be explored. The aim is to present a wider understanding of the role of multiliteracy in the science inquiry classroom. In broad terms the analysis of the video data and multiliteracy genre utilized by the students conducting scientific inquiry make it clear that the teacher has a pivotal role in the development of scientific knowledge. In relation to the current data set, it is not an exaggeration to say that scientific knowledge development in this specific scientific inquiry classroom was dependent on a series of multiliteracy roles that the teacher(s) enacted throughout the course. Five different teacher roles of significance were identified in the data analysed for this study: designing and implementing scientific inquiry; providing conceptual understanding of scientific inquiry; directing students to appropriate informational resources; exemplifying and explicating scientific thinking and providing literacy instruction and direction.

8.5.1 Designing and Implementing Scientific Inquiry

The scientific inquiry classroom is dependent on the ability of the teacher to clearly design and implement the science inquiry activities within the classroom setting. As with other aspects of scientific inquiry, this involves a multimodal design that addresses the physical setting, direction for the students' physical actions and appropriate oral and written discourse. Essentially, all the elements of the multimodal classroom design need to enhance one another in order for the science inquiry activities to be implemented with the most instructional value. The analysis of the video data in the current study provides some insight into the design of this specific science inquiry classroom. As a starting point the physical components of the classroom were considered. Scientific inquiry activities require enough space to be actually conducted. In practical terms, this meant combining desks and organizing them so that enough room existed among the desks in the classroom so that the teacher could easily move from desk to desk and children had enough room to do the required work. Since scientific inquiry instruction in the current context involved the communal discussion of findings and the provision of the teacher's informed understandings and summaries of material, a central focal spot for the teacher to discuss the experiments with the whole class was created. This space was used for the initial presentation of instructions on how to conduct the physical activities of scientific inquiry such as observations and experiments and final summarization of the scientific inquiry activities.

Scientific inquiry is not self-explanatory. The procedures, methods, tasks and aims of the scientific inquiry need to be clearly explicated to the students for any meaningful science activity to take place. In the current data set, this meant that time was directed to the initial and ongoing explanation of how to conduct the different science activities. In order to negotiate the complexities of verbally describing physical actions and conceptual meanings, a multimodal approach was used. Instructions were given orally and supported by written worksheets that moved the students through the various stages of the observation and design. In addition, the instructions were then further supported by the teaching moving from desk to desk while the students were working and providing more input on how to conduct the observations or experiments and making sure that students stayed on task while conducting hands-on science. Thus, as described above in section 8.2, science inquiry started from an oral presentation of instructions and was supported by on-line literacy in the form of a worksheet. This was further enhanced by the presence of the teacher at the group's table providing relevant feedback and making sure students stayed on task. Taken together, these measures attempted to ensure that scientific inquiry was conducted in a meaningful and appropriate way in the classroom.

8.5.2 Providing Conceptual Understanding of Scientific Inquiry

Scientific inquiry is conducted in order for students to acquire a substantive and procedural understanding of the scientific knowledge targeted within the science unit. The analysis of the current data makes it very clear that the teacher plays a significant role in the development of this knowledge. It is the teacher who actually directs the understanding of the various tasks conducted by the students and makes the scientific inquiry meaningful in relation to the aims of scientific knowledge development that underpins the design of the science inquiry classroom. Scientific inquiry is very engaging for students but it poses a danger for knowledge development in that it can stay on the level of just being 'fun things that were done in class' and have no intrinsic scientific value. The teacher and the multimodal and multiliteracy design of the materials were the way that the actual activities are transformed into a scientifically meaningful learning experience. This role is dependent to a certain extent on the teacher having a clear understanding of how the methods of scientific inquiry function both epistemologically and in practical terms in relation to the content being learnt.

The starting point of the conceptual direction of hands-on science is the initial introduction of the context for the science inquiry activity. In the current data set, this was carefully negotiated by the teacher who was a member of the original unit design team. The provision of a context for the science activity included addressing explicitly the scientific concepts that will be addressed while at the same time connecting these to the students' own experiences and understandings. As seen in the specific classroom explored in the current study, what might be considered basic understandings cannot be taken for granted and the teacher needs to be flexible in addressing the students' starting points. For example, in the current study, the ratio of land and water on earth was not well understood. This was addressed by the teacher in variety of ways, including a specific worksheet and looking at the globe. The context of the science inquiry conducted in the classroom needs to be explicitly understood by the students. They need to be able to connect the specific scientific simulations they are conducting with the scientific phenomenon that they are learning. The teacher's introduction is the first step in creating this direct connection.

A good introduction of context is important but does not guarantee that the scientific inquiry tasks will actually be understood in scientific terms by the students. In the current data set, a major role of the teacher consisted of on-line responses to the students' work while they were conducting the various science inquiry activities. The video data analysis revealed these verbal responses by the teacher to be crucial in directing the students understanding of what they were doing. The teacher's feedback in the form of oral responses directed and modified the students' understandings. Sometimes this was subtle in the form of a repetition in more scientifically termed statements than those used by the students, and sometimes it was more intrusive providing a summarizing statement that verbalized what the students were doing and what their findings should be. The teacher used language to make explicit the meaning of the tasks that the students were involved with.

The teacher also provided an authoritative final summary of the scientific meaning of the scientific inquiry. Although this science classroom was designed as a scientific inquiry that would imply that the students reach their own conclusions, in actual fact this unit can be seen as a series of simulations of scientific inquiry with the aim of promoting specific scientific understandings. The teacher's summary at the end of the activity made explicit the specific understandings and concepts that were to be remembered and learnt from the science activity. There is evidence in the current data analysis that the teacher's discourse was given a position of priority in describing and explaining the science activities that the students conducted. This discourse, whether oral, written or visual, was used in some cases verbatim, suggesting that the students may not have internalized the information provided to them.

At all three of these points, the initial contextualization, the on-line feedback and the final summarization, the teacher's discourse directed the students to a series of specific understandings and modifications of the science inquiry. Language functioned as an overlay that explicated the value of the tasks themselves and what they meant from a scientific perspective. This allowed the teacher and the course designers to ensure that specific understandings did emerge from the various activities conducted by the students.

8.5.3 Directing Students to Appropriate Informational Resources

By definition science is a historical, communal activity that has built a body of knowledge relating to a variety of natural phenomena. Students need to be aware of the existence, use and value of this body of knowledge, in particular those sources of knowledge that were designed specifically for children and can be useful in the development of scientifically-based knowledge. Within the framework of the current data set several different instances of this aspect of the teacher's role were identified. Essentially, the teacher functioned as the intermediary between the community of scientists and the students within the classroom.

The most basic role of this type performed by the teacher consisted of the presentation and explication of scientific vocabulary. Scientists use language in a specific way designed to provide a certain level of precision in the description of a process, object or phenomenon. This usage of language is different from the way everyday description is used. An understanding of these terms is central to the access to wider sources of information relating to the phenomenon being explored and to the way the object or process is understood by scientists. For example, in the current data set, the process of rock formation can be described in narrative terms as a journey through a variety of seasons and natural events. But to actually understand the process, the concepts of weathering and erosion need to be addressed. The use of these terms takes the description from the local personified description of a specific case to a discussion of the wider body of knowledge that describes this process and makes it applicable to a wider set of phenomena.

On a different level, there are a variety of materials that have been designed specifically with the aim of providing scientific information in a format suitable for children. Primary among these materials are encyclopedic format explanations of objects and processes. These can provide students with scientifically accurate descriptions that can be used to inform student work within the science unit. This can have a complementary position to the science inquiry activities conducted by the students. For example, in the current science unit, encyclopedic items were used to explore and describe animals living in the ecosystem of the shoreline. This provided additional information widening the understandings of the beach and its inhabitants. This also provides opportunities for reading non-fiction and exposure to different genres of writing, thus providing an exemplar of how to present and organize the students' own observations and understandings of scientific phenomena. By directing students to these authoritative sources of information, the teachers provided the students with the opportunity to conduct literacy research and see the connections between their own scientific inquiries and the knowledge that already exists in relation to the same phenomena.

8.5.4 Exemplifying and Explicating Scientific Thinking

In a very basic way, science is dependent on an understanding of the epistemology and thinking patterns of scientific inquiry. An epistemological understanding of science transforms the activities conducted in the classroom from a series of instructions to be followed into a way of constructing personal knowledge. On the most basic level, this means understanding that sensory data is used to evaluate claims and to describe the world. In many ways, this is counter to the usual interaction within the school setting that places the teacher as the centre of authority overriding all other sources of information. In this context, the teacher has an important role in explicating and exemplifying the types of thinking that underpin scientific inquiry.

As an initial step, scientific epistemology needs to be a topic of discussion within the science unit and as an introduction to the science inquiry activities. In the elementary classroom, this involves a discussion of the value of observation and the analysis of sensory data as a source of information. This is an aspect of how one answers a question and what one uses as an information source. In the current data set, epistemological classroom discussions were used by the teacher as an introduction to observation tasks. However, it was interesting to note that the teacher's authority was still more powerful than the students' ability to observe and report their observations.

Beyond explicit discussion of scientific epistemology, the actual patterns of scientific thinking and argumentation need to be exemplified by the teacher and pointed out explicitly to the students. This is a basic modelling process that tracks the movement of observation to stated conclusion. Through the science inquiry activities the teacher can model how a scientist thinks. This is similar to the way in which reading comprehension is taught with the teacher modelling processes such as prediction and inference while working through a shared reading. In the science inquiry classroom, there is enough data to model the types of process that are important for students to develop. In the current data set, this process was utilized in the context of teacher responses to student conclusions in relation to observation. For example, while considering some of the student groupings in an early categorization task, the teacher posed questions to the students relating to their categorizations, forcing the students to think why the objects were grouped together. She then provided an answer for the basis of the grouping, thus modelling the process of grouping and categorization according to material. Classroom discussion in conjunction with designed materials can also work in the same fashion of modelling epistemological thinking. For example, the oil on the beach prediction verification tasks directed students through a process of scientific thinking. The teacher's role consisted of making the scientific thinking pattern explicit once the task had been completed.

8.5.5 Providing Multiliteracy Instruction and Direction

Written, visual and physical representations are an intrinsic part of scientific inquiry. Specifically, visual and written genres fulfil the roles of recording observations, directing the process of scientific inquiry, summarizing understandings and allowing observations to be described. Scientific inquiry in the classroom cannot be conducted without multiliteracy. The importance and special aspects of scientific multiliteracy need to be addressed and negotiated by the teacher in the classroom both to enhance scientific knowledge development and multiliteracy knowledge. The teacher fulfils an important role in this context. Students in elementary school may have little experience of the types of visual and written literacy tasks involved in science and, therefore, these need to be taught and scaffolded by the teacher.

The data analysed for the current study reveals several points at which multiliteracy instruction and direction by the teacher becomes crucial. On the simplest level, the students must be able to follow written and oral instructions and provide adequate responses to a variety of different questions. As discussed in previous sections, the worksheet works in conjunction with the oral presentation of instructions for scientific inquiry. The teacher's role was to make sure worksheets were understood and to make sure they were being followed so that the scientific inquiry could be properly conducted and observations recorded.

On a different level, multiliteracy plays an important role in summarizing student understandings of scientific findings. The teacher's role consisted of directing this process and providing appropriate formats for the creation of summaries. As seen in the current data set, descriptive writing was found to be easier and more accessible to students than either informative or extended narrative writing. All three types of writing can be used for summarizing findings; however, the teacher needed to provide more direction and scaffolding for the informative and narrative texts. Of particular importance for all these genres as used in the context of scientific writing is the relationship between the written representation and the external observations that it is based on. The teacher's role as a science-literacy instructor is to make the form of representation reflect the actual empirical data of observation. This goes beyond the concerns usually represented in the discussion of literacy instruction.

The teacher also had the role of providing feedback on the formal aspects of the students' writing. As seen in the development of the students' written reports in the current data set, a process approach of drafting and revision was utilized. The teacher provided quite direct feedback on the formal aspects of the students' written drafts and was also observed working directly with the students to develop their knowledge of the syntactic, orthographic and textual conventions of writing.

8.6 Multiliteracy in the Science Inquiry Classroom

The process of learning science in a science inquiry classroom is a multimodal, multiliteracy enterprise. The physical, oral, written and visual modes of communication were seen in the current data set to work together to construct new understandings of scientific phenomena. The three progressions of multimodal direction of science inquiry, the multimodal and multiliteracy negotiation of the scientific understanding and multiliteracy summary all describe shifts from one mode of communication to the other and show some of the ways that these different modes of representation support each other and enhance the science learning process. These progressions of multiliteracy in the science inquiry classroom need to be considered in relation to the multiliteracy roles of the teacher. Taken together the progressions and the teacher's multiliteracy roles represent the basic ways in which multiliteracy develops scientific knowledge within the science inquiry classroom.

Chapter 9: Conceptualizing Scientific Discourse

9.1 Scientific Discourse in the Elementary Classroom

As reviewed in the theoretical introduction to this book, science is dependent on the presence and usage of scientific discourse. It is through discourse that professional scientific activities within the laboratory are negotiated, understood, circulated, contested and their ultimate scientific status evaluated. The aim of this final chapter is to discuss the characteristics of scientific discourse as represented and manifest within the specific early elementary science inquiry classroom studied within the research project presented in this book. As with other aspects of this book, the basic principle behind this description is to ground the statements made in relation to the characteristics of scientific discourse within the detailed analyses of the specific classroom that was explored. Specifically this chapter will attempt to answer the question:

1. What are the characteristics of scientific discourse?

9.1.1 Situated Pedagogical Scientific Discourse

A basic assumption of the current study of scientific inquiry in the elementary classroom is that literacy and by extension discourse are fully situated phenomena that need to be understood in relation to the context within which they appear. Scientific discourse is not considered to be a unitary term but rather that different contexts will empirically generate diverse types of discourse that fulfil the aims of the specific community that utilizes them. Accordingly the current discussion of scientific discourse describes the discourse of scientific inquiry within an elementary classroom.

This educational context has direct ramifications on the characteristics of scientific discourse. As with any educational context the aim is for students to reach a known set of goals. The educational context has made *a priori* decisions in relation to the desired outcomes for the discoursal interaction. In this sense, pedagogical discourse, as opposed to the assumptions of professional scientific discourse, differ in relation to the real aims of the discourse. Professional science aims to use discourse in a communal setting of scientists with a specific scientific domain and paradigm to find the most plausible explanations of phenomena in the world. Pedagogical scientific discourse aims to use discourse to provide those explanations that have already been accepted to students in the classroom. Professional scientific discourse is forward-looking and deals with the attempt to conceptually control the unknown. Pedagogical scientific discourse is backward-looking and deals with the presentation of accepted knowledge, positions and procedures.

As described in the initial chapters in this book scientific inquiry has been promoted as a central aim of the pedagogical scientific endeavour. The idea is that students will learn the basic epistemological and procedural components of professional scientific activity. In the educational framework, scientific inquiry is conceptualized as a range of activities that include making observations, posing questions and reaching conclusions based on empirical data. To a certain extent, this definition of scientific inquiry which is modelled on the work of professional scientists, does not take into account the discoursal intent of the educational framework. Conclusions presented in the classroom are based on the empirical data of established scientists but not necessarily on the work actually conducted by students in the classroom. As pointed out by both Millar (1998) and Nott and Smith (1995), educational settings may have difficulties in accepting the students' conclusions based on their own procedures of scientific inquiry in the classroom. In the data presented in the current study, a large proportion of the educational endeavour consists of guiding students towards established scientific knowledge. Situated pedagogical scientific discourse is a discourse that aims to direct students to a set of *a priori* defined, known and expected outcomes.

9.1.2 *Situated Pedagogical Scientific Discourse and the Art of Persuasion*

An aspect of any description of discourse is a discussion of the power relations manifest within that discourse. Professional scientific discourse is usually presented as a discourse of strife in which scientists argue over whether the most plausible explanation can be extrapolated from the data that has been collected (Harris 1997). Within professional scientific settings research is enacted within a framework of discourse that transforms the raw data into scientific arguments and evidentially supported theoretical positions. These scientific arguments and theories become written articles and conference presentations that are peer reviewed and evaluated in relation to the quality of the arguments. In other words, the work of a scientist is essentially that of a rhetorician who is trying to convince others of the correctness of her/his position (Prelli 1989).

This discoursal understanding of science is based to a large extent on Kuhn's (1970) sociological description of the development of scientific knowledge. In Kuhn's formulation, scientific knowledge is dependent on a community of researchers who have shared understandings of scientific procedure and knowledge. Thus scientific knowledge is contextualized within a specific scientific community and is the product of social construction. The evaluation of scientific knowledge requires direct access to the shared thinking of the scientific community and is not the result of some external objective criteria. Scientists within the net of relations that creates the scientific domain have vested interests and are committed to specific understandings within that community. Latour (1987), building on this description, points to the difference in the scientific discourse surrounding new scientific knowledge (science-in-the-making) and established scientific knowledge (science-once-made). New knowledge is embedded within the scientific discourse of conflict: argument, disagreement, dispute and evaluation; while established scientific knowledge is embedded with the scientific discourse of agreement: conformity, harmony and concurrence.

Most rhetorical and discoursal effort has been directed at describing the discourse of conflict that surrounds new scientific knowledge. Prelli (1989) conducted an analysis of the rhetoric used for the evaluation of new scientific knowledge in professional settings. Four contexts for scientific discourse concerning the evaluation of new knowledge were proposed by Prelli (1989): evidential, interpretive, evaluative and methodological. Evidential discourse deals with understandings concerning observations of the natural world. Counter positions and arguments within this discourse consist of questions relating to the nature of the evidence, the meaning of the evidence and the extension of data to potential claims. These arguments end when the evidential data is accepted as facts that need to be taken into consideration. Interpretive discourse deals with meaning of evidential data that has taken on the status of scientific facts. Counter positions and arguments within this context consist of questions relating to the nature of the interpretive theoretical construct that best addresses evidential data that has been presented. This is often a situation in which there is a multiplicity of competing potential interpretations and the scientific community needs to decide on the most plausible interpretation within the context of the community. Evaluative discourse deals with questions that arise in relation to the actual significance of the new scientific interpretations that are being proposed. Evaluative questions are posed within the context of the scientific community and address questions of whether the new knowledge has value within the research agenda of that community. Methodological discourse is directed towards issues concerning the procedures and scientific techniques used by the researcher in generating new scientific knowledge. Questions within this discourse involve questioning the appropriateness and validity of utilizing some methods over other potential methods. This discourse may question the way a particular technique was employed. When applied to the evaluation of new knowledge these four discourses provide a rhetorical framework for testing the strength of any new presentation of scientific knowledge.

A different approach to the same issue of evaluating new scientific knowledge has focused on the description of the rhetorical structure of empirical, scientific arguments. Most of these descriptions base themselves on the work of Toumlin (1958). Toumlin proposed a basic structure for substantive arguments that move from data to claims. The basic structure of this argument involves the presence of a warrant that provides rules of inference that legitimizes the claim made in relation to the data. Kelly *et al's* (1998) claim that scientific arguments are substantive arguments modifies Toumlin's original description in order to discuss students' use of scientific arguments in actual classroom discourse. In this study student's discourse was characterized by variability in the use of warrants to support scientific work. Claims that were concurred with established scientific understandings could be made with very little use of warrants. In some cases established claims were made on the basis of faulty warrants and in others a more significant number of warrants was presented but did not lead to substantive claims.

The current study of scientific inquiry in a second-grade elementary classroom sits in an ambiguous relationship with both the discourse of new and established scientific knowledge. Manifestations of both broad types of discourse can be found, however, the overall intent of the pedagogical discourse is directed towards creating harmony in relation to established scientific knowledge. In this sense pedagogical scientific discourse is a discourse of science-once-made that aims to ensure conformity of students' knowledge with canonical scientific understandings. As represented in the data analysed for the current study, many of the classroom tasks have the form of scientific inquiry in the sense that explorations were conducted, questions posed, tools used and aspects of measurement and observation utilized. As in the case of the beach bucket categorization tasks, these tasks can include aspects of questioning, countering existing decisions and regrouping and are reminiscent of the discourse of science-in-the-making. But within the wider context of the classroom, these forms do not have the discoursal authority that allows the establishment of new knowledge. As seen in the current analysis, authority rests with the teacher's discourse and is directed through the oral, written and visual materials that were presented.

Persuasion within this classroom consisted of the basic assumption that the teacher's discourse represents and summarizes the real meanings that are to be associated with the actions taken in the classroom. This aspect of teacher's discourse was found to function in the on-line responses to students during scientific inquiry tasks as well as within the wider envelope of discourse that introduced the tasks from a content and methodological perspective and the summarizing discourse that provided explicit oral, written and visual indicators of the meanings that are to be fixed to the tasks. The idea behind the use of scientific inquiry within this context consists of ensuring consistency between the conducted scientific inquiries and all statements made by the teacher and the materials based on established scientific knowledge. In this way the science inquiry activities become part of the rhetorical act of persuasion that the content of the established scientific knowledge is indeed correct and thus should be accepted. In this classroom, deference to the authority of the teacher's discourse and the use of scientific inquiry as a rhetorical tool of persuasion created a powerful structure for directing students' understandings towards established scientific knowledge.

9.1.3 The Multiliteracy of Situated Pedagogical Scientific Discourse

Recent discussions of scientific discourse have proposed that a wide representational base needs to be used in order to describe scientific activity (Kress *et al* 2001; Lemke 1998). The fundamental position presented in these works is that discussions of scientific literacy need to address the inherent multimodality of the scientific endeavour. From a theoretical perspective this is more than just recognition of the presence of different modes of representation. Cope and Kalantzis (2000) in a discussion of the conceptual foundations of multiliteracy state, 'Meaning is made in ways which are increasingly multimodal – in which written-linguistic modes of meaning are part and parcel of visual, audio, and spatial patterns of meaning' (p. 5). Meaning-making in this conception involves integration of these modes of representation into innovative textual and conceptual forms. Kress *et al* (2001) describe this as a process of 'reshaping' concepts within the internal cognitive system of the individual learner creating new scientific knowledge directly tied to the integration of different modes of representation. Multimodality does not just mean expressing the same concepts in different forms. The integration of different modalities creates new conceptual understandings that cannot be divorced from the integrated modalities that created them in the environment of the science classroom. In this sense the concept of the multiliteracy of science captures the idea of multimodal forms of representation which create new scientific understandings in a variety of novel representational genres.

Within the context of the current data set conceptual thinking was seen to be 'reshaped' through multimodal activity and multiliteracy representation. A clear example of this was the shift in the way objects were observed and described by students. At the beginning of the learning process, the beach itself and objects characteristic of the beach were described and represented in schematic terms based on prior learnt forms of representation. This form of representation ignored empirical sensory data in order to provide a description preferring the use of memorized accepted representations (such as using coloured circular shapes for rocks and coloured triangular shapes for shells). By being directed to observe a specific set of criteria in relation to rocks and shells, the way description was conducted changed. In both the written and visual formats an attempt was made to accurately represent the observed qualities of the objects being described. This resulted in innovative uses of language (such as using the analogy 'like a hammerhead shark' to describe a rock's shape or using the adjective 'twisty' to describe the shape of a shell). These new descriptions of the rocks and shells based on observed qualities and organized around these observed qualities consist of a significant cognitive shift. These multiliteracy representations result from a multi-modal movement from oral to written and visual formats which directed an increased emphasis on empirical observational abilities.

This reshaping of knowledge is even more pronounced in relation to the concept of sand. During the initial stages of this scientific inquiry classroom, sand was represented as a unitary single band of yellow colour. This representation basically represented an undifferentiated under-standing of the nature of sand. Following the use of both the magnifying glass and the microscope, sand changed from a single object into a collection of grains of eroded rock. As a set of multiliteracy representa-tions, this new concept was shown in the drawing of observed individual grains of sand, the pictorial representation of different narratives of a grain of sand's journey and the physical activity of grinding rock into sand while learning the vocabulary items of erosion and weathering and identification of rock. Together these multimodal forms of represen-tation reshaped knowledge of the concept of sand for the students in this classroom.

As documented in the previous chapter, multimodality plays a major role in guiding and directing the science inquiry process. Scientific discourse in the early elementary science inquiry classroom studied in the current research project was inherently multimodal. The inter-action among the teacher's verbal discourse, the written and visual materials of the worksheets and the physical activities of scientific inquiry constitute the components of the educational experience of the science inquiry classroom. These components functioned together to direct the activities and conceptualizations of the students in relation to the scientific knowledge being acquired. As discussed above this multimodal construction of the science inquiry classroom resulted in multiliteracy products that reformulated and reshaped the students' knowledge.

Within the current research project, scientific discourse was found to involve the development of several different multiliteracy genres. These genres covered written and visual forms of representation as well as oral interactions. In relation to visual formats, descriptive and narrative pictures, graphic organization of lists and symbolic notations were used. In relation to written representations, word lists, descriptive paragraphs, informational paragraphs, informational reports, written narratives and directed worksheets were all found to be part of the discoursal structure of scientific inquiry. In addition, genres of oral interaction such as the teacher triadic dialogue (teacher question, student answer and teacher evaluation), verbal introduction and summarization and explication of instructions were part of the educational context. Overall, scientific discourse within the current data set was found to be characterized by its use of multiliteracy in shaping and directing cognitive understanding of science. The interaction among the different modalities of scientific inquiry resulted in changes in representation expressed through multiliteracy.

9.1.4 The Epistemological Limitations of Situated Pedagogical Scientific Discourse

The theoretical introduction to this book proposed that epistemology is a crucial component of any scientific inquiry classroom (Kuhn 1993). As described by Latour and Woolger (1986), the process of transforming data into theory is a discoursal construct that involves understanding the scientific process of meaning-making. Specifically, the scientific process of knowledge construction requires the ability to fully evaluate evidence, to assess the value of competing theories of explanation and to construct arguments. A basic aspect of this epistemology is the ability to construct a valid scientific argument. Within the empirical context of scientific inquiry, a scientific argument allows conclusions to be reached based on empirical data. As described by Toumlin (1958) and later modified by Kelly *et al* (1998), the basic structure of this argument is of claims inductively drawn from data based on legitimate principles of inference. Thus the epistemology of science requires explicit understanding of the structure of the scientific argument and the ability to apply appropriate reasoning processes.

When broken down into components, there are several levels of understanding involved within the scientific argument. First, the epistemological status of evidence has to be recognized and differentiated from other components in the argument structure. Kuhn and Pearsall (2000) point out that there is a potential developmental aspect to understanding the role of evidence. In their research, kindergarten and first-grade children have difficulty differentiating evidence from explanation. Kuhn (2001) reveals a further difficulty in relation to the ontological status of evidence. From a developmental perspective, elementary age students tend to take an absolutist position in relation to both evidence and explanation. Both evidence and explanation are seen as objective and certain. This approach to the external world overrides the need for scientific argumentation. The world is just made of facts that exist. The conclusion from both these studies is that from a developmental perspective, recognizing and understanding the role of evidence may prove problematic.

The second level of understanding in relation to the scientific argument relates to the rules of inference that allow evidence-based claims to be constructed. Within the context of the epistemology of scientific arguments, clear rules of inference validate the construction of claims

(Toumlin 1958). The rules may be further contextualized by limiting circumstances or conditions under which certain claims can or cannot be made. Understanding the structure of the conditions under which the argument can be made is termed epistemic understanding (Kuhn 2001). The explicit understanding of the form of the argument that allows claims to be made and justified is unusual even with older students (Kuhn 2001). Without epistemic understanding it is impossible to evaluate the status of a claim made and it is impossible to differentiate between a valid or invalid claim. Only an understanding of the actual rules of inference would allow this to happen.

Kuhn (2001) points to a further developmental difficulty in relation to this argument structure. Children in early elementary school tend to see evidence not as generating claims but rather as supporting existing beliefs. From this perspective, children prefer theory certainty over indecision and ambiguity. Thus, without an explicit epistemic understanding of the scientific argument, this preference for theory certainty will direct the use of evidence to support existing ideas and concepts. The outcome of the problems with the different levels of understanding is the position that from a developmental perspective, enhancing early elementary school children's epistemological scientific understanding is a difficult task. As reviewed in the theoretical introduction to this book, children may have difficulty differentiating evidence from theory, have limited epistemic understanding and if evidence is used the tendency will be to support existing ideas and concepts rather than use empirical evidence as a way of qualifying or changing existing ideas.

Within the context of the current situated study of a second-grade science inquiry classroom, serious limitations on the understanding of scientific arguments were found. The clearest insight into the nature of the epistemological understanding of the students was found in the 'Making Inferences' worksheet activity. In this activity students were required to make an inference and then explicitly state the evidence that was used to make this particular inference. In responding to this task the only type of inference that was made was a world knowledge inference. This type of inference is based on existing world knowledge that has been activated. Once students identified an area of human activity presented in the task they just provided the continuation of that human activity from their schematic knowledge. When asked to explicitly state the nature of the evidence, this request was understood as the question 'How do you know this?' This question was answered by addressing personal experience or personal knowledge. In other words, there was no evidence of epistemic understanding that would allow the construction of a warrant to support the made inference. In the minds of the students the question was redundant because the answer was obvious – it comes from their personal knowledge. This is not the form of a scientific argument that provides a rule-based movement from evidence to claim. Essentially the evidence and the inference were part of the same pre-existing knowledge structure that the students already had.

In the last activity of the science inquiry unit studied in this project, students conducted small-group experiments in order to investigate the role of different materials in cleaning up oil spills. This activity was directed through a worksheet that allowed students to make predictions of outcomes, record observations and reach conclusions as to the best materials to use for cleaning oil spills. There was a direct request on the worksheet to explain the evidence used to reach the conclusion concerning the best material to use. Not a single student provided a response to this request. As with the making inference worksheet, this suggests that the students in this classroom did not possess an epistemic understanding of the structure of a scientific argument.

Early in the course, when asked to describe a photograph, students tended to use discourse which had come directly from the teacher and not trust their own sensory information. This predisposition to accept and utilize the teacher's discourse was a recurrent aspect of this science inquiry classroom. This predisposition combined with the absence of an epistemic understanding of the scientific argument creates a situation in which persuasion is easily achieved. While the class may aim to direct independent evidence-based conclusions, the epistemic understanding that would allow this does not seem to be present. Thus explicit statements made directly by the teacher, presented in written or visual form or indirectly represented in action carry very significant weight and the students are powerless to counter them through argumentation even if there is empirical evidence that is present. The development of scientific knowledge documented within this book would seem to result from this mechanism of direct discoursal multiliteracy guidance based on authority and not logical conclusions inferred from sensory data.

9.2 Multiliteracy Pedagogical Scientific Discourse and Cognitive Development

In the theoretical introduction to this book, the issue of the role of cognitive development was addressed. The proposed position was that of a neo-Piagetian stance that a specific situated learning experience has the potential to develop a child's knowledge and cognitive abilities in definite directions. Previous chapters have documented specific changes in the knowledge and abilities of the children who took part in the educational experience of the scientific inquiry of the shoreline ecosystem explored in this book. In this section a more underlying approach is taken to the question of cognitive development. Chapter 2 summarized a Piagetian and neo-Piagetian approach to cognitive development and proposed seven aspects of cognitive ability that need to be addressed at this age group. It is these seven aspects that will be used to organize the current discussion of cognitive development.

9.2.1 *Understanding the Role of Empirical Evidence*

Understanding the role of empirical evidence has a central position in the allowing of theoretical understandings to develop within an empirical context. In broad terms one of the main epistemological aims of any science inquiry classroom is the development of an understanding of how to use empirical evidence to develop theoretical understandings. In the current study, the data reveals an enhanced attentional presence for sensory evidence, but not a usage of empirical evidence within a personal scientific argument. There was no evidence of evidence being used to challenge and change established and stated scientific knowledge or to counter the authority of the teacher or written materials. There was evidence for the usage of sensory information in changing the personal understanding of natural phenomena within the shoreline ecosystem. As described above, understandings of sand were 'reshaped' and the description of rocks and shells were radically changed from schematic, memorized knowledge to realistic, observation-based descriptions. These are significant developments that utilize sensory evidence but they are mainly within the framework of observational developments and were directly supported by the authority of the teacher's discourse.

9.2.2 *Widened Perceptual Abilities*

Scientific knowledge is rarely limited to one perceptual variable. Problem solving within the realm of real world phenomena often requires the ability to recognize and address multiple sources of perceptual information. As discussed in the theoretical introduction to this book, in Piaget's classic conservation of liquid quantity task, younger children tend to focus only on the height of the liquid in the container while ignoring the perceptual quality of width. The ability to recognize the presence of more than one perceptual source of information is often a crucial cognitive component that allows more complex problems to be addressed. Within the current data set, as might be expected from a Piagetian perspective, students were seen to be able to address and utilize a range of perceptual stimuli. However, the specific tasks provided by the science inquiry tasks did have a significant influence on systematizing this aspect of observation. In the early observation tasks of shells and rocks, the students in this class were requested to address several different aspects of the objects. These requested aspects of observation then became the basis for the organization of written observations and the basis for later observations. In other words, the written and verbal request to observe a set of qualities became a global organizer for the observation of multiple characteristics of different objects. In this way, multiple sources of perceptual information were organized into a systematic approach to the observation of a variety of perceptual qualities of the same object.

9.2.3 Development of Historical Understanding of Process

Understanding science requires the basic understanding that the world perceived around us is the result of a series of states and transitions among these states. The understanding is that the current state of an object or being is transitory and that this is the result of an ongoing historical process. From a Piagetian perspective, younger children tend to address the current state of an object as a fixed reality and to ignore the transformative process that may have led to this end state. Older children have the ability to understand the role of a historical process in developing and changing the state of an object. Within the current data set, process was learnt through the multiliteracy activities of a shared reading of a science reader, discussion of the content and the creation of visual and written narratives of the process of sand formation. The students demonstrated through their visual representations an understanding of the specific process of sand formation. In later tasks with change in the concept of sand from a unitary, undifferentiated object to a collection of individual grains of sand, this knowledge of the process of sand formation provided the conceptual history of the relationship between the sand grain and the original material that the grain came from. The students also demonstrated an understanding of process in their final experiment on possible materials that can be used for cleaning oil spills. Support of the use of certain materials to clean up oil and the reporting of specific materials that did have this quality reinforces the underlying understanding of a causal relationship in transitions of the state of objects can occur. Beyond the acquisition of specific information, the multiliteracy products used to represent both the process of sand formation and the results and predictions in relation to oil spills demonstrate the students' understanding of the idea of scientific process.

9.2.4 Development of Systematic Observation

A basic aspect of any scientific inquiry is the ability to collect empirical evidence. For empirical data to emerge, a controlled process of systematic observation has to be conducted. Within the current data set, the ability to systematically collect observational data was clearly developed. During the early stages of this science inquiry unit, students were presented with photographs that they were required to describe. The students used the teacher's discourse to describe the content of the pictures often citing information that was not to be seen in the pictures themselves. In other words, they exemplified a behaviour that involved ignoring personal sensory information preferring to just cite the teacher's discourse. However, once students were directed to observe specific qualities in an organized manner, they quickly incorporated this behaviour and this had a profound influence on their descriptive abilities. As discussed in previous sections they developed an organized system of observation. In the later observational tasks, the students demonstrated the ability to use tools that allowed them to enhance their observational abilities. These included direct visual observation with tools such as magnifying glasses and microscopes and indirect observation through tools such as magnets. Over the period of the science inquiry tasks, clear developments in observational abilities were found.

9.2.5 Development of Inferential Processing

Inferential processing is a crucial component of scientific thinking. The ability to create an inference allows a student to move from direct observation of evidence to conclusions about the source or nature of the evidence and allows the construction of a scientific argument. As discussed above, in the current data set only one specific type of inference activity was observed. Students demonstrated the ability to construct world knowledge inferences. These inferences are dependent on existing background knowledge and consist of extending this knowledge beyond any explicit manifestations of it that are presented to the student. Thus while observing objects in the sand box, a student can infer that a white object may be a bone and when presented with a prompt stating that a crab was moving away from a dog on the beach, the suggestion that the dog will chase it can be offered. A real world inference does allow new information to be expressed but this new information is not the result of a logical argument structure. The lack of a logical argument structure inference severely limits the options of conducting scientific inquiry. Although several exercises and activities were directed exactly towards the development of this type of thinking, logical inferences were not produced by these students in the current data set. This suggests a cognitive parameter that was not overcome by the external input of the science inquiry classroom studied in this research project.

9.2.6 Focus on Meaning Construction

During the early years of elementary schooling a certain shift in relation to the concept of literacy needs to take place. While during the first year of school, the focus of instruction is literacy itself, during the next two subsequent years literacy needs to become a tool for the acquisition of knowledge of the world. This shift is usually termed the movement from 'learning to read' to 'reading to learn'. The understanding of the role of literacy in education is major component of the ability to become an autonomous and active learner within the educational framework. In the current data set, literacy and other forms of representation were used to enhance and guide the scientific learning process. For such an early grade level, literacy was used in a very mature context of actually allowing information to be recorded and utilized as part of the development of study. The science inquiry framework further situated literacy in the context of multiliteracy activities and thus widened the framework within which literacy was used for the real purpose of recording and developing understandings. One of the interesting aspects of literacy observed in the current data set was the way written description changed in light of observational developments. These changes were represented in the way literacy was used and resulted in creative usage of adjectives and description. In broad terms this usage of literacy is very mature and quite unusual within the early elementary curriculum which tends to be dedicated to the development of literacy knowledge for its own sake.

9.2.7 Development of Conventional Literacy Abilities

Learning conventional literacy requires several years of schooling. For students in second grade it is assumed that the process of acquiring conventional literacy abilities is still ongoing. Within the current data set, the teaching of conventional literacy was addressed through the direct feedback and rewriting of the different drafts of required classroom work. Within this context, issues of form such as spelling, syntax, handwriting and organization were addressed. Throughout the science inquiry classroom, the length of student work was seen to develop and new genres of literacy were acquired. Especially interesting was the development of the ability to write informative reports. The development of this type of writing was a significant achievement from a literacy perspective, especially since this type of writing is not usually addressed within the wider literacy instruction that is heavily directed towards the language arts.

9.2.8 Aspects of Situated Cognitive Development

A basic concept informing the current description of cognitive development is the neo-Piagetian idea of the situated learning experience within which specific cognitive abilities develop. Within the current study of the situated learning experience of a second-grade scientific inquiry classroom, certain abilities were seen to develop easily from the experience the students were exposed to. The prime example of this is the development of observational abilities and the ramifications of this on conceptual knowledge and representational abilities. Students' abilities to observe the world using their sensory information and utilizing appropriate tools can be seen as a major shift towards a more scientific examination of the world. However, not every situated learning experience of exposure has the desired outcome of the educational designers. Specifically epistemological knowledge in the form of an understanding of and ability to use a scientific argument was not found to develop. At the end of the course, although prompted several times and exposed to teacher's discourse and written, guided directions in the form of worksheets, students still had difficulty understanding the nature and role of evidence in constructing a scientific argument and did not use logical inferences. This suggests that in the present case, this type of thinking posed a cognitive boundary to what could be achieved with this specific group within the time frame of five weeks. From a cognitive developmental perspective the picture that emerges is that the science inquiry classroom with its emphasis on multimodal activities and multiliteracy products has a significant role in developing perceptual abilities (including using multiple sources of information, understanding process and the transformation and developing more systematic tool-based estimation of objects), but that the ability to logically manipulate information in order to construct scientific arguments or other types of rule-based inference was a cognitive parameter that was not overcome. Thus the situated learning experience of scientific inquiry was inhibited by this factor of developmental thinking.

9.3 Scientific Inquiry as Simulated Science

In the theoretical introduction to this book, the development of scientific inquiry as a preferred pedagogy for science education was discussed. One of the aspects addressed was the need for research on scientific inquiry within the early elementary school classroom (Britton *et al* 2000). Scientific inquiry as an educational method was modelled on adult, professional practices and evaluated in age groups from the end of elementary school through to high school. This opens the question as to the nature of scientific inquiry within the early elementary school. The aim of the current section is to discuss the nature of scientific inquiry as reflected within the data collected from one specific science inquiry classroom and based on this discussion to offer a revised definition of scientific inquiry that reflects the realities of the specific group studied.

Scientific inquiry as an educational method relates to a range of educational pedagogies that share the common assumptions that the learning of science needs to be an active process of learning with students fully involved in the discovery of scientific meaning. This is a constructivist approach to education that sees education as an outgrowth of the student's internal cognitive system and requires full engagement with that system in order for real in-depth learning to take place. Taking professional scientific practice as a core model, the educational practice of scientific inquiry aimed to make students think like scientists by doing such things as asking questions, posing solutions, designing experiments and collecting and analysing data. In an early formulation, Karplus and Thier (1967) describe scientific inquiry as a three-stage process in which students first explore a problem or issue proposing tentative hypotheses about the processes and objects involved, then gather evidence and information relating to their hypotheses defining and refining their concepts and hypotheses and finally apply their newly constructed knowledge to new and novel situations. This type of process moves from personal exploration of the problem to the application of solutions to new situations and clearly involves sophisticated autonomous thinking.

In relation to real school practice it has been noted that the science inquiry classroom may not in actuality be modelled on the procedures of practicing scientists. Both Millar (1998) and Nott and Smith (1995) make the point that teachers have the ability to modify and manipulate the actual classroom experiences to reflect established understandings of science. Thus science inquiry becomes more of a directed than open process. Thier and Daviss (2002) integrate this idea of direction into their concept of science education. Using the term 'guided science' instead of scientific inquiry, Thier and Daviss (2002) see science instruction as 'a series of structured, sequenced scientific investigations that integrate appropriate processes and information (or of activities and rigorous academic content, to use education's preferred terms), chosen through research, to fashion meaningful learning experiences for students' (p. 12). Thus science inquiry is a structured event designed by science educators to enhance the learning of science. Thier and Daviss do, however, hold on to the earlier idea of the importance of scientific knowledge application. In their words 'A feature that distinguishes guided inquiry from hands-on science is that, after students complete an assigned activity, they are encouraged to design their own projects and investigations to continue exploring the topic' (2002:12–13). Thus, what was once guided established knowledge ultimately has the aim of becoming knowledge applied to new research questions within the context of the topic area.

As described in the previous two sections, within the current study of an early elementary school science inquiry classroom, two main factors constrain the manifestation of open scientific inquiry: 1. the rhetorical aims of situated pedagogical scientific discourse; and 2. the stage of development of epistemological scientific understanding. Both these factors, although having very different starting points, lead to the same conclusion: open scientific inquiry is neither feasible nor really desirable within the early elementary science classroom. It is not feasible because open inquiry would require the ability to construct scientific arguments and rule-based inferences. This ability although coaxed and addressed by the educational team was not found within the current classroom. It is not desirable because on a very basic level, the educational system desires to direct students to established scientific knowledge and does not wish to entertain scientific ideas that are unconventional (and probably incorrect in relation to established understandings). The educational team wishes to develop a very specific and defined scientific knowledge base. Thus most of the efforts of this science inquiry classroom were directed to the fulfilment of this aim and in the current case there is documented evidence of their success.

In this context, science inquiry is close to the basic definition of guided inquiry – a set of structured activities designed to integrate appropriate scientific information and processes into a meaningful learning experience. As such, these structured activities do actively involve the students in doing and engage them on an emotional and conceptual level.

The study presented in this book shows how multimodality and multiliteracy directed the process of meaning construction directly guiding the physical, representational and conceptual components of the educational process. Here, scientific discourse in its broadest conceptualization means a process of utilizing all the representational means (including the physical manipulation of objects) to persuade students of a specific and known *a priori* outcome. The actual inquiries become part of a rhetorical persuasive structure designed to produce a specific understanding in students.

Where the current description of scientific inquiry differs from Thier and Daviss' (2002) description of guided inquiry is in the fact that the last stage of personal extension of knowledge to new situations was not directly part of the classroom and it seemed that students did not have the epistemological understandings that would really allow this. Thus the main body of the scientific inquiry classroom consisted of the carefully designed, implemented and guided science tasks and activities. These tasks and activities did create a situation of science inquiry for the individual students. But this inquiry was a physical simulation of real scientific inquiry and not a manifestation of it. In a physical simulation like a digital simulation, aspects of the real world are replicated but the outcomes are bound within the definitions of the simulation. In the physical simulations of scientific inquiries conducted by the students of this science inquiry class, the multimodal and multiliteracy structure of the classroom directed students to required outcomes. While working within the science simulation the student is active and has the sense and excitement of exploration and discovery. But the outer boundaries of what can be discovered, how it can be discovered and the meaning of the discovery are predefined by the design and multimodal implementation of the science inquiry unit.

Scientific inquiry as simulated science is a practical and creative educational solution to how to teach science to early elementary school students. This method does reflect the practices of scientists and researchers and does create a situation in which students are actively engaged in investigating and understanding the world. But it is not a process of open inquiry in which new scientific discoveries are made. It is a process in which old discoveries are carefully formed into simulated research experiences that guide students to specific and known outcomes. These simulated experiences enhance the student's scientific knowledge on procedural, substantive and representational levels and as such have the potential to grow into personal explorations of the world at a later developmental stage.

9.4 Scientific Discourse

The aim of this book was to describe the characteristics of scientific discourse in an elementary science inquiry classroom. The description of scientific discourse that emerges from the current study is of a pedagogical multiliteracy discourse directed at presenting students with established scientific knowledge. This discourse utilizes a series of multimodal forms of representation and multiliteracy products and has some of the conceptual aspects of professional scientific inquiry. But this discourse is bound within the inherent power structures of the educational setting in which the teacher's discourse is seen as the conceptual authority. Thus educational scientific inquiry does not have the authority of professional scientific inquiry and is not capable of qualifying, challenging or adding to scientific knowledge. As described in this chapter, this is a case of the simulation of scientific activity and not the manifestation of open scientific inquiry. What this book documents is that this approach does indeed develop student knowledge of the specific scientific ideas and processes that the science unit was interested in developing. While conducting the specific science inquiry tasks described in this book, students' knowledge of science did develop. The book shows how multimodality and multiliteracy carefully direct and guide this process both from a physical and conceptual perspective.

Bibliography

AAAS, American Association for the Advancement of Science (1993), *Benchmarks for Science Literacy*. New York: Oxford University Press.

Adams, M. J. (1990), *Beginning to Read: Thinking and Learning about Print*. Cambridge, MA: MIT Press.

Anderson, D. and Helms, J. (2002), *Open Questions in Science Education*. Available online at http//:www.stemworks.org/digests/dse02-09.html.

Atkinson, D. (1999), *Scientific Discourse in Socio-Historical Context: The Philosophical Transactions of the Royal Society of London 1675–1975*. Mahwah, NJ: Lawrence Erlbaum.

Barron, J. (1977), 'Mechanisms for pronouncing printed words: Use and acquisition', in D. LaBerge and S. J. Samuels (eds), *Basic Processes in Reading: Perception and Comprehension*. Hillsdale, NJ: Erlbaum.

Barton, D. (1994), *Literacy: An Introduction to the Ecology of Written Language*. Oxford, UK: Blackwell.

Barton, D., Hamilton, M. and Ivanic, R. (2000), *Situated Literacies: Reading and Writing in Context*. London, UK: Routledge.

Bazerman, C. (1988), *Shaping Written Knowledge: The Genre and Activity of the Experimental Article in Science*. Madison, WI: University of Wisconsin Press.

Berninger, V. W. (1994), *Reading and Writing Acquisition: A Developmental Neuropsycholigical Perspective*. Madison, WI: Brown & Benchmark.

Biggs, J. and Collis, K. (1982), *Evaluating the Quality of Learning; the Solo Taxonomy*. New York, NY: Academic Press.

Britton, E., Raizen, S., Kaser, J. and Porter, A. (2000), *Beyond description of the problems: Directions for research on diversity and equity issues in K-12 mathematics and science education*. Retrieved from http://www.wcer.edu/nise/News_Activities/Forums/5th_Annual_Forum.

Carey, S. (1985), *Conceptual Change in Children*. Cambridge, MA: MIT Press.

Carver, R. P. (1992), *Reading Rate: A Review of Research and Theory*. New York, NY: Academic Press.

Case, R. (1978), 'A developmentally based theory of and technology of instruction.' *Review of Education Research* 48, (3), 439–63.

—— (1985), *Intellectual Development: Birth to Adulthood*. New York, NY: Academic Press.

—— (1992), 'The role of central conceptual structures in the development of children's scientific and mathematical thought', in A. Demetriou, M. Shayer and A. Efklides (eds), *Neo-Piagetian Theories of Cognitive Development: Implications and Applications for Education*. New York, NY: Routledge.

Chi, M. T. H., Glaser, R. and Farr, M. J. (eds) (1988), *The Nature of Expertise*. Hillsdale, NJ: Erlbaum.

Chi, M. T. H., Hutchinson, J. E. and Robin, A. F. (1989), 'How inferences about novel domain-related concepts can be constrained by structured knowledge'. *Merrill Palmer Quarterly*, 35, 27–62.

Cope, B. and Kalantzis, M. (eds) (2000), *Multiliteracies: Literacy Learning and the Design of Social Futures*. New York, NY: Routledge.

Dunbar, K. (1995), 'How scientists really reason: Scientific reasoning in real world laboratories', in R. J. Sternberg and J. Davidson (eds), *Mechanisms of Insight*. Cambridge, MA: MIT Press.

—— (1997), 'How scientists think: Online creativity and conceptual change in science', in T. B. Ward, S. M. Smith and S. Vaid (eds), *Conceptual Structures and Processes: Emergence, Discovery and Change*. Washington DC: APA Press.

Ehri, L. (1991), 'Development of the ability to read words', in R. Barr, M. Kamil, P. Mosenthal and P. Pearson (eds), *Handbook of Reading Reasearch* (Vol. 2). New York, NY: Longman.

—— (1994), 'Development of the ability to read words: Update', in R. Ruddell, M. Ruddell and H. Singer (eds), *Theoretical Models and Processes of Reading*. Newark, DE: International Reading Association.

Ehri, L. and Wilce, L. S. (1987), 'Cipher versus cue reading: An experiment in decoding acquisition'. *Journal of Educational Psychology*, 79, 3–13.

Fischer, K. W. (1980), 'A theory of cognitive development: the control and construction of hierarchies of skills'. *Psychological Review*, 87, 477–531.

Fischer, K. W. and Canfield, R. L. (1986), 'The ambiguity of stage and structure in behavior: Person and environment in the development of psychological structures', in I. Levin (ed.), *Stage and Structure: Reopening the Debate*. Norwood, NJ: Ablex.

Flavell, J. H., Miller, H. M. and Miller, S. (1993) *Cognitive Development*. Englewoods Cliffs, NJ: Prentice Hall Inc.

Freedman, A. and Medway, P. (1994a), *Learning and Teaching Genre*. Portsmouth, NH: Boynton/Cook Publishers Inc.

—— (1994b), *Genre and the New Rhetoric*. London: Taylor & Francis.

Gee, J. (1996), *Social Linguistics and Literacies: Ideology in Discourses*. London, UK: Falmer Press.

Giere, R. (1991), *Understanding Scientific Reasoning*, (3rd edn). Fort Worth, TX: Holt, Rinehart & Winston.

Hanauer, D. (1997), 'Student teacher's knowledge of literacy practices in school'. *Teaching and Teacher Education*, 13, (8), 847–62.

—— (1998), 'A genre approach to graffiti at the site of Prime Minister Rabin's assassination', in D. Zissenzwein and D. Schers (eds), *Present and Future: Jewish Culture, Identity and Language*. Tel-Aviv: Tel-Aviv University Press.

Harris, R. A. (1997), *Landmark Essays on Rhetoric of Science: Case Studies*. Mahwah, NJ: Erlbaum.

Henderson, E. H. (1992), *Teaching Spelling*. Boston, MA: Houghton Mifflin.

Karplus, F. and Thier, H. D. (1967), *A New Look at Elementary School Science*. Chicago, IL: Rand-McNally.

Kelly, G. J. and Bazerman, C. (2003), 'How students argue scientific claims: A rhetorical-semantic analysis' *Applied Linguistics*, 24, (1), 28–55.

Kelly, G. J., Druker, S. and Chen, C. (1998), 'Student's reasoning about electricity: Combining performance assessments and argumentation analysis'. *International Journal of Science Education*, 20, (7), 849–71.

Kress, G., Jewitt, C., Ogborn, J. and Tsatsarelis, C. (2001), *Multimodal Teaching and Learning: The Rhetorics of the Science Classroom*. London: Continuum.

Kuhn, D. (1989), 'Children and adults as intuitive scientists'. *Psychological Review* 96, 674–89.

—— (1993), 'Science as argument: Implications for teaching and learning scientific thinking'. *Science Education*, 77, (3), 319–37.

—— (2001), 'How do people know?' *Psychological Science*, 12, (1), 1–8.

Kuhn, D., Amsel, E. and Loughlin, M. (1988), *The Development of Scientific Thinking Skills*. Orlando, FL: Academic Press.

Kuhn, D. and Pearsall, S. (2000), 'Developmental origins of scientific thinking. *Journal of Cognition and Development*, 1, 113–29.

Kuhn, T. S. (1970), *The Structure of Scientific Revolutions*. Chicago, IL: University of Chicago Press.

LaBerge, D. and Samuels, S. J. (1974), 'Toward a theory of automatic information processing in reading' *Cognitive Psychology*, 6, 293–323.

Langenberg, D. N., Correro, G., Ferguson, G., Kamil, M. L., Samuels, S. J., Shaywitz, S. E., Williams, J., Yatvin, J., Ehri, L., Garza, N., Bagley-Marrat, C., Shanahan, T., Trabasso, T. and Willows, D. (2000), *National Reading Panel: Teaching Children to Read*. Washington, DC: National Institute of Child Health and Human Development.

Latour, B. (1987), *Science in Action*. Cambridge, MA: Harvard University Press.

Latour, B. and Woolgar, S. (1986), *Laboratory Life: The Construction of Scientific Facts*. Princeton, NJ: Princeton University Press.

Lemke, J. L. (1990), *Talking Science: Language, Learning and Values*. Norwood, NJ: Ablex.

—— (1998), 'Multiplying meaning: Visual and verbal semiotics in scientific text', in J. R. Martin and R. Veel, (eds), *Reading Science: Critical and Functional Perspectives on Discourses of Science*. London, UK: Routledge.

Llyod, C. V. and Contreras, N. J. (1987), 'What research says: Science inside-out'. *Science and Children*, 25, (2), 30–1.

Lowe, R. K. (1993), *Successful Instructional Diagrams*. London, UK: Kogan Page.

—— (2000), 'Visual Literacy and Learning in Science'. *Eric Educational Digest, SE 064 310*.

Marsh, G., Friedman, M., Welch, V. and Desberg, P. (1981), 'A cognitive-developmental theory of reading acquisition', in G. E. Mackinson and T. G. Waller (eds), *Reading Research: Advances in Theory and Practice*. New York, NY: Plenum.

Mattheis, F. E. and Nakayama, G. (1998), 'Effects of a laboratory centered inquiry program on laboratory skills, science process skills, and understanding of science knowledge in middle grade students'. *Eric Educational Digest, 320 755*.

Millar, R. (1998), 'Rhetoric and reality: What practical work in science education is really for', in J. Wellington (ed), *Practical Work in School Science: Which Way Now?* London, UK: Routledge.

NCES, National Center for Educational Statistics (1996), *Pursuing Excellence: A Study Of US Eight Grade Mathematics and Science Teaching, Learning, Curriculum and Achievement in International Context*. Washington, DC: US Government Printing Office.

—— (1998), *Pursuing Excellence: A Study of US Twelfth Grade Mathematics and Science Teaching, Learning, Curriculum and Achievement in International Context*. Washington, DC: US Government Printing Office.

Nott, M. and Smith, R. (1995), '"Talking your way out of it", "rigging" and "conjuring": What science teachers do when practicals go wrong'. *International Journal of Science Education*, 17, (3), 399–410.

NRC, National Research Council (1996), *National Science Education Standards*. Washington, DC: US Government Printing Office.

NSB, National Science Board (1991), *Science and Engineering Indicators – 1991*. Washington, DC: US Government Printing Office.

Osbourne, J. (2002), 'Science without literacy: a ship without a sail'. *Cambridge Journal of Education*, 32, (2), 203–18.

Pare, A. and Smart, G. (1994), 'Observing genres in action: Towards a research methodology', in A. Freedman and P. Medway (eds), *Genre and the new rhetoric*. London: Taylor & Francis.

Piaget, J. (1954), *The Construction of the Reality in the Child*. New York, NY: Basic Books.

—— (1962), *The Origin of Intelligence in the Child*. New York, NY: Norton.

Prelli, L. J. (1989), *A Rhetoric of Science: Inventing Scientific Discourse*. Columbia, SC: University of South Carolina Press.

Pressley, M. (1998), *Reading Instruction that Works*. New York, NY: Guilford Press.

Qin, Y. and Simon, H. A. (1990), 'Laboratory replication of scientific discovery processes'. *Cognitive Science*, 14, 281–312.

Read, C. (1986), *Children's Creative Spelling*. New York, NY: Allen and Unwin.

Reiss, M. (2000), *Understanding Science Lessons: Five Years of Science Teaching*. Buckingham, UK: Open University Press.

Rodriguez, I. and Bethel, L. J. (1983), 'An inquiry approach to science and language teaching'. *Journal of Research in Science Teaching*, 20, (4), 291–6.

Skehan, P. (1998), *A Cognitive Approach to Language Learning*. Oxford, UK: Oxford University Press.

Stanovitch, K. E. and West, R. F. (1989), 'Exposure to print and orthographic processing'. *Reading Research Quarterly*, 24, 402–33.

Street, B. (1995), *Social Literacies*: London, UK: Longman.

Swales, J. (1990), *Genre Analysis*. Cambridge: Cambridge University Press.

Thier, M. and Daviss, B. (2002), *The New Science Literacy: Using Language Skills to Help Students Learn Science*. Portsmouth, NH: Heinemann.

Toumlin, S. E. (1958), *The Uses of Argument*. Cambridge, UK: Cambridge University Press.

Wellington, J. and Osbourne, J. F. (2001), *Language and Literacy in Science Education*. Buckingham: Open University Press.

Wellman, H. M. and Gelman, S. A. (1992), 'Cognitive development: Foundational theories of core domains', in M. R. Rozenzweig and L. W. Porter (eds), *Annual Review of Psychology* 43. Palo Alto, CA: Annual Reviews Inc.

Index